EYEWITNESS TRAVEL

MA

Main Contributors **Adam Hopkins,
Mark Little and Edward Owen**

Penguin
Random
House

Project Editor Helen Townsend

Art Editors Gillian Andrews

Editor Elizabeth Atherton, Sophie Warne

Designers Carolyn Hewitson, Nicola Rodway

DTP Designer Pamela Shiels

Picture Researchers Monica Allende

Main Contributors

Adam Hopkins, Mark Little, Edward Owen

Photographers

Peter Wilson and Kim Sayer

Illustrators

Richard Bonson, Stephen Gyapay, Claire Littlejohn,
Isidoro González-Adalid Cabezas (Acanto, Arquitectura y Urbanismo S.L.),
Maltings Partnership, Chris Orr & Associates

Printed and bound in Malaysia

First published in the UK in 1999
by Dorling Kindersley Limited
80 Strand, London WC2R 0RL

16 17 18 19 10 9 8 7 6 5 4 3 2 1

Reprinted with revisions 2000, 2001, 2002, 2003, 2004, 2005,
2006, 2007, 2009, 2010, 2012, 2014, 2016

Copyright © 1999, 2016 Dorling Kindersley Limited, London
A Penguin Random House Company

A CIP catalogue record is available from the British Library.

ISBN 978-0-24120-873-1

Floors are referred to throughout in accordance with
European usage i.e., the "first floor" is the floor above ground level.

MIX
Paper from
responsible sources
FSC
www.fsc.org   FSC™ C018179

Front cover main image: The historic gateway, Puerta de Alcalá, erected by Carlos III

◀ Panoramic view of the main shopping street, Gran Vía

Contents

How to
Use this Guide **6**

Beautifully sculpted Fuente de
Cibeles *(see p71)*

Introducing
Madrid

Great Days
in Madrid **10**

Putting Madrid on
the Map **14**

The History of
Madrid **18**

Madrid at
a Glance **28**

Madrid Through
the Year **38**

*Madrileños enjoying the May-time Fiesta
de San Isidro (see p38)*

The 13th-century church of San Esteban in Segovia *(see p134)*

The bustling Plaza Mayor *(see pp48–9)*

Chorizo

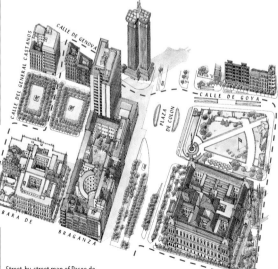

Street-by-street map of Paseo de Recoletos *(see pp94–5)*

ʌV TO USE THIS GUIDE

..s Eyewitness Travel Guide helps you get the most from your stay in Madrid with the minimum of difficulty. The opening section, *Introducing Madrid*, locates the city geographically, sets modern Madrid in its historical context and describes events through the entire year. *Madrid at a Glance* is an overview of the city's main attractions. Madrid *Area by Area* starts on page 42. This is the main sightseeing section, which covers all the important sights, with photographs, maps and illustrations. It also includes day trips from Madrid and three walks around the city. Carefully researched tips for hotels, restaurants, cafés and bars, markets and shops, entertainment and sports are found in *Travellers' Needs*. The *Survival Guide* contains practical advice, from how to make a telephone call to using the transport system and its ticket machines.

Finding your way around the sightseeing section

Each of the six sightseeing areas in the city is colour-coded for easy reference. Every chapter opens with an introduction to the part of Madrid it covers, describing its history and character, followed by a Street-by-Street map illustrating a typical part of the area. Finding your way around each chapter is made simple by the numbering system used throughout. The most important sights are covered in detail in two or more full pages.

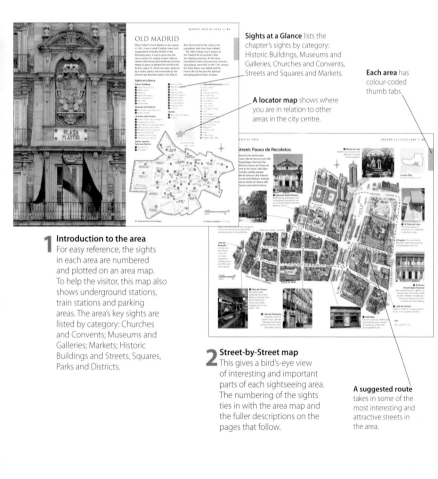

Sights at a Glance lists the chapter's sights by category: Historic Buildings, Museums and Galleries, Churches and Convents, Streets and Squares and Markets.

Each area has colour-coded thumb tabs.

A locator map shows where you are in relation to other areas in the city centre.

1 Introduction to the area
For easy reference, the sights in each area are numbered and plotted on an area map. To help the visitor, this map also shows underground stations, train stations and parking areas. The area's key sights are listed by category: Churches and Convents; Museums and Galleries; Markets; Historic Buildings and Streets, Squares, Parks and Districts.

2 Street-by-Street map
This gives a bird's-eye view of interesting and important parts of each sightseeing area. The numbering of the sights ties in with the area map and the fuller descriptions on the pages that follow.

A suggested route takes in some of the most interesting and attractive streets in the area.

Madrid Area Map

The coloured areas shown on this map *(see inside front cover)* are the six main sightseeing areas used in this guide. Each is covered in a full chapter in *Madrid Area by Area (pp42–107)*. They are highlighted on other maps throughout the book. In *Madrid at a Glance (pp28–37)*, for example, they help you locate the top sights. They are also used to help you find the location of the three guided walks *(pp118–23)*.

Numbers refer to each sight's position on the area map and its place in the chapter.

Practical information provides all the information you need to visit every sight. Map references pinpoint each sight's location on the *Street Finder* map *(pp210–17)*.

The visitors' checklist provides all the practical information needed to plan your visit.

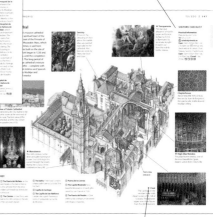

3 Detailed information on each sight
All the important sights in Madrid are described individually. They are listed in order, following the numbering on the area map at the start of the section. Practical information includes a map reference, opening hours, telephone numbers, admission charges and facilities available for each sight. The key to the symbols used is on the back flap.

4 Madrid's major sights
Historic buildings are dissected to reveal their interiors; museums and galleries have colour-coded floorplans to help you find important exhibits.

Stars indicate the features no visitor should miss.

INTRODUCING MADRID

GREAT DAYS IN MADRID

Madrid is a city packed with an array of things to see and do. The following pages list itineraries for some of the best attractions Madrid has to offer, arranged first by theme, and then by length of stay. The first three suggestions for a day out can all be undertaken on foot. The price guides on pages 10–11 show the cost for two adults or for a family of four, and include expenses for travel and food.

Palm trees in the Real Jardín Botánico

History and Art

Two adults allow at least €70

- **Fabulous art at the Prado**
- **Relaxing Real Jardín Botánico**
- **Picasso at the Reina Sofía**
- **Cocktails at the Westin Palace hotel**

The Museo Reina Sofía, a museum of modern art

Morning

Start at the **Museo Thyssen-Bornemisza** *(see pp74–7)* and enjoy the world's greatest private art collection, acquired by Spain thanks in part to the late Baron Thyssen-Bornemisza's Spanish wife. There is also a good bookshop on the premises. Then head to the **Museo del Prado** *(see pp82–5)*, whose small size belies the treasures within. Make sure you get a plan at the entrance to find your way around and to be able to enjoy fully the best that Spanish art has to offer. Among the highlights are works by Goya and El Greco. There is also a café near the far exit, making an ideal lunch stop, and it is opposite the entrance to the **Real Jardín Botánico** *(see p86)*, a lovely oasis in central Madrid.

Afternoon

Next, walk across to the **Museo Reina Sofía**, a modern art collection *(see pp88–91)*, whose highlight is Picasso's *Guernica*. Walk back towards the Thyssen for a cocktail in the lovely **Westin Palace** hotel *(see p73)*.

Old Madrid

Two adults allow at least €70

- **Art treasures and monasteries**
- **Tapas on Plaza de Oriente**
- **The majestic Palacio Real**
- **Explore Cava Baja**

Morning

Start at the **Monasterio de las Descalzas Reales** *(see p56)* to see the fabulous art treasures collected by Felipe II's sister, Juana, and her royal nuns, then continue to see more at the **Monasterio de la Encarnación** *(see p57)*, opened by Felipe III's spouse, Margaret of Austria. Walk to **Plaza de Oriente** *(see p62)* and have a tapas lunch at either the Taberna del Alabardero (Felipe V 6) or the **Café de Oriente** *(see p164)*.

Afternoon

Cross the Plaza de Oriente to the **Palacio Real** *(see pp58–61)*. A visit to the amazing armoury is essential. After the palace head for the vast and majestic **Plaza Mayor** *(see p48)*. This was once the scene of Spanish

Allegorical paintings on the Casa de la Panadería, Plaza Mayor

◀ Depiction of King Charles III entering Madrid in 1760, by Lorenzo Quiros

Smart boutiques along Calle de Serrano

Inquisition trials, as well as bullfights, and you can see gory bullfighting photos in the Torre del Oro bar while you enjoy a drink. Today it is an altogether calmer place. Also don't miss the murals on the Casa de la Panadería. Continue straight on and pass Casa Botín (Cuchilleros 17), purportedly the world's oldest restaurant, cross to Cava Baja and explore the streets of the city's Old Quarter off to the right.

Fashion and Shopping

Two adults allow at least €90

- Nineteenth-century mansions
- Exclusive boutiques
- Stop for a wine bar lunch
- Enjoy archeological finds

Morning
Before you begin your day's shopping, step back in time and see what stylish people wore and how they lived at two private houses, now museums, dedicated to their 19th-century owners: **Joaquín Sorolla**, the painter *(see p104)* and **Lázaro Galdiano**, the collector *(see pp102–3)*. For a quick snack, opposite the second museum in Calle de Serrano is José Luis, a popular tapas bar for the well heeled. Walk a short way down Calle de Serrano to the ABC shopping centre on the right

and the smart Zara Home shop on the left for trendy household goods. Then, for a relaxed lunch in a fashionable wine bar walk a few blocks to Lagasca 74 and O'Caldino, a traditional Galicían tapas bar.

Afternoon
The area bordered by Lagasca, Serrano and Goya streets is packed with fashion boutiques, including designer names, as well as two branches of the **El Corte Inglés** department store *(see p172)*. Expensive Serrano shops continue alongside the **Plaza de Colón** *(see p100)* and opposite the excellent **Museo Arqueológico Nacional** *(see pp98–9)*, which displays a treasure-trove of archeological finds. End the day with a gourmet dinner at the Mallorca restaurant (Calle de Serrano 6).

A Family Day

Family of 4 allow at least €200

- Real Madrid stadium
- Dinosaurs at the Natural History Museum
- Lunch in the park
- Interactive science and technology

Morning
Start at Calle de Alfonso XII 3, where you can visit the old **Real Observatorio Astronómico de Madrid** *(see p86)*. Join a guided tour (weekends only; booking essential) to see the Foucault pendulum and the collection of telescopes. Then take a short taxi ride to Real Madrid's **Estadio Santiago Bernabéu** (open daily) just off the Paseo de la Castellana *(see p111)*. The trophy room and shop are both worth a look. Next, visit the **Museo de Ciencias Naturales** *(see p111)* with its impressive displays, including a reproduction of a dinosaur skeleton.

Afternoon
For lunch you could visit the **Parque del Retiro** *(see p81)* which has lovely cafés near the lake, and afterwards take a turn in one of the rowing boats that can be hired here. Alternatively, eat in a 1930s dining car in the café at the **Museo del Ferrocarril** *(see p114)*. The museum displays engines, trains and detailed model train layouts.

Dinosaur skeleton, Museo de Ciencias Naturales

Two Days in Madrid

- Explore Plaza Mayor
- Enjoy art at the Prado
- Make a trip to Museo Reina Sofía

Day 1
Morning Take a stroll around the historic heart of the capital, **Old Madrid** *(pp46–7)*, admire the splendid **Plaza Mayor** *(pp48–9)*, a grand 17th-century square fringed with arcades. Note the allegorical paintings that decorate the Casa de la Panadería. Have lunch at one of the restaurants in **Mercado de San Miguel** *(p49)*, a fabulous gourmet glass-and-iron market.

Afternoon Spend the afternoon with Velázquez, Goya and the other great artists represented in the **Museo del Prado** *(pp82–5)*, one of the world's finest and largest museums. Then head to the **Ritz** *(p72)*, the extravagant, *belle époque*-style hotel, handily situated next door to the museum, for a well-deserved post-museum cocktail.

Day 2
Morning Go shopping along the **Gran Vía** *(p52)*, Madrid's biggest shopping and entertainment street, lined with extraordinary early 20th-century

Monument of Alfonso XII and the boating lake in the Parque del Retiro

architecture including some of the first Spanish skyscrapers including the **Edificio Grassy** *(p53)* and the **Telefónica** *(p53)* buildings. Then linger over lunch in **Malasaña** *(p105)*, a traditional neighbourhood with cobbled streets and charming squares, now full of arty cafés and vintage shops.

Afternoon See Picasso's *Guernica* and other modern masterpieces at the spectacular **Museo Reina Sofía** *(pp88–91)*, perhaps pausing for coffee at the fashionable café in its stunning Nouvel building. You could spend the evening enjoying tapas in the buzzy bars around the **Plaza de Santa Ana** *(p51)*.

Three days in Madrid

- Relax in Parque del Retiro
- Marvel at Palacio Real
- Admire art at Museo Thyssen-Bornemisza

Day 1
Morning Start with a visit to the **Prado** *(pp82–5)*, choosing the highlights beforehand to avoid being overwhelmed by its immense collection. Then, head to the lovely **Parque del Retiro** *(p81)*, picking up picnic goodies in nearby **Salamanca** *(p101)* to enjoy on one of the lawns.

Afternoon Stroll around the statue-lined **Plaza de Oriente** *(p62)*, overlooked by the opera house, **Teatro Real** *(p62)*. Then head across the square to visit **Palacio Real** *(pp58–61)*, one of Europe's largest palaces.

Day 2
Morning Visit **Museo Thyssen-Bornemisza** *(pp74–7)* and admire its fine art collection. Then stroll along **Paseo del Prado** *(pp68–9)*, admiring the grand façades and fountains.

Afternoon Soak in the atmosphere of **Old Madrid** *(pp46–7)*, stopping for coffee on the **Plaza Mayor** *(pp48–9)*, a beautiful arcaded square. Visit the **Monasterio de las Descalzas Reales** *(p56)*, founded as a convent for blue-blooded nuns, and still full of treasures.

Day 3
Morning This morning's art feast is at the **Museo Reina Sofía** *(pp88–91)*, which houses Picasso's *Guernica*. Drop in at the **Círculo de Bellas Artes** *(p73)*, an elegant café and cultural centre.

Afternoon Go shopping along the glittering **Gran Vía** *(p52)*, and stop for a drink at **Museo Chicote** *(p52)*, a classic cocktail bar that has become a city institution. Wander through the Chueca neighbourhood's trendy boutiques and cafés. It's a great place to enjoy drinks and dinner.

Bustling Plaza Mayor with its outdoor cafés

Five days in Madrid

- Enjoy the bustle of El Rastro and tapas in La Latina
- Chill out at Real Jardín Botánico
- Check out Museo Arqueológico Nacional

Mouthwatering dishes on display at a tapas bar

Day 1

Morning Begin with Madrid's most celebrated attraction: the **Prado** museum *(pp82–5)*, home to an outstanding collection of art, including the celebrated painting *Las Meninas* by Velázquez. Follow it up with a wander along **Paseo del Prado** *(pp68–9)*, admiring landmark buildings such as the 19th-century Bolsa de Comercio, the Stock Exchange, and a stroll in **Parque del Retiro** *(p81)*.

Afternoon Enjoy the beautiful gardens of **Real Jardín Botánico** *(p86)*, an idyllic oasis in the heart of the city, and peek into the church, **Iglesia de San Jerónimo el Real** *(p80)*, scene of many aristocratic weddings.

Day 2

Morning Rummage for bargains in the Sunday market at **El Rastro** *(p65)*; if you're not around on a Sunday, you can still visit the area's appealing antique shops. Afterwards, follow the crowds to the tapas bars of **La Latina** *(p65)*, part of a Madrileño Sunday tradition.

Afternoon Wander through the lavish salons of **Palacio Real** *(pp58–61)* – perhaps

fortunately, only a few of its almost 3,000 rooms are open to the public – then climb the enormous dome of **Catedral de la Almudena** *(p63)* for stunning views that stretch across the city and out to the Guadarrama mountains.

Day 3

Morning Choose some highlights from the immense **Thyssen-Bornemisza** collection *(pp74–7)* to enjoy during the morning, then head up to the **Plaza Mayor** *(pp48–9)*, in the heart of the city's enticing historic quarter, for lunch.

Afternoon Explore **Old Madrid** *(pp46–7)*, admiring the ancient palaces and narrow streets, then take in the bright lights, vast variety of shops, and striking early 20th-century architecture of the **Gran Vía** *(p52)*.

Day 4

Morning Visit 20th-century masterpieces at **Museo Reina Sofía** *(pp88–91)*, the city's most

fashionable museum, then head up to **Parque del Retiro** *(p81)* to find a shady corner for a picnic, or perhaps take a boat trip on the lake.

Afternoon Check out the **CaixaForum** *(p80)*, a fantastic cultural centre with a wide-ranging programme of events, and an amazing vertical garden designed by Patrick Blanc. Head up to the **Puerta del Sol** *(p48)*, to see the 18th-century Casa de Correos (Post Office), crowned with a bell tower that has become the focus of Madrid's New Year's celebrations.

Day 5

Morning Spend the morning admiring the astonishing treasures contained in the **Museo Arqueológico Nacional** *(pp98–9)*, including a 2,000-year-old bust, the Dama de Baza, which is one of the finest Iberian artworks ever discovered. Then join the fashionistas in **Salamanca** *(p101)*, the city's most upmarket neighbourhood, shopping at designer boutiques and enjoying lunch at one of the trendy cafés.

Afternoon While away the afternoon in the fascinating **Museo Lázaro Galdiano** *(pp102–3)*, which occupies an elegant Neo-Renaissance mansion and has a vast, eclectic collection of artworks. You'll be spoilt for choice when it comes to dining, as Salamanca is packed with some of the city's top restaurants.

Visitors at the Prado museum

Putting Madrid on the Map

Spain, in southwestern Europe, covers the greater part of the Iberian
Peninsula. Madrid lies geographically in the centre of the country,
some 650 m (2,130 ft) above sea level. With a population of over
three million, Madrid is Europe's third largest city. A major economic
and cultural centre, the city is also home to the Spanish
government and monarchy.

*Portsmouth,
Plymouth*

*Bay
of Biscay*

*Atlantic
Ocean*

See next page

MADRID

Madrid

Key

━━━ Highway/Motorway
━━━ Major road
━━━ Minor road
━━━ International border
━━━ Provincial border

For keys to symbols *see back flap*

Canary Islands

Melilla

Europe and North Africa

Genoa, Livorno, Civitavecchia

Melilla, Nador
Ghazaouet

Beyond Madrid

Madrid lies in the centre of the Spanish *meseta* (high plain).
The surrounding area is known as the Comunidad de Madrid, while
further afield are the provinces of Guadalajara, Cuenca, Toledo,
Avila and Segovia. This beautiful, varied region is scattered with
historic towns, mountains, lakes, forests and arid plains.

Key

- ▭▭ Highway/Motorway
- ▬▬ Major road
- ─── Minor road
- ─── Main railway line
- ▪▪▪ Province boundary

For keys to symbols *see back flap*

THE HISTORY OF MADRID

Although archeological evidence suggests that humans were attracted to the area in prehistoric times, the story of Madrid doesn't begin until AD 852, when the Moors built a fortress near the Manzanares river. By Spanish standards, the city is a mere adolescent – it was born 21 centuries after the Phoenicians founded Cádiz and six centuries after the Romans constructed Itálica near Seville.

In the early 8th century, a Moorish army from North Africa landed at Gibraltar and, within a few years, conquered most of the Iberian Peninsula. The Moors established an independent emirate based in Córdoba, southern Spain and, in 852, under Emir Mohamed I, they built a fortress (alcázar) to protect the northern approach to Toledo; it stood on the site of Madrid's present-day Royal Palace. Named Mayrit (later corrupted to Magerit, then Madrid), a small community arose around the alcázar.

Christian Conquest

Timidly at first, then with gathering strength, the Christians to the north rallied against the Moorish invaders, pushing southward in the so-called Reconquest. By the middle of the 11th century, the kingdom of Castile had arisen as the major Christian power, its territory extending as far south as the Cordillera central mountain range, within sight of Mayrit. In 1085, the Castilians under Alfonso VI mustered for the decisive thrust against Toledo. Mayrit stood in the path of the advancing army. According to one story, the troops mistook it for the much larger Toledo, which is why they bothered laying siege to it. Another legend has it that the Christian attackers subdued the town after some of the more intrepid soldiers clambered up the defence walls.

Once all the excitement was over, the town of Madrid settled back into its sleepy rural existence. Many of its earliest inhabitants were monks, encouraged by the Spanish rulers to establish monasteries there and thus breathe new life into the community. Before long, Madrid had 13 churches, more than enough to serve the spiritual needs of its small population.

Among the first *Madrileños* was San Isidro Labrador, a local farmer who founded a *cofradía* (religious brotherhood). It is also said he performed miracles, but little else is known about Madrid's rustic patron saint.

In the 13th century a dispute arose over hunting rights on land owned by the Church. It was agreed that, while the Church owned the soil, *Madrileños* had rights to all that was above it, namely, game. Thus Madrid acquired its symbol – a bear (the Church's emblem) sniffing a tree.

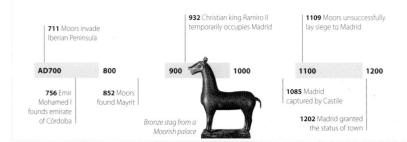

711 Moors invade Iberian Peninsula

932 Christian king Ramiro II temporarily occupies Madrid

1109 Moors unsuccessfully lay siege to Madrid

| AD700 | 800 | 900 | 1000 | 1100 | 1200 |

756 Emir Mohamed I founds emirate of Córdoba

852 Moors found Mayrit

Bronze stag from a Moorish palace

1085 Madrid captured by Castile

1202 Madrid granted the status of town

◄ Tiled mural showing San Isidro Labrador, Madrid's patron saint, and another farmer tilling the soil

Columbus setting foot in the Americas in the late 15th century

Royal Hunting Ground

Madrid's reputation as a hunting paradise attracted the attention of Castilian royals, whose visits became increasingly frequent. The city was especially favoured by Enrique IV de Trastamara who was, by all accounts, physically repellent, politically inept and morally perverted. Enrique was married to Juana of Portugal, but most people doubted that their daughter, Juana, was actually the king's; it was assumed her real father was the queen's lover, Beltrán de la Cueva, thus earning her the sobriquet, La Beltraneja (Beltrán's little one). On Enrique's death in 1474, a dynastic struggle ensued between supporters of La Beltraneja and those of Enrique's half-sister, Isabel, who went down in history as Isabel la Católica.

Madrid's nobility threw its support behind La Beltraneja, and the forces of Isabel and her husband Fernando of Aragón laid siege, conquering Madrid with the help of supporters within the town. Although Isabel and Fernando visited often, most of the momentous events of the age, such as the final war against the Moors and Columbus' encounter with the queen, took place elsewhere.

When Isabel died in 1504, her daughter Juana "la Loca" ("the Mad") was deemed unfit to rule. She and her husband, the Archduke of Austria, who were living in Burgundy, returned to Spain to reassert their rights. But the archduke soon died, leaving Juana to slip further into dementia. Fernando of Aragón acted as regent until the couple's son, Charles of Ghent, acceded to the throne in 1516 as Carlos I, the first of the Spanish Habsburgs (later Holy Roman Emperor Charles V).

Carlos I (1516–56)

Carlos I ruled over a European empire that included the Low Countries, parts of Italy and Germany, and Spain's newly conquered possessions in the Americas. But he had been brought up in France, spoke no Spanish when he arrived to claim the throne and, although his reign lasted 40 years, he spent only 16 of them in Spain. The European wars and the Counter-Reformation kept him busy elsewhere. Finally, spiritually exhausted and plagued with gout, Carlos I retired to the monastery of Yuste in western Spain, where he died at the age of 58.

1309 First royal Cortes (parliament) held in Madrid

1391 Pogroms sweep through Madrid's Jewish quarter

1498 Pigs banned from roaming freely in Madrid streets

1492 Moorish Granada falls; Columbus reaches America; Jews are expelled from Spain

1300	1350	1400	1450	150

1339 Alfonso XI holds Cortes in Madrid

1434 Madrid buffeted by rain, hailstorms and floods for nine weeks

1474 Supporters of Queen Isabel besiege Madrid

1478 Start of Spanish Inquisition

Brotherhood of Death

A City is Born

Since the beginnings of the kingdom of Castile, its rulers travelled ceaselessly from one part of the realm to another, with the entire court tagging along. Fed up with this migrant existence, Carlos I's successor, Felipe II, established a permanent capital in Madrid in 1561. It was centrally located in the Iberian Peninsula and small enough to lack the complex web of loyalties and intrigues of larger cities, such as Toledo. Artisans, cooks, poets, soldiers, thieves and hangers-on from around the peninsula flocked to the new capital. Within four decades, the population swelled from some 20,000 to 85,000.

Unlike his father, Felipe II spent most of his reign in Spain. Under him, the Inquisition became a major force, and the unsuccessful Spanish Armada was launched against England. The "Black Legend" has painted a dark picture of Felipe II, yet whatever his shortcomings, laziness and dishonesty were not among

Felipe V, the first
Bourbon king

them and, during his reign, Spain's world power was virtually unchallenged.

Due to its sudden rise to prominence, Madrid's growth was haphazard. Yet under the Habsburgs the city acquired some of its most notable constructions. The best examples were built in the reigns of Felipe's successors, a period when the country enjoyed an age of cultural brilliance (the *Siglo de Oro*) just as Spain's military and political strength was declining. The Plaza Mayor *(see pp48–9)*, the epitome of Habsburg Madrid, was built during the reign of Felipe III. His successor, Felipe IV, built a stylish new palace at El Retiro. At the same time, Cervantes, Lope de Vega, Velázquez, Zurbarán and Murillo *(see pp32–3)* were active in Madrid. Money poured in from the New World and, although most of it financed Spain's foreign wars and increasing debt, enough was left to fuel an artistic boom.

The Bourbon Zenith

It was too good to last. The inbred Habsburg dynasty produced the gentle but dim-witted Carlos II who died without an heir in 1700, leaving the Spanish throne in dispute. France favoured Philippe of Anjou, the grandson of Louis XIV. Alarmed at the implications of a French-Spanish alliance, England, Austria and Holland supported the Archduke Charles of Austria. This dispute led to the 14-year-long War of Spanish Succession. At the end of the conflict Philippe was crowned as Felipe V – the first Bourbon king – and Spain was securely in the French orbit.

Bullfighting in Madrid's Plaza Mayor in the 17th century

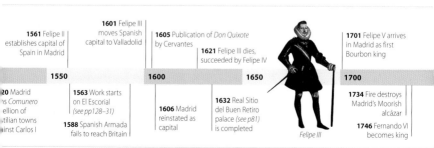

1561 Felipe II establishes capital of Spain in Madrid

1601 Felipe III moves Spanish capital to Valladolid

1605 Publication of *Don Quixote* by Cervantes

1621 Felipe III dies, succeeded by Felipe IV

1701 Felipe V arrives in Madrid as first Bourbon king

1550

1600

1650

1700

20 Madrid …s Comunero ellion of …tilian towns …inst Carlos I

1563 Work starts on El Escorial *(see pp128–31)*

1588 Spanish Armada fails to reach Britain

1606 Madrid reinstated as capital

1632 Real Sitio del Buen Retiro palace *(see p81)* is completed

1734 Fire destroys Madrid's Moorish alcázar

1746 Fernando VI becomes king

Felipe III

The Bourbons were able administrators, availing themselves of French and Italian advisers who introduced modern improvements to Spain. Felipe V spoke little Spanish and his main concern was making Madrid look as French as possible. When the alcázar burned down in 1734, he ordered the construction of a royal palace *(see pp58–61)* modelled on Versailles, but died before it was completed. The first occupant was Carlos III, under whose rule the Bourbon dynasty, and Madrid, reached their greatest splendour. At this time the centre of the city shifted from the old Plaza Mayor to the new Paseo del Prado, and many new buildings were constructed. Such was Carlos's urbanistic zeal that he is still cited as the best "mayor" Madrid ever had.

The presence of foreign advisers did not sit well with *Madrileños*, however, and the Church encouraged sentiment against interloping outsiders. The most famous incident was the 1766 Esquilache affair in which the Marqués de Esquilache, adviser to the king, banned the traditional broad-brimmed hat and long cape, as they enabled weapons to be concealed. His men roamed the streets armed with scissors to trim the offending garb. The people took this as an attempt to make them conform to foreign fashions, and fierce riots ensued. The Jesuits were thought to be behind the disturbances, and the order was expelled from Spain. On his death in 1788, Carlos was succeeded by his vacillating son, Carlos IV, who ushered in the decline of the monarchy.

Carlos III

The real power sat with his domineering wife, María Luisa of Parma, and chief minister, Manuel Godoy.

A City in Arms

Godoy struck a deal with the France of Napoleon (who had declared himself emperor in 1804) to allow French troops to cross Spain to conquer Portugal. In the end, however, the French occupied Spain itself. *Madrileños* blamed the royals and their hated counsellor, Godoy, and riots broke out in March 1808. The king was forced to abdicate in favour of his son, Fernando VII, though with the French occupying Madrid he ruled in name only.

On 2 May, *Madrileños* turned on the occupying troops in front of the Palacio Real. This popular uprising was met with bloody reprisals by the French the following day.

After the May riots Napoleon, increasingly impatient with events in Spain, installed his brother Joseph Bonaparte (José I) on the Spanish throne. Spanish sentiment against the occupying French could not be stopped, however, and the country rose up in arms. In the face of organized, well-armed

Goya's *The 3rd of May* (1814) with the French executing Spanish patriots

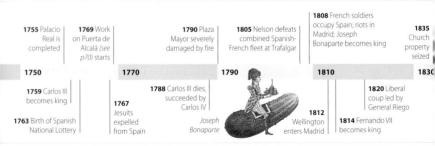

French troops, Spaniards resorted to terrorist tactics, with small bands mounting surprise attacks on the enemy before vanishing into mountain hiding places.

In 1810, the army of the British Duke of Wellington landed in Portugal and started the two-year campaign to drive the French from the Iberian Peninsula.

Liberals versus Conservatives

A century of close contact with the French left its mark on Spain. Liberal ideas found fertile soil among the Spanish enlightened classes and, while the war was at its peak, delegates in Cádiz drafted Spain's first constitution. Yet when Fernando VII was restored to the throne in 1814, he rejected the Cádiz document and ruled as an absolute monarch. This rift between reactionary and progressive sides would plague the country for the next century and a half. When an army uprising headed by the liberal Rafael de Riego in 1820 forced the king to accept the constitution, the exercise ended with Riego's execution.

After Fernando VII's death in 1833, Spanish politics became a complicated succession of coups d'état and uprisings. To make matters worse, the choice of his young daughter Isabel II as successor angered supporters of his brother Carlos, leading to a civil war in which 140,000 died. During Isabel's 35-year reign, Spanish politics were dominated by military brass, conservative or liberal.

Against this background of instability, Madrid was slowly becoming a modern European capital with a growing middle class. It was expanding relentlessly with the *Ensanche* (widening), with fashionable residential areas replacing overcrowded working-class districts.

In 1868 liberals joined forces with disgruntled military to oust Isabel II under the pretext of her corrupt and lascivious behaviour. But Spaniards still favoured a monarchy, and placed Amadeo of Savoy, son of Italy's King Victor Emmanuel, on the throne. The king received the cold shoulder from *Madrileños*, however, and abdicated after two years, at which point the Cortes (parliament) proclaimed a republic. The First Republic lasted only 11 months. In 1874, General Manuel Pavia ended it all by riding up the steps of the Cortes, declaring support for Isabel II's son, Alfonso. Under Alfonso XII (1875–85) and, later, the regency of his wife, María Cristina, who reigned on behalf of her son Alfonso XIII until 1902, Madrid enjoyed a period of prosperity and unstoppable growth, culminating with the inauguration of the Gran Vía *(see p52)* by Alfonso XIII in 1910.

Isabel II

The Battle of Madrid

Alfonso XIII felt it his duty to meddle in political affairs. Ministers were sacked by the dozen, and there were 33 governments between 1902 and 1923. Finally, the king resorted to General Miguel Primo de Rivera, who installed a dictatorship. It was relatively benign and had support among much of the working class. Spain underwent a flurry of public works, but Primo de Rivera was a disaster when it came to economics.

1840 Radical coup by General Espartero

1843 Conservative coup by General Narváez

1850

1850 Inauguration of Cortes building and Teatro Real *(see p62)*

1868 Coup by General Prim ends reign of Isabel II; the peseta becomes the Spanish monetary unit

1870

1873 First Spanish Republic

1875 Bourbon monarchy restored under Alfonso XII

1876 New Spanish constitution

Alfonso XII

1885 Alfonso XII dies

1890

1906 Ritz hotel opens

1897 Prime minister Cánovas del Castillo assassinated by Italian anarchist

1910 Work starts on Gran Vía

1910

Poster for the Nationalist cause in the Civil War

controlled the city. But, with much of the Spanish army's troops and weapons in the hands of insurgent Nationalists, the rebellion gathered increasing territory, and by November 1936 the Nationalists had reached the outskirts of Madrid. The city was to be on the front line for the duration of the Civil War until it finally fell in March 1939.

General Franco, who had manoeuvred himself into position as the uprising's *generalísimo*, was installed as dictator. Although Spain had remained nominally neutral during World War II, Franco's sympathies for Hitler and Mussolini were not forgotten, and for more than a decade the country was ostracized from the community of nations. Farms suffered a devastating drought, the black market thrived and Franco taught "autarchy" – his extreme form of isolationism and self-sufficiency. Yet the nation was starving, and millions were forced to emigrate to work in factories in France and Germany.

General Francisco Franco

Within six years the country was bankrupt. After the dictator stepped down in 1930, Republicans forced Alfonso XIII to call elections. The vote went overwhelmingly to the Republicans, and the king headed for exile after an angry Madrid crowd demanded his abdication.

During the brief Second Republic, the bourgeoisie, landowners and military were increasingly alarmed by the spread of left-wing ideas. The assassination of conservative member of parliament, José Calvo Sotelo, in July 1936 precipitated events. On 18 July news reached Madrid that a military uprising had taken several Andalusian cities, including Seville.

Madrileños flocked to the army barracks, demanding arms to defend the Republic, and within a day the working-class militia

By the 1950s geopolitics came to the rescue. The US forgave Franco's past sins in return for support in the Cold War against the Soviet Union, in the form of US military bases in Spain. The door was open to foreign aid and investment. The first adventurous travellers soon followed.

Dictatorship to Democracy

Franco's twilight years were devoted to securing the continuity of his regime. Alfonso XIII's grandson Juan Carlos was

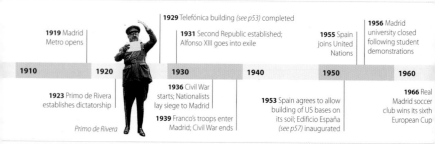

1919 Madrid Metro opens

1923 Primo de Rivera establishes dictatorship

Primo de Rivera

1929 Telefónica building *(see p53)* completed

1931 Second Republic established; Alfonso XIII goes into exile

1936 Civil War starts; Nationalists lay siege to Madrid

1939 Franco's troops enter Madrid; Civil War ends

1953 Spain agrees to allow building of US bases on its soil; Edificio España *(see p57)* inaugurated

1955 Spain joins United Nations

1956 Madrid university closed following student demonstrations

1966 Real Madrid soccer club wins its sixth European Cup

1910   1920   1930   1940   1950   1960

The Cortes being held at gunpoint in the coup d'état on 23 February 1981

a world fair in Seville and Madrid's stint as the "European Capital of Culture". The 1980s were a time of euphoria and cultural ferment, especially in Madrid. Under mayor Enrique Tierno Galván, the arts experienced a flurry of creativity, and the city revelled in a spirit of optimism and confidence, known as *La Movida (see p106)*.

The party couldn't last forever. Creative verve can only go so far, and a series of scandals involving some people serving in high offices chipped away at the public's faith in the governing powers, ultimately costing the PSOE the 1996 elections.

Like their counterparts in other European capitals, *Madrileños* complain about traffic, never-ending public works and pollution. Yet despite this they retain a fiercely individualistic spirit, a refusal to conform to European hours and, above all, a sardonic sense of humour that sets them apart from other Spaniards. They are living in one of the world's most lively and attractive cities and they know it.

groomed as his nominal successor, while the real power was to be wielded by the hardline prime minister, Admiral Luis Carrero Blanco. But in 1973, the militant wing of the Basque separatist group ETA assassinated Carrero Blanco. When Franco died in November 1975, all eyes turned on his heir apparent, who was sworn in as king. Juan Carlos had been planning for Spain's reunion with the modern world while lending lip service to the Franco regime, and in a series of bold moves, he manoeuvred the country into its first post-Franco democratic elections in 1977. When die-hard supporters of the old regime seized the Cortes in 1981, the coup failed largely due to Juan Carlos's intervention.

The next year the government passed bloodlessly from the centrists to the social democratic PSOE, under long-serving prime minister Felipe González. The first half of his tenure coincided with a period of economic buoyancy, crowned in 1992 with the Olympic Games in Barcelona,

Present-day Madrid, a thriving metropolis

			1996 Conservative Partido Popular wins relative majority in general elections	2004 PSOE (Spanish Socialist Party) wins General Election	
Carrero Blanco sinated by ETA	1976 *El País* newspaper founded in Madrid				
	1977 General elections held; centrist UCD (Unión de Centro Democrático) party wins			2011 PP (People's Party) comes to power	
1970	**1980**	**1990**	**2000**	**2010**	**2020**
975 Franco Juan Carlos omes king; rd Bourbon restoration	EL PAÍS — El País newspaper	1986 Spain joins EC and NATO		2008 PSOE wins General Election again	
		1982 Felipe González's PSOE wins general elections			2017 International LGBT festival, WorldPride, will be hosted in July
		1981 Right-wing coup fails; Picasso's *Guernica (see p89)* returns to Spain	2002 Real Madrid makes soccer history winning its ninth European Cup		

Rulers of Spain

Spain became a nation-state under Isabel and Fernando, whose marriage eventually united Castile and Aragón. With their daughter Juana's marriage, the kingdom was delivered into Habsburg hands. Carlos I and Felipe II were both capable rulers, but in 1700 Carlos II died without leaving an heir. After the War of the Spanish Succession, Spain came under the French Bourbons, who have ruled ever since – apart from an interregnum, two republics and Franco's dictatorship. The current Bourbon king, Juan Carlos I, a constitutional monarch, is respected for his support of democracy.

1665–1700
Carlos II

1479–1516
Fernando, King
of Aragón

1474–1504 Isabel,
Queen of Castile

1516–56 Carlos I of Spain
(Holy Roman Emperor
Charles V)

1598–1621 Felipe III

1400	1475	1550	1625
Independent Kingdoms		**Habsburg Dynasty**	
1400	1475	1550	1625

1469 Marriage of Isabel
and Fernando leads to
unification of Spain

1504–16 Juana la
Loca (with Fernando
as regent)

1621–65
Felipe IV

Fernando and Isabel, the Catholic Monarchs

Unification of Spain

In the late 15th century the two largest kingdoms in developing Christian Spain – Castile, with its military might, and Aragón (including Barcelona and a Mediterranean empire) – were united. The marriage of Isabel of Castile and Fernando of Aragón in 1469 joined these powerful kingdoms. Together the so-called Catholic Monarchs defeated the Nasrid Kingdom of Granada, the last stronghold of the Moors. With the addition of Navarra in 1512, Spain was finally unified.

1556–98 Felipe II

1701–24 Felipe

THE HISTORY OF MADRID | 27

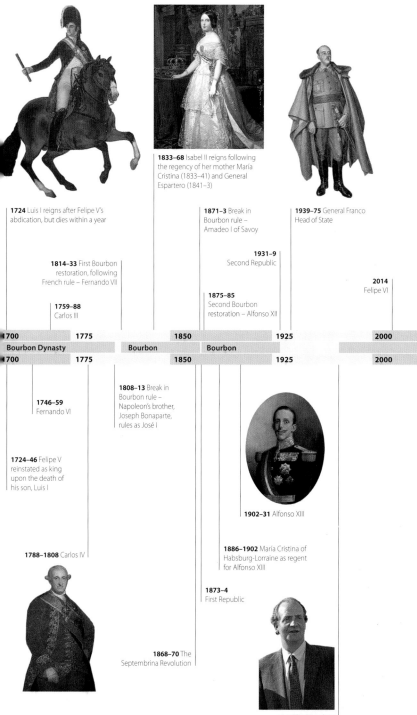

1833–68 Isabel II reigns following the regency of her mother María Cristina (1833–41) and General Espartero (1841–3)

1724 Luis I reigns after Felipe V's abdication, but dies within a year

1871–3 Break in Bourbon rule – Amadeo I of Savoy

1939–75 General Franco Head of State

1814–33 First Bourbon restoration, following French rule – Fernando VII

1931–9 Second Republic

2014 Felipe VI

1759–88 Carlos III

1875–85 Second Bourbon restoration – Alfonso XII

| 1700 | 1775 | 1850 | 1925 | 2000 |

Bourbon Dynasty | **Bourbon** | **Bourbon**

| 1700 | 1775 | 1850 | 1925 | 2000 |

1808–13 Break in Bourbon rule – Napoleon's brother, Joseph Bonaparte, rules as José I

1746–59 Fernando VI

1902–31 Alfonso XIII

1724–46 Felipe V reinstated as king upon the death of his son, Luis I

1886–1902 María Cristina of Habsburg-Lorraine as regent for Alfonso XIII

1788–1808 Carlos IV

1873–4 First Republic

1868–70 The Septembrina Revolution

1975 Third Bourbon restoration – Juan Carlos I

MADRID AT A GLANCE

Over 100 places of interest are described in the *Madrid Area by Area* and *Beyond Madrid* sections of this book. The detailed catalogue of significant buildings and monuments traces the history of the city – beginning with the 16th- and 17th-century Habsburg Madrid ("Madrid de los Austrias"), as exemplified by the medieval Plaza de la Villa *(see p49)* and the Colegiata de San Isidro *(see p50)*. From here, it follows the development of Madrid from the Bourbon city of the 18th century with its Parque del Retiro and Plaza de Cibeles *(see p71)*, to the upmarket 19th-century Barrio de Salamanca and the modern skyscrapers in the Azca area. The list also includes recreational sights, such as Casa de Campo *(see p116)*. Pictured below are some attractions no visitor should miss.

Madrid's Top Tourist Attractions

Plaza Mayor
See pp48–9.

Plaza de Toros de Las Ventas
See p112.

Parque del Retiro
See p81.

Museo Thyssen-Bornemisza
See pp74–7.

Museo Lázaro Galdiano
See pp102–3.

Museo Arqueológico Nacional
See pp98–9.

Museo Reina Sofía (MNCARS)
See pp88–91.

Palacio Real
See pp58–61.

Museo del Prado
See pp82–5.

◀ Flowers in bloom at the gorgeous Plaza de la Villa

Madrid's Best: Museums and Galleries

For a city of its size, Madrid boasts an exceptional number of world-class museums and galleries. Heading the list are the Prado, with the world's largest collection of Spanish art, the Thyssen-Bornemisza, which traces the development of Western art from the 14th century, and Reina Sofía, with its outstanding display of modern art. But there are many smaller, more intimate museums, too. Some, such as the Museo Lázaro Galdiano, are gems both for the sumptuous mansions housing the collections and for the untold treasures within. When planning your itinerary, note that many museums are closed on Mondays.

Museo de Historia de Madrid
Anyone with an interest in Madrid's evolution, from prehistoric to present times, will be fascinated by this museum, which features a captivating scale model of 19th-century Madrid *(see p105)*.

Museo Cerralbo
Entering this 19th-century mansion, with its eclectic array of artifacts, paintings and sculptures, gives an uncanny sense of stepping back in time and experiencing aristocratic life in Madrid at the turn of the 20th century *(see pp56–7)*.

Real Academia de Bellas Artes
Goya's *Entierro de la Sardina* is one of more than 1,000 paintings and sculptures, from the 16th–20th centuries, which can be seen at this arts academy *(see p51)*.

PLAZA DE ESPAÑA

CALLE DE SAN BERNARDO

GRAN VIA

PLAZA DEL CALLAO

CALLE DE BAILEN

OLD MADRID

PUERTA DEL SOL

CALLE MAYOR

PLAZA MAYOR

CALLE DE SEGOVIA

CALLE DE TOLEDO

Museo Thyssen-Bornemisza
Sold to the nation in 1993, this vast private art collection traces Western art through the ages, with major works by Titian, Goya, Picasso and Rubens *(see pp74–7)*.

Museo Lázaro Galdiano
The collection of the late José Lázaro Galdiano includes paintings, sculptures, jewellery, archeological finds and ceramics in his Neo-Renaissance mansion *(see pp102–3).*

Museo Arqueológico Nacional
This museum, situated at the back of the Biblioteca Nacional, is second only to the Prado in terms of the importance of its collection. Exhibits date from prehistoric times to the 19th century *(see pp98–9).*

AROUND LA CASTELLANA

Museo del Prado
Recognized as one of the world's greatest art galleries, the Prado is particularly notable for its collections by Velázquez and Goya *(see pp82–5).*

BOURBON MADRID

Museo Thyssen-Bornemisza

0 kilometres   0.5
0 miles   0.5

Museo Reina Sofía (MNCARS)
A former hospital, the Reina Sofía now houses an outstanding collection of 20th-century art *(see pp88–91),* including *Retrato de Josette,* by the Spanish Cubist Juan Gris (pictured), and *Guernica,* Picasso's famous depiction of the horrors of the Civil War.

Famous People of Madrid

Ever since Felipe II made Madrid the capital of Spain in 1561 (see p21), the city has attracted the best artistic and literary talent in the country. Painters, writers, composers and architects in search of fame and fortune left behind their rural dwellings and migrated to Madrid, where they could take advantage of royal sponsorships and subsidies, publish their works and sell their wares to the city's ever-growing population. Thus Madrid became the cultural centre of Spain, a distinction that grew in times of political and economic stability, and flourished – as great art usually does – following times of turmoil and strife.

Novelist Camilo José Cela (1916– 2002), painted by Alvaro Delgado

The prolific Golden Age dramatist, Félix Lope de Vega (1562–1635)

Writers

Spanish writers were the first to make their mark in Madrid, and throughout the 17th century the city acted as a magnet for the country's most famous scribes. The Barrio de las Letras (Writers' Quarter), or Huertas district, was where Spain's greatest literary figure, Miguel de Cervantes Saavedra (1547–1616), produced part of his comic masterpiece, *Don Quixote*. In the local taverns he would argue with his rival, Félix Lope de Vega (1562–1635), Spain's most prolific dramatist. The Huertas area was also home to Cervantes' and Lope's 17th-century contemporaries, writer Francisco de Quevedo y Villegas (1580–1645) and dramatist Pedro Calderón de la Barca (1600–81).

In the following centuries, this small area of Madrid continued to be the haunt of famous writers. The 18th-century Madrid native Leandro Fernández de Moratín was influenced by the French Enlightenment, as evidenced by his popular comedy *El Sí de las Niñas*. José Zorrilla y Moral (1817–93) was raised in the Huertas area, and his world-famous Romantic play, *Don Juan Tenorio* (1844), had its first showing in Madrid. In the same century, Madrid's most beloved writer, Benito Pérez Galdós (1843–1920), wrote his famous novel, *Miau* – a literary masterpiece that takes the reader on a journey through the streets and society of the Spanish capital during the city's most vibrant years. Madrid was at the centre of the "Generation of [19]27" writers that included poet and playwright Federico García Lorca (1899–1936) who, during his student years in Madrid, found inspiration as well as the theatres he needed to showcase his creations. The 20th century also produced Nobel Prize-winning novelist Camilo José Cela (1916–2002), whose novel *La Colmena* depicted everyday life in hungry, postwar Madrid. And while 20th-century American writer Ernest Hemingway could not be mistaken for a *Madrileño*, his novels helped the world fall in love with Spain, and his antics in the city after long nights of sipping gin at the Ritz hotel (see p72) made him a local favourite. Today it is difficult to walk through Madrid's Plaza Mayor without imagining the writer swaggering down the narrow steps of the Arco de Cuchilleros on his way to a roast suckling pig dinner at Botín (see p34).

José Zorrilla (1817–93)

Painters

All of Spain's most famous artists had an impact, one way or another, on Madrid. But it was 17th-century artist Diego Velázquez (1599–1660) and 18th-century painter Francisco de Goya (1746–1828) who actually formed part of the city's history. Both were Spanish court painters whose works were inspired by their surroundings in the capital. Each weekend *Madrileños* brave traffic jams to escape the grey city in search of the blue skies made famous by Velázquez, many of whose works have been brought together by Madrid's Museo del Prado (see pp82–5). There you can see his 1656 masterpiece, *Las Meninas*. Goya began his stint at the Spanish court in 1763 at the age of 17, and stayed on and off until 1826, two years before his death. He depicted life during one of the city's most violent times and was the painter of four kings – Carlos III, Carlos IV, José I (Joseph Bonaparte) and Fernando VII. While his works can be seen at several museums in Madrid, his masterpieces *The 3rd of May, Saturn Devouring One of his Sons* and *Naked Maja* are all displayed at the Prado.

Velázquez Bosco's Palacio de Cristal

Las Meninas (1656) by Diego Velázquez

Architects

Architecture is an art form of which *Madrileños* are especially proud. Some of the best architects in the world have contributed to turning the capital into the "city of a thousand faces". Francesco Sabatini designed the Palacio Real *(see pp58–61)*, the grand Puerta de Alcalá *(see p70)* and the 18th-century extension wing to the Palacio de El Pardo *(see p140)*. Juan Gómez de Mora was the architect responsible for the beautiful Plaza Mayor *(see pp48–49)*, which was completed in 1619. Gómez de Mora learned his trade from Juan de Herrera, the designer of Felipe II's palace

El Escorial *(see pp128–31)*. In the 1640s, Gómez de Mora designed the Monasterio de la Encarnación *(see p57)* and the old *Ayuntamiento* (town hall) in the Plaza de la Villa. A balcony was added to the town hall by Juan de Villanueva, the architect of the Prado museum. In 1781 Villanueva and Sabatini, along with botanist Gómez Ortega, designed the Real Jardín Botánico, or Royal Botanical Gardens *(see p86)*. In the Parque del Retiro *(see p81)* there are two pavilions built by architect Velázquez Bosco: the Neo-Classical Palacio de Velázquez (1883) and the Palacio de Cristal (1887), constructed of glass and iron. Noteworthy contemporary architects include Rafael Moneo Valles, who designed the extension to the Museo del Prado *(see pp82–5)* and redesigned the 18th-century Palacio de Villahermosa, home to the Museo Thyssen-Bornemisza *(see pp74–7)*. Also notable are Luis Gutiérrez Soto for the Ministerio del Aire in the Plaza de la Moncloa and Antonio Lamela for the Torres de Colón in the Plaza de Colón *(see p100)*.

Although not an architect, the Marqués de Salamanca, a flamboyant banker and speculator, had a profound effect on the design of the upmarket Barrio de Salamanca *(see p101)*. When investors

shied away from much-needed expansion plans in the 1860s, the Marqués stepped in and began work on what is today a fashionable line of housing blocks along Calle de Serrano.

Politicians

Since Madrid is the Spanish capital, there is a tendency here to claim or disclaim national figures as the city's own. Kings, dictators and prime ministers, while ruling from Madrid, did not always have a popular impact on the city. Felipe II *(see p21)*, for example, made Madrid the capital but then promptly left for his palace at El Escorial.

One of the best-loved political figures was the 18th-century *rey-alcalde* (king-mayor) Carlos III *(see p22)*. He took a personal interest in the city and set out to improve it with monuments, fountains, arches, street lighting and sewers. Another favourite politician was 20th-century (civilian) Socialist Mayor Enrique Tierno Galván, who became mayor in 1979, and died in 1986. He helped bring Madrid out of the grey dictatorial years by throwing his full support behind cultural events and progressive causes. He was instrumental in making Madrid's San Isidro festival *(see p38)* the popular cultural event it is today.

Enrique Tierno Galván, mayor of Madrid in the post-Franco era

Madrid's Best: Tabernas

It could be assumed that the first business establishment in Madrid was a *taberna* (tavern). In the 14th century, the area around Plaza Mayor and Plaza de la Villa was home to over 50 *tabernas*. Two hundred years later, their number had risen to 800. But, of the classical *tabernas* that took shape in the early to mid-19th century, only about 100 remain. Although each is unique, they share common features, such as a large clock standing guard over a carved wooden bar with a zinc counter, and wine flasks cooled by water running through a polished filter on the bar. Table tops tend to be of marble, and ceramic tiles often line the façade or interior.

Casa Perico
Once a humble bar selling *cazalla* (aniseed-flavoured spirit) and wine to local workmen, Casa Perico is a local favourite today, famed for its delicious traditional cuisine *(see p168)*.

La Bola
This small, bright red *taberna* was founded nearly 200 years ago. It has a beautifully carved wooden bar and, since 1873, it has been serving some of Madrid's best *cocido* *(see p185)*.

Restaurante Botín
Established in 1725, this is the oldest restaurants in the world, and is considered by many to be one of Madrid's finest. It serves traditional Castilian fare, including roast suckling pig, and was, at one time, favoured by the writer Ernest Hemingway *(see p166)*.

0 kilometres 0.5

0 miles   0.5

Taberna Antonio Sanchez
Madrid's *tabernas* take their cue from this classical 1830s watering hole, where the character of the place is just as important as the service. Many later *tabernas* have emulated its decor *(see p185)*.

PLAZA DE ESPAÑA

CALLE DE SAN BERNARDO

GRAN VIA

PLAZ DEL CA

CALLE DE BAILEN

OLD MADRID

CALLE MAYOR

PLAZA MAYOR

CALLE DE SEGOVIA

CALLE DE TOLEDO

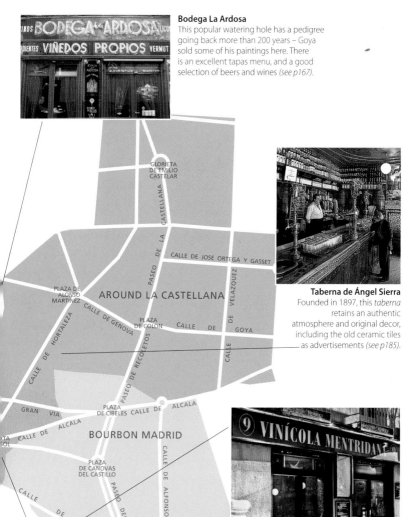

Bodega La Ardosa
This popular watering hole has a pedigree going back more than 200 years – Goya sold some of his paintings here. There is an excellent tapas menu, and a good selection of beers and wines *(see p167)*.

Taberna de Ángel Sierra
Founded in 1897, this *taberna* retains an authentic atmosphere and original decor, including the old ceramic tiles as advertisements *(see p185)*.

Vinícola Mentridana
This atmospheric wine bar in Lavapiés has been around since the 1890s. Although the interiors have been transformed, the wood panelling, the marble-topped bar and the lines of dusty bottles still exude old-fashioned charm *(see p185)*.

La Casa del Abuelo
This diminutive *taberna* more than makes up for its lack of size with its larger-than-life atmosphere. Founded in 1906, it specializes in sweet red wine and prawns cooked in four different ways *(see p164)*.

Madrid's Best: Architecture

Madrid has been described as the "city of a thousand faces", an image reflected in the diversity of its architectural styles. Among these are the rich and highly ostentatious buildings that mark the 16th-century areas of Old Madrid around the Plaza Mayor and the Plaza de la Villa. Northwest of Madrid, in El Escorial (see pp128–31), the architecture of Felipe II's palace is characterized by unornamented severity of style. The 18th century brought with it the Bourbon urge to break with the previous mould, introducing new, ornate styles of Baroque architecture. In the mid-18th century, with the arrival of Carlos III (see p22), more sedate Neo-Classical lines became fashionable. And, as the city expanded outwards, so did its love for new styles of architecture. Today Madrid's architects continue to experiment with adventurous building styles and techniques.

Contemporary
The Puerta de Europa twin towers survived a financial scandal and now seem to defy gravity as they lean over Paseo de la Castellana.

Art Deco
This landmark building, at Gran Vía 39, was built by architect Luis Sainz de los Terreros between 1926 and 1928. It now houses the Allianz insurance company.

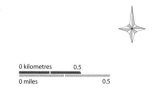

Habsburg
Since 1560 the red brick and granite Monasterio de las Descalzas Reales (see p56) has been home to a society of cloistered nuns – the Royal Barefoot Sisters.

Baroque
Built in the 1720s by Baroque architect José de Churriguera, this residence was stripped of its elaborate Baroque detail after being acquired by the Real Academia de Bellas Artes in 1773.

OLD MADRID

CALLE DE SAN BERNARDO
PLAZA DE ESPAÑA
GRAN VÍA
PLAZA DEL CALLAO
GRAN VÍA
CALLE DE BAILEN
PUERTA DEL SOL
CALLE MAYOR
PLAZA MAYOR
CALLE DE TOLEDO
CALLE DE SEGOVIA

0 kilometres   0.5
0 miles   0.5

Art Nouveau
An eye-catching example of Madrid's version of this art form is the Sociedad General de Autores de España.

AROUND LA CASTELLANA

BOURBON MADRID

Neo-Mudéjar
The Antiguas Escuelas Aguirre is a good example of this late 19th-century Moorish style, characterized by its extensive use of fine brickwork, balconies and row of vantage points along its bevel.

Bourbon
Influenced by French architecture, the grand Puerta de Alcalá *(see p70)* was erected by Carlos III as part of his plan to improve eastern Madrid. He effectively moved the centre of the city from the Plaza Mayor to the Paseo del Prado.

Francoesque
The Instituto de Crédito Oficial is in the Neo-Herreriano style, invented in the Franco years and named after 16th-century architect, Juan de Herrera.

Neo-Classical
Designed in 1785 by Juan de Villanueva, the Museo del Prado *(see pp82–5)* illustrates the Neo-Classical move towards dignity and away from the excesses of Baroque architecture.

MADRID THROUGH THE YEAR

A wide selection of fiestas, sports competitions and cultural events crowds the calendar in Madrid. Every neighbouring district, town and village also has its own fiestas, especially during the summer, with hair-raising bull runs, music and dancing until the early hours and spectacular fireworks which rank among the best in the world. There are vibrant street processions to celebrate Christmas and Easter, and at other times the capital's roads are completely taken over by bicycles, marathon runners and even sheep. Check with the tourist offices to see if your visit coincides with any public holidays, local festivals or special fairs.

Colourful tulips in a park,
signalling the start of spring

Spring

In late March the boulevards of the capital are lined with tulips, and on the first warm day in April the cafés open their terraces. But the weather is changeable, and it may be warm one day and cold the next. May's San Isidro fiestas, which herald the start of the bullfighting season, are often marred by rain, but the country-side also looks its best at this time. Many *Madrileños* leave town for the Easter Semana Santa holiday, and the deserted streets of Madrid resound with solemn religious processions.

March

Cristo de Medinaceli *(first Fri)*, Iglesia de Medinaceli, Calle del Duque de Medinaceli. Thousands of people come to this church to make three wishes before the image of Christ, one of which will hopefully come true.

April

Semana Santa *(Easter week)*. On Holy Thursday and Good Friday evening processions are held in Toledo *(see pp142–7)* and all over Madrid. On Easter

Saturday there are church services and a passion play in Chinchón *(see p141)*. Easter Sunday is marked in Tiermes by the symbolic burning of a tree and an effigy of Judas at noon. **El Día de Cervantes** *(23 April)*, Alcalá de Henares. Book Day commemorates the death of Cervantes with a book fair and literary discussions in Alcalá de Henares and celebrations throughout Spain.
Madrid Marathon *(last Sun)*.

May

Labour Day *(1 May)*. Public holiday and rally held in the Puerta del Sol *(see p48)*.
Fiestas de Mayo *(1 May)*, Ajalvir, Casarrubuelos, Fresno de Torote and Torrelaguna. Local fiestas celebrating May.
Las Mayas *(first Sun)*, around Iglesia de San Lorenzo in the Lavapiés district *(see p65)*. Each street elects a May Queen *(maya)* who sits in her best clothes surrounded by flowers in a spring fertility ritual.
La Maya *(2 May)*, Colmenar Viejo. Similar fiesta to above.

Día de la Comunidad *(2 May)*. Public holiday in Madrid and the surrounding area with a military parade in the Puerta del Sol and street festivals in Móstoles.
Artisans & Ceramic Fair *(mid-May)*, Plaza de las Comendadoras.
Fiestas de San Isidro *(15 May)*. Public holiday in Madrid and the feast of the city's patron saint. For a week either side of 15 May, the city vibrates with fiestas, music and dance, including the *chotis*. Bands play nightly in the Jardines de las Vistillas, Calle de Bailén.
San Isidro Corridas *(15 May–end Jun)*. Daily bullfight fiesta at Plaza de Toros de Las Ventas *(see p112)*.
Corpus Christi *(end May or beginning Jun)*. Religious holiday with processions in Madrid and Toledo.
Romería Alpina *(last Sun)*, Lozoya. Country procession with La Virgen de la Fuensanta.
Feria del Libro *(end May–mid-Jun)*, Parque del Retiro *(see p81)*. Book fair.

Semana Santa (Easter Week) observed with solemn religious processions

Average Daily Hours of Sunshine

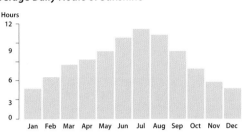

Hours

12
9
6
3
0

Jan Feb Mar Apr May Jun Jul Aug Sep Oct Nov Dec

Sunshine Chart
Madrid is a sunny place and, even in the depths of winter when temperatures plummet, there are usually a few hours of sunshine to brighten the skies. At the height of summer you can expect an average of 12 hours of blistering sun a day, so come prepared with a hat and a high-factor sun cream, and avoid the midday sun.

Summer

Madrid's outdoor swimming pools and aqua parks open in June *(see p188)*. By August, the fierce dry heat settles in and entire families escape to the cool of the mountains, the coast or outlying villages to visit relatives. Most offices work intensively from 8am to 3pm. Many bars and restaurants close in August, but those that stay open are thronged until the early hours. With a fraction of the usual traffic on the roads, it is a pleasant month in Madrid.

June

Fiesta de San Antonio de la Florida *(13 Jun)*, Ermita de San Antonio, Paseo de la Florida. *Señoritas* throw pins in a font, dip in their hands and ask St Anthony for a boyfriend. If any pins stick to their hands they will have that many boyfriends in the year ahead.

July

Concierto de las Velas *(first two Sats of Jul)*, Pedraza, Segovia. Candlelit fiesta.
Fiestas de la Virgen del Carmen *(around 16 Jul)*. District fiestas in Chamberí.
Fiestas de Santiago Apóstol *(25 Jul)*. Public holiday for Spain's patron saint.
Romería Celestial *(26 Jul)*, Alameda del Valle, Lozoya. Procession climbs 3 km (2 miles) to La Ermita de Santa Ana. Bring your own picnic.
Veranos de la Villa *(Jul–Aug)*, numerous venues across Madrid. Performing arts festival offering a varied programme

Candles lit along Mayor Street in Pedraza for the Concierto de las Velas

of open-air evening events including concerts, theatre, dance, flamenco, cinema, opera and *zarzuela*.

August

Castizo Fiestas *(6–15 Aug)*. Traditional *castizo (see p107)* fiestas in La Latina and Lavapiés. Traditional *Madrileño* fiestas of San Cayetano *(3 Aug)*, San Lorenzo *(5 Aug)* and La Virgen de la Paloma *(15 Aug)*.
Fiesta de San Lorenzo *(10 Aug)*, El Escorial *(see pp128–31)*.
Fiesta de San Roque, *(12–18 Aug)*, Chinchón. A bullfight in Plaza Mayor and *anís* tastings.
Asunción *(15 Aug)*. Assumption Day national holiday.
Fiestas de San Bartolomé *(24 Aug)*, Alcalá de Henares. Fiestas with giants, classical theatre and bullfights.

Encierros *(last week)*, Cuellar, Segovia. Spain's oldest known bull run, dating back to 1546.
Encierros *(end Aug)*. Bull runs in San Sebastián de los Reyes.
El Motín de Aranjuez *(end Aug or early Sep)*, Aranjuez. Carlos IV's abdication (1808), commemorated with bullfights, outdoor concerts and fireworks.

Decorations for La Virgen de la Paloma fiesta

Average Monthly Rainfall

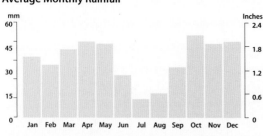

Rainfall Chart
Madrid has two main rainy periods – one from March to May, and the other from October to December. During the autumn, the skies tend to open in short thundery bursts, bringing the year's highest rainfall. Summers are dry and hot, and you are very unlikely to see much rain from June to September.

View of the Plaza de España (see p57) in autumn

Autumn

With the onset of autumn, the first rains for months relieve the parched countryside and begin to replenish depleted reservoirs. *Madrileños* love foraging in pine forests for the wild mushrooms produced by damp nights. The hunting season begins in October, and wild *níscalos* (fungi), boar, partridge and pheasant begin to appear on restaurant menus.

Wild mushrooms

September

Encierros *(first 12 days)*, Torrelaguna. Exciting bull runs and local celebrations.
Procesión de la Virgen de la Ciguiñuela *(6 Sep)*, Fuente de Saz de Jarama. Procession honouring the Virgin of the Stork amid burning scrub.

Romería de la Virgen de los Hontanares *(10 Sep)*, Riaza, Segovia. Local pilgrimage and fiesta of the Virgin of Springs.
Virgen de la Fuencisla *(27 Sep)*. Segovia fiesta.
Procesión Fluvial *(second Sat)*, Fuentidueña de Tajo. A river procession with beautiful illuminated barges.
Romería Panorámica *(second Sun)*, San Lorenzo de El Escorial. Procession with La Virgen de la Gracia (Grace) to a picnic in La Herrería woods.

October

International Book Fair: Liber *(first week)*. International publishers gather here annually. Cultural activities are held.
Festival Taurino *(around 12 Oct)*, Chinchón. Bullfights.
Día de la Hispanidad *(12 Oct)*. Spanish National Day.
Virgen de Pilar *(12 Oct)*, Plaza Dalí, Salamanca. Various district fiestas are held.
Festival de Otoño a Primavera *(mid-Oct to mid-May)*. Annual drama, ballet and opera festival.

November

Todos los Santos *(1 Nov)*. On All Saints' Day flowers are taken to graves of relatives.
La Almudena *(9 Nov)*. Old Madrid honours its patron saint La Virgen de la Almudena.
Romería de San Eugenio *(14 Nov). Castizo* procession in open carriages to El Monte de El Pardo for picnics.
Procesión de San Andrés *(30 Nov)*, Rascafría. Procession in honour of the local saint.

Celebration of Mass in Plaza Mayor to honour La Virgen de la Almudena

Average Monthly Temperature

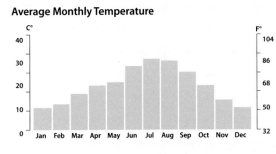

Temperature Chart
Scorching hot summers and freezing winters make Madrid a place of extremes, with averages giving scant indication of the heights and depths of temperature the city can achieve. For many people, the most comfortable months to visit Madrid, in terms of milder temperatures, are June and October.

Winter

The first snow usually falls in the Sierra de Guadarrama (see p132), heralding the start of the skiing season, and traffic jams form on the way up to its small resorts. Madrid, and the higher parts of central Spain, can become very cold. Christmas is a special time of celebration – an occasion for families to reunite, share food and attend religious services. On New Year's Eve, crowds gather in the Puerta del Sol.

Skiers in the Sierra de Guadarrama, north of Madrid (see p132)

December
Día de la Constitución (6 Dec). Constitution Day.
Inmaculada Concepción (8 Dec). Immaculate Conception.
Christmas Fair (mid-Dec– 5 Jan), Madrid's Plaza Mayor.
Nochebuena (24 Dec). Christmas Eve – an important night of family celebrations.
Día de Navidad (25 Dec). Christmas Day celebration.
Belén Viviente (last eves Dec), Buitrago del Lozoya. Nativity play on horseback.
Nochevieja (31 Dec). New Year's Eve. Crowds in Puerta del Sol eat a grape each midnight chime.

January
Cabalgata de Reyes (5 Jan). Evening (6pm) procession from Parque del Retiro (see p81) with floats, animals and celebrities.
Los Reyes Magos (6 Jan). Epiphany is celebrated with the giving of gifts.
San Antón (17 Jan), Calle de Hortaleza 63. Animals blessed at Iglesia de San Antón.
Vaquillas (20 Jan), Pedrezuela and Fresnedillas. Fiesta in which youths dress up as bulls.

San Sebastián (20 Jan), Villaviciosa de Odón. Procession, fiestas and dancing.
FITUR Tourist Fair (end Jan), Parque Ferial Juan Carlos I.

February
La Vaquilla Premiada (2 Feb), Colmenar Viejo. Amateur bullfighting contest and fiesta.
La Romería de San Blas (3 Feb), Madrid and Miraflores. Costumed celebrations.
Alcadesas de Zamarramala (around first Sun), Segovia. For a day village women boss their men around.
Mercedes Benz Madrid Fashion Week (mid-Feb), Parque Ferial Juan Carlos I. International fashion week.
ARCO (mid-Feb), Parque Ferial Juan Carlos I. International contemporary art fair.
Carnaval (run up to Lent). Fancy-dress parties; parade in the city centre.
Entierro de la Sardina (Shrove Tue), Casa de Campo. "Burial of the Sardine" parade to mark the changeover from Carnaval to Lent.

National Public Holidays

Año Nuevo
(New Year's Day) (1 Jan)
Los Reyes Magos
(Epiphany) (6 Jan)
Jueves Santo
(Maundy Thursday) (Mar/Apr)
Viernes Santo
(Good Friday) (Mar/Apr)
Domingo de Pascua
(Easter Sunday) (Mar/Apr)
Día del Trabajo
(Labour Day) (1 May)
Asunción
(Assumption Day) (15 Aug)
Día de la Hispanidad
(National Day) (12 Oct)
Todos los Santos
(All Saints' Day) (1 Nov)
Día de la Constitución
(Constitution Day) (6 Dec)
Inmaculada Concepción
(Immaculate Conception) (8 Dec)
Navidad (Christmas Day) (25 Dec)

The spectacular Fuente de Cibeles ▶

MADRID AREA BY AREA

OLD MADRID

When Felipe II chose Madrid as his capital in 1561, it was a small Castilian town with a population of barely 20,000. In the following years, it was to grow into the nerve centre of a mighty empire. Narrow streets with houses and medieval churches began to grow up behind the old Moorish fortress *(see p19)*, which was later replaced by a Gothic palace and eventually by the present-day Bourbon palace, the Palacio

Real. By the end of the century the population had more than trebled.

The 16th-century city is known as the "Madrid de los Austrias", after the Habsburg dynasty. At this time, monasteries were endowed and churches and palaces were built. In the 17th century, the Plaza Mayor was added and the Puerta del Sol became the spiritual and geographical heart of Spain.

Sights at a Glance

Historic Buildings
- **7** Palacio de Santa Cruz
- **11** Edificio Grassy
- **12** Telefónica
- **19** Palacio del Senado
- **21** Palacio Real *pp58–61*
- **23** Teatro Real
- **27** Muralla Árabe

Museums and Galleries
- **9** Real Academia de Bellas Artes
- **17** Museo Cerralbo

Churches and Convents
- **5** Basílica Pontificia de San Miguel
- **6** Colegiata de San Isidro
- **14** Monasterio de las Descalzas Reales
- **15** Iglesia de San Ginés de Arlés
- **20** Monasterio de la Encarnación
- **24** Iglesia de San Nicolás
- **25** Catedral de la Almudena
- **28** San Francisco el Grande

Streets, Squares, Parks and Districts
- **1** Puerta del Sol
- **2** Plaza Mayor
- **4** Plaza de la Villa
- **8** Plaza de Santa Ana
- **10** Gran Vía
- **13** Plaza del Callao
- **16** Calle de Preciados
- **18** Plaza de España
- **22** Plaza de Oriente
- **26** Campo del Moro
- **29** Plaza de la Paja
- **30** La Latina

Markets
- **3** Mercado de San Miguel
- **31** El Rastro

Selected Restaurants *pp164–6*
1. Ana La Santa
2. Botín
3. Café de los Austrias
4. La Carbonería
5. La Casa del Abuelo
6. Casa Alberto
7. Casa Ciriaco
8. Casa Jacinto
9. La Ciudad Invisible
10. Delic
11. Donnafugata
12. El Abrazo de Vergara
13. El Club Allard
14. El Cucurucho del Mar
15. Julián de Tolosa
16. Malaspina
17. La Musa Latina
18. Naïa
19. Prada a Tope
20. Taberna del Chato

See also Street Finder maps 1, 3, 4 & 7

0 metres 500
0 yards 500

◀ Ornate exteriors in the Plaza Mayor

For keys to symbols *see back flap*

Street-by-Street: Old Madrid

Stretching from the charming Plaza de la
Villa to the busy Puerta del Sol, the compact
heart of Old Madrid is steeped in history
and full of interesting sights. Trials by the
Inquisition and executions were once held
in the Plaza Mayor. This porticoed square is
Old Madrid's finest piece of architecture, a
legacy of the Habsburgs *(see p21)*. Other
noteworthy buildings include the Colegiata
de San Isidro and the Palacio de Santa Cruz.
For a more relaxing way of enjoying Old
Madrid, sit in one of the area's numerous
cafés or browse among the colourful stalls
of the Mercado de San Miguel.

❷ ★ **Plaza Mayor**
This beautiful
17th-century square
competes with
the Puerta del Sol
as the focus of Old
Madrid. The arcades
at the base of the
impressive buildings
are filled with cafés
and craft shops.

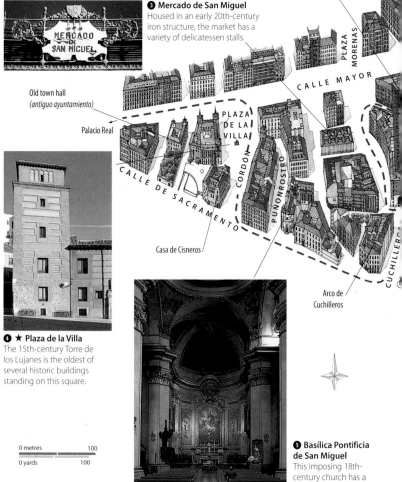

❸ **Mercado de San Miguel**
Housed in an early 20th-century
iron structure, the market has a
variety of delicatessen stalls.

Old town hall
(antiguo ayuntamiento)

Palacio Real

PLAZA MORENAS

CALLE MAYOR

PLAZA DE LA VILLA

CORDÓN

PUÑONROSTRO

CALLE DE SACRAMENTO

CUCHILLEROS

Casa de Cisneros

**Arco de
Cuchilleros**

❹ ★ **Plaza de la Villa**
The 15th-century Torre de
los Lujanes is the oldest of
several historic buildings
standing on this square.

0 metres		100
0 yards		100

❺ **Basílica Pontificia
de San Miguel**
This imposing 18th-
century church has a
beautiful façade and a
graceful Baroque interior.

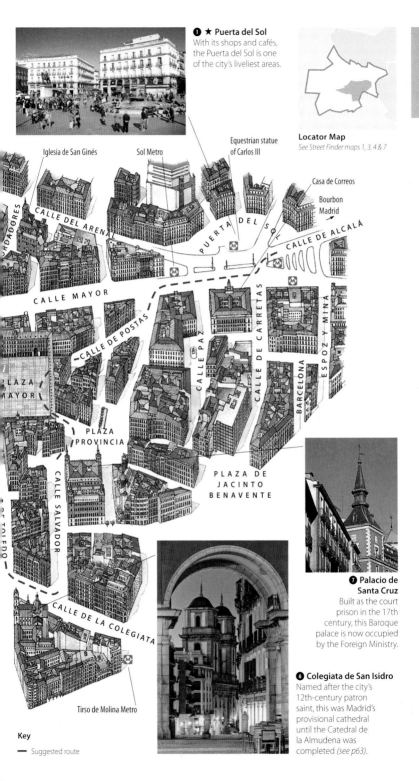

❶ ★ Puerta del Sol
With its shops and cafés, the Puerta del Sol is one of the city's liveliest areas.

Locator Map
See Street Finder maps 1, 3, 4 & 7

Iglesia de San Ginés

Sol Metro

Equestrian statue of Carlos III

Casa de Correos

Bourbon Madrid

CALLE DEL ARENAL

PUERTA DEL SOL

CALLE DE ALCALÁ

CALLE MAYOR

CALLE DE POSTAS

CALLE PAZ

CALLE DE CARRETAS

ESPOZ Y MINA

BARCELONA

PLAZA MAYOR

PLAZA PROVINCIA

PLAZA DE JACINTO BENAVENTE

CALLE SALVADOR

CALLE DE LA COLEGIATA

Tirso de Molina Metro

❼ Palacio de Santa Cruz
Built as the court prison in the 17th century, this Baroque palace is now occupied by the Foreign Ministry.

❻ Colegiata de San Isidro
Named after the city's 12th-century patron saint, this was Madrid's provisional cathedral until the Catedral de la Almudena was completed *(see p63)*.

Key

— Suggested route

Kilometre Zero, the centre of Spain's road network, at the Puerta del Sol

❶ Puerta del Sol

Map 4 F2. Ⓜ Sol.

Noisy and crowded, the Puerta del Sol ("Gateway of the Sun") makes a fitting centre for Madrid. It is one of the city's most popular meeting places; huge crowds converge on this famous square, which is now mostly pedestrianized, on their way to the shops and sights in the old part of the city.

The square marks the site of the original eastern entrance to Madrid, once occupied by a gatehouse and castle. These disappeared long ago and in their place came a succession of churches. In the late 19th century the area was turned into a square and became the centre of café society.

Today the "square" is shaped like a half moon. The equestrian statue of Carlos III in its centre is a recent addition. The square's southern side is occupied by the austere red-brick Casa de Correos, once the city's post office, built in the 1760s under Carlos III. In 1847 it became the headquarters of the Ministry of the Interior. In 1866 the clocktower, which gives the building much of its identity, was added. During the Franco regime (see p24), the police cells beneath the building were the site of many human rights abuses. In 1963, Julián Grimau, a member of the underground Communist party, allegedly fell from an upstairs window and miraculously survived, only to be executed shortly afterwards.

The building is now home to the regional government and is the focus of many festive events. At midnight on New Year's Eve dense crowds fill the square and people swallow a grape on each stroke of the clock, a tradition supposed to bring good luck for the rest of the year. Outside the building, a symbol on the ground marks Kilometre Zero, considered the centre of Spain's road network.

The buildings opposite are arranged in a semicircle and contain modern shops and cafés. At the start of Calle Alcalá is a bronze statue of the symbol of Madrid – a bear reaching for the fruit of a *madroño* (strawberry tree).

The Puerta del Sol has witnessed many important historical events. On 2 May 1808 the uprising against the occupying French forces began here, but the crowd was crushed (see p22). In 1912 the liberal prime minister José Canalejas was assassinated in the square and, in 1931, the Second Republic (see p24) was proclaimed from the balcony of the Ministry of the Interior.

❷ Plaza Mayor

Map 4 E3. Ⓜ Sol.

The Plaza Mayor forms a splendid rectangular square, complete with balconies, pinnacles,

Allegorical paintings on the Casa de la Panadería, Plaza Mayor

dormer windows and steep slate roofs. The square, with its theatrical atmosphere, has a noticeably Castilian character. Much was expected to happen here and a great deal did – bullfights, executions, pageants and trials by the Inquisition *(see p21)* – all watched by crowds, often in the presence of the reigning king and queen.

The first great public scene in the Plaza Mayor was the canonization of Madrid's patron, San Isidro, in 1622. A year earlier, the execution of Rodrigo Calderón, secretary to Felipe III, was held here. Although hated by the Madrid populace, Calderón bore himself with such dignity on the day of his death that the phrase "proud as Rodrigo on the scaffold" survives to this day. Perhaps the greatest occasion of all, however, was the arrival – from Italy – of Carlos III in 1760.

Construction of the square started in 1617, and was completed in just two years, replacing slum houses on the site. Its architect, Juan Gómez de Mora, was successor to Juan de Herrera, designer of El Escorial *(see pp128–31)*, Felipe II's austere monastery-palace. Mora echoed the style of his master, softening it slightly. The square was later reformed by Juan de Villanueva. The fanciest part of the arcaded construction is the **Casa de la Panadería** (bakery). Its façade is decorated with allegorical paintings.

The **equestrian statue** in the centre is of Felipe III, who ordered the square to be built. Begun by the Italian Giovanni de Bologna and finished by his pupil Pietro Tacca in 1616, the statue was moved here in 1848 from the Casa de Campo *(see p116)*. Nowadays the square is lined with cafés and hosts a collectors' market on Sundays. The southern exit leads into the Calle de Toledo towards the streets where El Rastro, Madrid's famous flea market *(see p65)*, is held. A flight of steps in the southwest corner of the square takes you under the Arco de Cuchilleros to the Calle de Cuchilleros, where there are a number of *mesones*, traditional restaurants.

The 20th-century Mercado de San Miguel

❸ Mercado de San Miguel

Plaza de San Miguel. **Map** 4 D3.
Tel 91 542 49 36. 🚇 Sol. **Open** 10am–midnight daily (to 2am Thu–Sat).

Although there are larger markets in Madrid, the Mercado de San Miguel is the last surviving example in the capital of a marketplace constructed from iron. The unique single-level, glassed-in market was built in 1914–15. It stands on the site of the former Iglesia de San Miguel de los Octoes, which was demolished in 1810 during the reign of Joseph Bonaparte. The market boasts excellent delicatessen stalls selling cheese, ham and seafood. There are also a number of bars and restaurants. At weekends it gets crowded.

❹ Plaza de la Villa

Map 4 D3. 🚇 Ópera, Sol.

This much restored and remodelled square is one of Madrid's most atmospheric spots, surrounded by many historic buildings.

The oldest building is the early 15th-century **Torre de los Lujanes**, with its Gothic portal and Mudéjar-style horseshoe arches. France's François I was allegedly imprisoned in it following his defeat at the Battle of Pavia in 1525. The **Casa de Cisneros** was built in 1537 for the nephew of Cardinal Cisneros,

founder of the historic University of Alcalá *(see p137)*. The façade on Calle de Sacramento is an excellent example of the Plateresque style – early Spanish Renaissance with fine detail.

Linked to this building by an enclosed bridge is the **old town hall** *(antiguo ayuntamiento)*. Designed in the 1640s by Juan Gómez de Mora, architect of the Plaza Mayor, it exhibits the same combination of steep roofs with dormer windows, steeple-like towers at the corners and an austere brick-and-stone façade. Before construction was completed, more than 30 years later, the building had acquired handsome Baroque doorways. A balcony was later added by Juan de Villanueva, architect of the Prado *(see pp82–5)*, so that the royal family could watch Corpus Christi processions passing by.

Portal of the Torre de los Lujanes

❺ Basílica Pontificia de San Miguel

Calle de San Justo 4. **Map** 4 D3. **Tel** 91 548 40 11. 🚇 Sol. **Open** 10am–1:15pm, 6–9pm daily. ✉ 🌐 **bsmiguel.es**

Standing on the site of an old Romanesque church dedicated to two local child-martyrs put to death by the Romans, this building is a rare example of Bourbon-inspired Baroque in the middle of old Madrid. It was built for Don Luis de Borbón y Farnesio, the youngest son of Felipe V and Archbishop of Toledo at only five years of age.

Several architects had a hand in its design and construction between 1739 and 1746. The pediment and twin bell towers topping its convex façade were, however, added later. Four allegorical statues, representing Charity, Fortitude, Faith and Hope, grace the elegant façade. There are also carvings depicting the two child-martyrs, Justo and Pastor.

Inside, there is a single nave, and the roof is supported only by the curved and crossing arches sprouting from the exterior walls. The decor is a curious mixture of old and new – the frescoes on the ceiling and the organ in the choir date from the 18th century, but many of the paintings and stained-glass windows are

Statue of Charity gracing the façade of Basílica Pontífica de San Miguel

contemporary. Today the church is administered by the Catholic organization, Opus Dei, who use it for some of their activities. One of the side chapels, which is dedicated to the organization's founder, Monsignor José María Escrivá de Balaguer (1902–75), houses an eerily lifelike statue of him. Concerts of classical music are held some evenings.

Ornate altar in the Colegiata de San Isidro

❻ Colegiata de San Isidro

Calle de Toledo 37. **Map** 4 E3. **Tel** 91 369 20 37. 🚇 La Latina. **Open** 9am–1pm, 7–9pm daily.

This twin-towered church was built in the Baroque style for the Jesuits in the mid-17th century. It was used as Madrid's unofficial cathedral until 1993 when Nuestra Señora de la Almudena (see p63) was finally completed and consecrated by the pope.

After Carlos III (1759–88) expelled the influential Jesuit order from Spain in 1767 (see p22), he commissioned Ventura Rodríguez to redesign the church's interior. It was then rededicated to St Isidore, Madrid's patron saint and, two years later, the saint's remains were brought here from the Iglesia de San Andrés. The Colegiata was returned to the Jesuits during the reign of Fernando VII (1814–33).

❼ Palacio de Santa Cruz

Plaza de Santa Cruz. **Map** 4 E3. **Tel** 91 522 44 41. 🚇 Sol. **Closed** to the public.

Commissioned by Felipe IV and constructed between 1629 and 1643 by Juan Bautista Crescendi, this Baroque building is one of the jewels of Habsburg architecture. Since 1901 it has been the Ministry of Foreign Affairs, but has also housed the Overseas Ministry, law courts and, originally, the Carcel de la Corte (city prison). It was here that the luckless participants in the autos-da-fé (Spanish inquisition trials), held in the nearby Plaza Mayor (see p48), awaited their fate. Its more famous inmates include the playwright Lope de Vega (1562–1635), imprisoned for libelling his former lover, the actress Elena Osorio. The English writer and travelling Bible salesman, George Borrow, who was accused of instigating liberal ideas, also spent three weeks here. General Rafael de Riego, who led an uprising against Fernando VII in 1820, and the famous bandit Luis Candelas spent their last hours in its cells. Candelas was a colourful Robin Hood-like character, educated in Greek and Latin, who rubbed shoulders with the aristocracy (and stole their jewels). He was executed on 6 November 1837; today one of Madrid's tourist restaurants, situated on nearby Cava de San Miguel, is named after him.

The palace underwent an extensive restoration in 1846, following a fire, and further renovations in the aftermath of the Spanish Civil War (see p24), but its original architecture remains essentially intact. The style of the building is in keeping with the area around the Plaza Mayor, with spired towers on its corners and two interior courtyards. The building only became known as the Palacio de Santa Cruz after 1846, when it was made the headquarters of Spain's Overseas Ministry.

The 17th-century Palacio de Santa Cruz – a jewel of Habsburg architecture

❽ Plaza de Santa Ana

Map 7 A3. Ⓜ Sevilla, Antón Martín.

This large pedestrian square, just four blocks southeast of the Puerta del Sol (see p48), is a popular gathering place with a lively, at times rowdy, atmosphere. Built during the reign of Napoleon Bonaparte's brother Joseph (1808–13), the square took its name from the 16th-century Convent of Santa Ana that stood here. It was demolished to make way for the square.

Monuments to two of Spain's most famous writers testify to the square's strong literary connections. At one end is the brooding marble figure of Pedro Calderón de la Barca (1600–81). Madrid-born, he was the leading playwright in the twilight years of Spain's *Siglo de Oro* (Golden Century) of arts. His best-known work is *La Vida es Sueño* (Life is a Dream). The monument, with scenes from four of Calderón's plays adorning the pedestal, was sculpted by Juan Figueras in 1878. At the other end of the square, a statue of the poet Federico García Lorca (see p32), erected in 1998, commemorates the centenary of his birth and faces the **Teatro Español**

Scene from a play by Calderón de la Barca adorning his statue

(see p80). Built in 1745, the theatre was originally known as the Teatro del Príncipe. It had to be restored in 1980 after a devastating fire.

The square's theatrical links go back even earlier, as the theatre stands on the spot of the Corral del Príncipe, one of Madrid's popular, 16th-century *corrales de comedias* (open courtyards where plays were staged). These tended to be boisterous affairs, often culminating in fights between the actors and the audience. Across from the theatre are the glassed-in balconies of **ME Madrid** (see p155), one of Madrid's classic hotels. Before the Meliá chain acquired it, the hotel's then-modest lodgings were used by bullfighters who could not afford luxurious city rooms. Now, it's a luxury modern hotel.

The other two sides of Plaza de Santa Ana and adjoining streets are home to some of the city's most popular bars and restaurants. The classic **Cervecería Alemana**, built in 1904 and once frequented by author Ernest Hemingway, is always packed with customers.

Around the corner from the theatre is the **Viva Madrid** (see p184). This well-known *taberna*, near Plaza de Santa Ana, is popular with the young and

fashionable and boasts extraordinary 19th-century ceramic tableaux. Tile landscapes also adorn the Villa Rosa, a nightclub on the corner of Plaza de Santa Ana and Calle Núñez de Arce.

❾ Real Academia de Bellas Artes

Calle de Alcalá 13. **Map** 7 A2.
Tel 91 524 08 64. Ⓜ Sevilla, Sol.
Open 10am–3pm Tue–Sun and some public hols. **Closed** some public hols.
🎟 (free Wed). 📷 11am Tue, Thu & Fri; for groups by appt. ♿
🌐 rabasf.insde.es

Dalí and Picasso are among the former students of this arts academy, housed in an 18th-century building by Churriguera. Its art gallery displays a large selection of works, including drawings by Raphael and Titian. A superb collection of old masters includes paintings by Rubens and Van Dyck. Spanish artists from the 16th to the 19th centuries are particularly well represented, with magnificent works by Ribera, Murillo, El Greco and Velázquez. One of the highlights is Zurbarán's *Fray Pedro Machado*, typical of his paintings of monks.

An entire room is devoted to Goya, a former director of the academy. On show here are his painting of Carlos IV's chief minister, Manuel Godoy, the *Burial of the Sardine*, the grim *Madhouse*, and a self-portrait painted in 1815.

Fray Pedro Machado by Zurbarán

⑩ Gran Vía

In the mid-1800s, Madrid's burgeoning middle class was pushing the city's limits outwards, destroying houses and poor districts to allow for the *Ensanche* (widening). The city fathers saw the need for a new thoroughfare – a *Gran Vía*. Departing from the haphazard growth of the past, this street was to follow a plan and be a symbol of modern Madrid. On the drawing board since 1860, with even a satirical *zarzuela (see p79)* devoted to it, the project was not approved until 1904. Inaugurated by Alfonso XIII in 1910 *(see p23)*, the street was built in three stages, each segment bearing a different name, although they are no longer used. The first, and most elegant – Avenida Conde de Peñalver (after the Mayor) – ran from Calle de Alcalá to Red de San Luis. The second phase, to the Plaza de Callao, was completed in 1922, while the final segment, ending in the Plaza de España, was built between 1925 and 1929. The new street gave architects an opportunity to prove their skill, providing a survey of early 20th-century design trends, including some of the best examples of modern architecture in the city.

The rounded Art Deco façade of this building, like many along the Gran Vía, displays a style and grandeur befitting the city's most impressive thoroughfare. Many Art Deco buildings were built as cinemas, several of which are clustered around Plaza del Callao.

The Museo Chicote cocktail bar, on the ground floor of Gran Vía 12, has an immaculately preserved Art Deco interior. It opened in 1932 and was patronized by Salvador Dalí, Frank Sinatra, Ava Gardner and Orson Welles.

Behind La Gran Peña's curved façade (No. 2) is a luxurious, increasingly popular men's club. In 1926, attempts to make Franco a member caused such a stir that the club was later taken over and used by the militia during the Civil War *(see p24)*.

Edificio la Estrella (No. 10) is a good example of the eclectic mix of Neo-Classical design and ornamental touches evident in the first buildings to have appeared along Gran Vía.

Today's Gran Vía continues to be a throbbing main artery for the city of Madrid, lined with theatres and cinemas, hotels, shops and restaurants.

The two-tiered colonnade of the Edificio Grassy on Gran Vía

⓫ Edificio Grassy

Gran Vía 1. **Map** 7 B1. **Tel** 91 532 10 07. Ⓜ Banco de España, Sevilla. Museum: **Open** 5–6pm Thu, noon–1pm Fri. 📷 book by phone. 🅦 grassy.es

Designed by Eladio Laredo on a small sliver of land between the Gran Vía and the Calle de Caballero de Gracia, the Grassy building boasts a circular end-tower similar to that of the nearby Edificio Metrópolis (see p78). It is crowned by a round, two-tiered colonnade. It was built in 1917, but became known as the Grassy building in the 1950s, after the jewellery shop that has occupied the ground floor since then. The prestigious jewellery firm, established in 1923, specializes in watches and, in the basement, is the **Museo de Reloj Grassy**, a collection of 500 timepieces from the 16th to 19th centuries, including rare clocks which belonged to European royalty.

Clock at the Grassy museum

⓬ Telefónica

Gran Vía 28. **Map** 4 F1, 7 A1. Ⓜ Gran Vía, Callao. Museum: **Tel** 91 580 87 00. **Open** 10am–8pm Tue–Sun. 📷 ♿ 📷 call to arrange. 🅦 espacio. fundaciontelefonica.com

If the Telefónica building has an American look to it, it is because it was inspired by Manhattan's skyscrapers and designed by an American – Louis S Weeks – although the Spanish architect Ignacio de Cárdenas was made officially responsible in order to secure planning permission. Built between 1926 and 1929 to house the Spanish telephone company, it was Madrid's tallest building. Its façade consists of tapered setbacks, ending in a central tower 81 m (266 ft) tall. The little exterior ornamentation it has was added by Cárdenas so that the building would seem less out of place amid the neighbouring architecture. The clear view from the upper floors enabled the Republican defenders of the city to monitor the movements of besieging Nationalists in the Spanish Civil War (see p24).

Part of the building, which is entered from Calle de Fuencarral, is used for temporary and permanent exhibitions. There is a permanent exhibition of the evolution of telecommunications. Displays range from old phones, including the one used by Alfonso XIII to inaugurate Madrid's automatic telephone service in 1926, to a bank of switchboards with 19 life-size operators and sound effects. The exhibition rooms are arranged around a gallery that overlooks the main foyer. Some of the Foundation's formidable collection of modern art is now on long-term loan to the Museo Reina Sofía (see pp88–91).

The Telefónica – a Manhattan-style skyscraper from the 1920s

⓭ Plaza del Callao

Plaza del Callao. **Map** 4 E1. Ⓜ Callao.

Situated at the junction of Gran Vía and Calle de Preciados, the Plaza del Callao was named after a naval battle off the coast of Callao, Peru, in 1866. This square was once the movie mecca of film-loving Madrid, but today the only two surviving cinemas are the Art Deco Cine Callao, completed in 1927, and the Capitol (see below). Most of the other cinemas along the Gran Vía have been converted into musical theatres or shops.

Housed in the Capitol building is the Capitol cinema, built in 1933. A superb example of Art Deco architecture, its features include a covered entrance and a vast, box-like interior, 35 m (115 ft) wide, adorned with simple lines and curves.

The Capitol cinema, a good example of Art Deco architecture

Chapel with ornate altar in the Monasterio de las Descalzas Reales

⓮ Monasterio de las Descalzas Reales

Plaza de las Descalzas 3. **Map** 4 E2. **Tel** 91 454 88 00. Sol, Callao. **Open** 10am–2pm, 4–6:30pm Tue–Sat, 10am–3pm Sun & public hols (last adm 1 hour before closing). **Closed** 1 & 6 Jan, Easter week, 1 & 15 May, 1 & 9 Nov, 24–25 & 31 Dec. (free for EU residents on Wed & after 4pm on Thu). **patrimonionacional.es**

Madrid's most notable religious building is also a rare surviving example of 16th-century architecture in the city. Around 1560, Felipe II's sister Doña Juana converted the medieval palace which stood here into a convent for nuns and women of the royal household. Her rank, and that of her fellow nuns, accounts for the vast store of art and wealth of the Descalzas Reales (Royal Barefoot Sisters).

The stairway has a fresco of Felipe IV with his family, and a fine ceiling by Claudio Coello. It leads to a first-floor cloister, ringed with chapels containing paintings and precious objects. The main chapel houses Doña Juana's tomb. The Sala de Tapices (Tapestries Room) contains a series of 17th-century tapestries. There are also works by Brueghel the Elder, Titian, Zurbarán, Murillo and Ribera.

⓯ Iglesia de San Ginés de Arlés

Calle Arenal 13. **Map** 4 E2. **Tel** 91 429 70 52. Ópera. **Open** 9:30am–1pm, 6–8:30pm Mon–Sat, 6–8:30pm Sun.

This 17th-century church has numerous chapels with some of Madrid's most outstanding frescoes, sculptures and paintings. Luca Giordano, El Greco, and Alonso Cano are a few of the artists on display.

Legend has it that an alligator, brought by Alonso de Montalbán (Isabel la Católica's admiral) in 1522, rested under the altar. The stuffed animal now stands in the Capilla del Lagarto (Chapel of the Alligator), and is a popular attraction for visitors.

⓰ Calle de Preciados

Map 4 F2. Sol, Callao.

This pedestrian street leading north from Puerta del Sol to the Plaza de Santo Domingo is now the domain of shoppers. It was originally a humble country path from the centre of old Madrid to the orchards and threshing floors of the Convent of San Martín which, until 1810, faced the

Monasterio de las Descalzas Reales. In the 17th century two brothers, the Preciados, purchased land from the convent to build their homes. They were in charge of controlling official weights and measures used for trade in Madrid.

Calle de Preciados acquired its contemporary look during the *Ensanche* (urban renewal) of the mid-19th century. It is the birthplace of Spain's most successful department store chain, El Corte Inglés. Adjoining the Plaza del Callao is a modern building occupied by FNAC, one of the city's best sources for music, videos and books. Between the two superstores, trendy boutiques share space with old-fashioned shops.

⓱ Museo Cerralbo

Calle de Ventura Rodríguez 17. **Map** 1 C5. **Tel** 91 547 36 46. Plaza de España, Ventura Rodríguez. **Open** 9:30am–3pm Tue–Sat, 5–8pm Thu, 10am–3pm Sun. (free Sun). **Closed** public hols. except summer (by appt). **museocerralbo.mcu.es**

This 19th-century mansion is a monument to Enrique de Aguilera y Gamboa, the 17th

Main staircase of the exuberant Museo Cerralbo

Marquis of Cerralbo. He bequeathed his lifetime's collection of art and artifacts to the nation in 1922, which ranges from Iberian pottery to 18th-century marble busts.

One of the star exhibits is El Greco's *The Ecstasy of Saint Francis of Assisi*. There are also paintings by Ribera, Zurbarán, Alonso Cano and Goya.

The focal point of the main floor is the ballroom, lavishly decorated with mirrors.

⑱ Plaza de España

Map 1 C5. Ⓜ Plaza de España.

One of Madrid's busiest traffic intersections and most popular meeting places is the Plaza de España. In the 18th and 19th centuries the square was occupied by military barracks, built here because of the square's proximity to the Palacio Real *(see pp58–61)*. However, further expansion of Madrid resulted in it remaining a public space.

The square acquired its present appearance during the Franco period with the construction of the massive **Edificio España**. Commissioned by the Metropolitana real estate developers, the 26-floor concrete structure was built between 1947 and 1953, when Spain was isolated from the Western world and materials were scarce. It was seen as a triumph of "autarchy" *(see p24)*. The imposing main tower is flanked by two 17-floor wings. The building is no longer in use.

Metropolitana also built the 33-floor **Torre de Madrid** on the corner of Plaza de España and Calle de la Princesa. Completed in 1957 and nicknamed La Jirafa (the Giraffe), for a time it was the tallest concrete structure in the world.

The most attractive part of the square is its centre, with a massive stone obelisk built in 1928. In front of it is a statue of Cervantes *(see p137)*. Below him, Don Quixote rides his horse while Sancho Panza trots alongside on his donkey.

⑲ Palacio del Senado

Plaza de la Marina Española. **Map** 3 C1.
Tel 91 538 13 75. Ⓜ Plaza de España,
Ópera. **Open** tours by appt
(email: visitas@senado.es).
✉ ♿ Ⓦ **senado.es**

The upper house of the Cortes (Spanish parliament) is installed in a 16th-century monastery, adapted in 1814 for the purpose. It became the Senate headquarters when a two-chamber system was introduced 23 years later.

The monastery's courtyards were covered to create more meeting rooms. Some, such as the Salón de los Pasos Perdidos (Hall of the Lost Footsteps), contain enormous paintings depicting great moments in Spanish history. Among these are the surrender of Granada and Queen Regent María Cristina swearing to uphold the Constitution in 1897.

The library is a magnificent example of English Gothic style, dating from the turn of the 20th century. Ornate tiers of black metal bookcases contain 14,000 volumes, including a copy of Nebrija's *Gramática*, the first Spanish grammar.

In 1991 a modern granite-and-glass circular wing was added at the back of the building to create more space.

The Palacio del Senado is open to the public for three days, free of charge, in early December each year, to mark the establishment of the 1978 Constitution on 6 December.

Old assembly hall of the Palacio del Senado, housed in the church of the monastery

Imposing entrance to the Monasterio de la Encarnación

⑳ Monasterio de la Encarnación

Plaza de la Encarnación 1. **Map** 3 C1.
Tel 91 454 88 00. Ⓜ Ópera, Santo
Domingo. **Open** 10am–2pm,
4–6:30pm Tue–Sat, 10am–3pm
Sun & public hols (last adm1 hour
before closing). **Closed** 14 May, 24,
25 & 31 Dec. 🎫 (free for EU residents
on Wed & after 4pm on Thu). ♿ 📷
Ⓦ **patrimonionacional.es**

Set in a lovely tree-shaded square, this Augustinian convent was founded in 1611 for Margaret of Austria, wife of Felipe III. The architect, Juan Gómez de Mora, also built the Plaza Mayor *(see pp48–9)*.

Still inhabited by nuns, the convent has the atmosphere of old Castile, with its Talavera tiles, exposed beams and portraits of royal benefactors. It also contains a collection of 17th-century art, with paintings by José de Ribera and Vicente Carducho and a polychrome wooden statue *Cristo Yacente* (*Lying Christ*) by Gregorio Fernández. The main attraction is the reliquary chamber which is used to store the bones of saints. There is also a phial of St Pantaleon's dried blood which, according to legend, liquifies every 27 July, the saint's birthday. The church, rebuilt by Ventura Rodríguez after a fire in 1767, has paintings by Francisco Bayeu and frescoes by González Velázquez.

㉑ Palacio Real

Madrid's vast and lavish Royal Palace was built to impress. The site, on a high bluff overlooking the Río Manzanares, had been occupied for centuries by a royal fortress but, after a fire in 1734, Felipe V commissioned a truly palatial replacement. Construction lasted 17 years, spanning the reign of two Bourbon monarchs, and much of the exuberant decor reflects the tastes of Carlos III and Carlos IV *(see p22)*. The palace was used by the royal family until the abdication of Alfonso XIII in 1931. The current royal family live in the more modest Zarzuela Palace outside Madrid, but the Royal Palace is still used for state occasions. The Museum of Royal Collections is due to open near the palace in late 2016. It will house paintings, tapestries and carriages.

★ Dining Room
This gallery was decorated in 1879. Its chandeliers, ceiling paintings and tapestries evoke the grandeur of Bourbon and Habsburg entertaining.

★ Porcelain Room
The walls and ceiling of this room, built on the orders of Carlos III, are entirely covered in royal porcelain from the Buen Retiro factory. Most of the porcelain is green and white, and depicts cherubs and wreaths.

First floor

★ Gasparini Room
Named after its Neapolitan designer, the Gasparini Room is decorated with lavish Rococo chinoiserie. The adjacent antechamber, with painted ceiling and ornate chandelier, houses Goya's portrait of Carlos IV.

The Hall of Columns, once used for royal banquets, is decorated with 16th-century bronzes and Roman imperial busts.

Plaza de Armas
The square forms the entrance to the Pharmacy, the Palace and the Royal Armoury. At noon, on the first Wednesday of each month, visitors can see the changing of the guard.

VISITORS' CHECKLIST

Practical Information
Calle de Bailén. **Map** 3 C2.
Tel 91 454 88 00.
W patrimonionacional.es
Open Apr–Sep: 10am–8pm daily; Oct–Mar: 10am–6pm daily (last adm 1 hour before closing).
Closed 11 May, 12 Oct & 25 Dec.
(free for EU residents: Apr–Sep: Wed & Thu after 6pm, Oct–Mar: Wed & Thu after 4pm).

Transport
Ópera. 3, 25, 39, 148.

Entrance Hall
A marble staircase by Sabatini, next to the statue of Carlos III as a Roman emperor, leads to the main floor. The painted Rococo ceiling by Giaquinto vividly depicts allegorical scenes.

Billiards·room

Pharmacy
This unique collection includes decorated Talavera pottery storage jars and herb drawers. The Pharmacy Museum has recipe books detailing medications prescribed for the royal family.

Hall of the Halberdiers

Entrance

Key to Floorplan

☐ Exhibition rooms
☐ Entrance rooms
☐ Carlos III rooms
☐ Chapel rooms
☐ Carlos IV rooms

Visitors' centre

Plaza de Armas

★ Throne Room
This room is unique in the palace as it retains the original decor from the days of Carlos III. The huge mirrors were made in the royal glass factory of La Granja.

Royal Armoury

The Museum of Royal Collections

Exploring the Palacio Real

This splendid Royal Palace stands on the site of the original Moorish fortress, or alcázar, which served as a residence for visiting royals after the Christian conquest of Madrid in 1085 *(see p19)*. Following extensive modifications in 1561, it became the residence of Felipe II until the completion of El Escorial *(see pp128–31)* in 1584. The alcázar was destroyed by fire on Christmas Eve 1734, during the reign of Felipe V. This suited Spain's first Bourbon king well – his idea of a royal palace was the Versailles of his childhood, and so he commissioned a new royal palace decorated in the French style.

Stately façade of the Palacio Real, seen from the Plaza de Armas

The Palace

Most of the limestone and granite building is the work of Italian Giovanni Battista Sachetti, with later modifications by other architects like Sabatini. So vast was the plan that construction lasted from 1738 to 1755, by which time Felipe V

was dead. His son, Carlos III, became the first royal resident. The palace remained the official home of the Spanish royal family until Alfonso XIII left for exile in 1931. The distribution of rooms and the interior decoration were altered by successive monarchs.

General Franco *(see p24)* also used the palace – known at the time as the Palacio de Oriente – for official business, and would address the crowds from the balcony overlooking the Plaza de Oriente *(see p62)*. Today it is used for state functions.

Visitors enter the palace from the **Plaza de Armas**. The main entrance is crowned by a pediment with a clock and two bells, one of which dates from 1637 and is a survivor of the fire which destroyed the old alcázar. The interior is remarkable for its size and for the exuberant decor, carpets, tapestries and antique furnishings in many of the rooms.

Grand entrance stairway with 72 steps in Toledo marble

Entrance Rooms

The Toledo marble in the main stairway, presided over by ceiling frescoes by Corrado Giaquinto, provides a regal taste of what is to follow. The first port of call is the **Salón de los Alabarderos** (Hall of the Halberdiers, or palace guards), decorated with a fresco by Tiépolo. Adjoining it is the **Salón de Columnas** (Hall of Columns), which served as the banquet hall until the new dining hall was incorporated in the 19th century. Today it is used for receptions and functions – the charter by which Spain joined the EU was signed here, on the 19th-century table supported by sphinxes. There are five tapestries of the Deeds of the Apostles, based on cartoons by Raphael and originally commissioned by the Vatican.

Finally, visitors enter the Carlos III rooms through the 18th-century Rococo **Salón del Trono** (Throne Room), whose decor has remained constant throughout generations of rulers. Completed in 1772, it has two rock crystal chandeliers, numerous candelabra and mirrors, and walls of crimson velvet with silver embroidery. The twin thrones are recent (1977), while the bronze lions that guard them date from 1651. The room is used for functions, such as the royal reception on 12 October (the Día de la Hispanidad) or the yearly reception for the diplomatic corps posted in Madrid.

Regal crimson-and-gold Throne Room with a rock crystal chandelier

Carlos III Rooms

Leading off from the Throne Room are three smaller halls named after Mattia Gasparini, the original decorator. These were the king's private chambers. He would take his meals in the **Sala de Gasparini** – lonely affairs considering the queen had her own dining room. The **Ante-cámara de Gasparini** contains four paintings by Goya of Carlos IV and María Luisa de Parma. In the **Cámara de Gasparini** the king would be dressed, usually in the presence of courtiers. This is the only room to retain its original decor – Rococo and Oriental, with a stucco ceiling and embroidered silk walls.

A small room, the **Tranvía de Carlos III**, leads into the former bedroom of Carlos III. In the Baroque **Sala de Porcelana** (Porcelain Room), 18th-century porcelain from the Buen Retiro factory covers the walls. The **Salita Amarilla** (Yellow Room), named after the tapestry covering the walls, leads to the Gala Dining Hall.

Portrait of *Carlos IV* by Goya in the Antecámara de Gasparini

Dining Room

This 400-sq m (4,300-sq ft) banquet hall was formed in 1879 when the queen's private chambers were joined together, during the reign of Alfonso XII. It is richly adorned with gold plate decoration on the ceiling and walls, frescoes, chandeliers, Flemish tapestries, Chinese

The lavish dining room, formerly the queen's private chambers

vases and embroidered curtains. The table can accommodate up to 160 diners.

The rooms leading off from the dining room house exhibits of royal household possessions. The room immediately off the dining hall is devoted to commemorative medals, and also contains the elaborate centrepiece used during banquets. Other rooms contain the silverware, china, crystal and an extraordinary collection of musical instruments, including unique Stradivarius examples.

Chapel Rooms

Built in 1749–57, the chapel is still used for religious services, and also for musical soirées. While the decor is luxurious, it is the dome, with its murals by Giaquinto, that immediately catches the eye.

Next, visitors pass through the **Salón de Paso** and into María Cristina's chambers (originally Carlos IV rooms). During the reign of Alfonso XII these four small rooms served as an American-style billiards room, Oriental-style smoking room, the **Salón de Estucos** (queen's bedroom) and the **Gabinete de Maderas de Indias**, used as an office.

Pharmacy and Armoury

Returning to the Plaza de Armas, near the ticket office you come to the **Real Farmacia** (Royal Pharmacy) founded by Felipe II in 1594. The pharmacy is a warren of rooms, with jars and vials bearing the names of different potions and medicinal plants.

On the other side of the plaza is the **Real Armería** (Royal Armoury), housed in a pavilion built in 1897 after the original armoury was destroyed by fire. It contains weapons and royal suits of armour. On display is an elaborate suit of armour which once belonged to Carlos I, the Holy Roman Emperor Charles V. The armoury could be considered as Madrid's first museum because it has been open to the public since Felipe II inherited the collection from his father. It originally contained weapons used by Spanish kings and those from defeated enemy armies.

Armour of Carlos I

Equestrian statue of Felipe IV, by Pietro Tacca, Plaza de Oriente

㉒ Plaza de Oriente

Map 3 C2. 🚇 Ópera.

During his days as King of Spain, Joseph Bonaparte (José I) carved out this stirrup-shaped space from the jumble of buildings to the east of the Palacio Real *(see pp58–61)*, providing the view of the palace enjoyed today.

The square was once an important meeting place for state occasions: kings, queens and dictators all made public appearances on the palace balcony facing the plaza. The many statues of early kings which stand here were originally intended to adorn the roofline of the Palacio Real, but proved to be too heavy. The equestrian statue of Felipe IV in the centre of the square is by Italian sculptor Pietro Tacca, and is based on drawings by Velázquez.

In the southeast corner of the plaza is the **Café de Oriente** *(see p164)*, with outdoor tables for enjoying the view.

㉓ Teatro Real

Plaza de Oriente. **Map** 4 D2. **Tel** 91 516 06 60 (info); 90 224 48 48 (tickets). 🚇 Ópera. **Open** 10:30am–1pm daily. **Closed** Aug. 🎫 🅿 ♿ 🅰 🌐 teatro-real.com

Madrid's opera house stands opposite the Palacio Real *(see pp58–61)* on the Plaza de Oriente. It is an imposing six-sided grey building, made all the more impressive by the six floors below street level as well as the nine floors visible above ground.

It was originally built around 1850. However, much of the structure that exists today is the result of a massive project to renovate the theatre, which took place between 1991 and 1997. The horseshoe-shaped main theatre area, decorated in red and gold with seating on five levels, holds 1,630 spectators and the stage area measures 1,430 sq m (15,400 sq ft). This, together with the curtain and the magnificent crystal chandelier weighing 2.5 tonnes, are among the theatre's noteworthy features.

On the second floor, there are four large foyers arranged around the main hall. They contain tapestries, paintings, mirrors, chandeliers and antiques. All of them are laid with carpets produced especially for the theatre by the Manuel Morón workshop in Ciudad Real, south of Madrid.

The second-floor restaurant is also worth seeing. It has a ceiling representing Madrid's starlit sky as it was on the night of the theatre's inauguration. It is open for both lunch and dinner (at 9pm), but is reserved for theatre-goers on nights when there are performances. The restaurant is located in

Costume used in *Anne Boleyn*

what was originally the ballroom, where Isabel II would often throw lively parties. On display are costumes from the operas *Aïda* and *Anne Boleyn*.

On the sixth floor there is a pleasant cafeteria which has a good view overlooking the Plaza de Oriente and the Palacio Real, but it is reserved for those who attend a performance.

The site has always been associated with the stage. In 1708, an Italian company built a small theatre here, which was demolished in 1735 to be replaced by a more ambitious building. However, due to the presence of underground streams, this theatre suffered severe structural problems. In 1816, it was torn down to make way for a modern opera house instigated by Fernando VII. Construction dragged on in fits and starts for 32 years. The theatre was finally inaugurated

Awe-inspiring interior of Madrid's opera house, the Teatro Real

in 1850 by Isabel II on her 20th birthday. A production of Gaetano Donizetti's *La Favorita* marked the occasion, and the theatre became a centre of Madrid culture until the late 1920s. It appeared, however, that the new building was beset with problems just like its predecessor, and needed constant repair work to keep it upright. In the Spanish Civil War *(see p24)* it was used as a weapons depot and suffered further damage from an explosion. It was finally closed in 1988.

In 1991, an ambitious project to renovate the building was also plagued with problems. The architect died of a heart attack while inspecting the works and, when the theatre finally opened in October 1997 with a performance of Falla's *The Three-Cornered Hat*, it was way over budget and five years behind schedule.

㉔ Iglesia de San Nicolás

Plaza de San Nicolás 1. **Map** 3 C2. **Tel** 91 559 40 64. 🚇 Ópera. **Open** 8:30–9:30am, 6:30–8:30pm daily. ✝ Mass in Italian Oct–Jun noon Sun. 📷 by appt.

The first mention of the church of San Nicolás de Bari is in a document written in 1202. Its brick tower, which is decorated

The 12th-century Mudéjar-style brick tower of the Iglesia de San Nicolás

View of the Catedral de la Almudena and the Palacio Real

with horseshoe arches, is the oldest surviving religious structure in Madrid. Thought to date from the 12th century, the tower is Mudéjar in style, and may well have originally been the minaret of a Moorish mosque.

㉕ Catedral de la Almudena

Calle de Bailén 8–10. **Map** 3 C2. **Tel** 91 542 22 00. 🚇 Ópera. Cathedral: **Open** 9am–8:30pm daily (Jul & Aug: 10am–9pm). Museum: **Open** 10am–2:30pm Mon–Sat. Crypt: **Open** 10am–8pm daily. ♿

The building of Madrid's cathedral began in 1883, but it was not until 1993 that it was completed and subsequently inaugurated by Pope John Paul II. The slow construction, which ceased completely during the Spanish Civil War, involved several architects. The cathedral's Neo-Gothic grey and white façade resembles that of the Palacio Real, which stands opposite. The crypt houses a 16th-century image of the *Virgen de la Almudena*.

㉖ Campo del Moro

Map 3 A2. 🚇 Príncipe Pío. **Open** Oct–Mar: 10am–6pm daily; Apr–Sep: 10am–8pm daily. **Closed** 11 May, 12 Oct & 25 Dec. 🌐 patrimonionacional.es.

The Campo del Moro (Field of the Moor) is a pleasing park, rising steeply from the Río Manzanares to offer one of the finest views of the Palacio Real *(see pp58–61)*. The park has a varied history. In 1109, a Moorish army, led by Ali ben Yusuf, set up camp here – hence the name. The park later became a jousting ground for Christian knights.

In the late 19th century, it was used as a playground for royal children and landscaped in what is described as the English style – with winding paths, grass and woodland, as well as fountains and statues.

In 1931, under the Second Republic *(see p24)*, the Campo del Moro was opened to the public. Under Franco it was closed again and was not reopened until 1978.

The Muralla Árabe – archeological remains of Madrid's Moorish heritage

㉗ Muralla Árabe

Parque del Emir Mohamed I, Cuesta de la Vega. **Map** 3 C3. 🚇 Opera. **Open** dawn–sunset.

Other than the city's name, which comes from the Arabic *Mayrit*, a small stretch of outer defence wall is all that is left of Madrid's Moorish heritage. The Muralla Árabe (Arab Wall) stands to the south of the Catedral de Nuestra Señora de la Almudena, down the steep Cuesta de la Vega street. It is believed that one of the main gateways to the Moorish town stood near this site *(see p19)*. The wall, constructed from flintstone blocks of various shapes and sizes, rises over 3 m (10 ft) along one side of the Parque del Emir Mohamed I. The park is named after the Moorish leader who founded Madrid.

The site was discovered while excavations were being carried out in 1953. As well as Moorish ruins dating from the ninth century, there is also a segment of a 12th-century Christian wall. On the other side of the wall are examples of typically Moorish brick horseshoe arches.

Across the street, a plaque and an image of the Virgin identify this as the spot where the statue of the Virgen de la Almudena was discovered in 1085 (*almudena* is from the Arabic for "outer wall"), possibly hidden from the Moors.

During the summer, outdoor concerts and plays have been held in Parque del Emir Mohamed I. At other times, this treeless area is not well patrolled, and you should not visit the park on your own or after dark.

㉘ San Francisco el Grande

Plaza de San Francisco. **Map** 3 B4. **Tel** 91 365 38 00. 🚇 La Latina, Puerta de Toledo. Museum: **Open** 10:30am–12:30pm, 4–6pm Tue–Fri (Jul & Aug: 5–7pm). 🅿 for guided tours. Capilla del Cristo de los Dolores: **Open** 10am–1pm Sat. 🗎

The site of this basilica was previously occupied by a Franciscan convent founded, according to legend, by St Francis of Assisi in 1217. When Felipe II made Madrid the capital of Spain in 1561 (*see p21*), the convent's wealth and status grew, and it was made custodian of the "Holy Places" conquered by the crusaders.

In 1760 Carlos III ordained that the convent be replaced by a Neo-Classical basilica. The architect, Francisco Cabezas, designed a dome to measure over 33 m (108 ft) in diameter. However, in 1768, work had to be halted due to complications with the size. It was finally completed in 1784 by Francesco Sabatini.

The basilica was taken over by the Foreign Ministry in 1835 and used as an army barracks. A few years later it was made into a national pantheon. The Franciscan friars had to leave, and they only returned in 1926.

In 1878, a renovation project was initiated and the church decorated extravagantly. The façade is dominated by the dome and twin towers, which house 19 bells, 11 of which form the church's carillon.

The seven main doors were carved in walnut by Juan Guas, under the direction of sculptor Antonio Varela. The central image above the doors is of Christ crucified with Faith and Hope at his feet. On either side are the two thieves who were crucified with him. The panels on the doors show biblical scenes. Just inside the basilica, supported by bronze angels, are huge scallop-shaped marble bowls containing holy water.

The main chapel contains five large paintings executed by Manuel Domínguez and Alejandro Ferrant depicting the life of St Francis. The Four Evangelists, made from wood and plaster but imitating bronze, are by Sanmartí and Molinelli. The roof of the basilica and the frescoes inside have undergone restoration work. On each side of the basilica are three chapels, the most famous being the one to the left of the main entrance. This chapel boasts an early painting (dating from 1784) by Goya of San Bernardino de Siena, with the painter

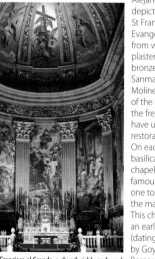

Interior of San Francisco el Grande, a church richly endowed with the work of great artists

himself appearing on the right of the picture. Work by Andrés de la Calleja and Antonio González Velázquez is also featured here. The sacristy and old cloisters can also be visited.

The adjoining Capilla del Cristo de los Dolores, dating from 1162, was designed by architect Hermano Francisco Bautista. In it is the remarkable sculpture of *Cristo de los Dolores*, with bleeding holes in Christ's hands from the nails on the cross. This polychrome statue was created in 1643 by Diego Rodríguez but is, in fact, a copy of Domingo de la Rioja's original sculpture. This statue, now in Serradilla, was venerated for its association with miracles and spent some time in the alcázar, taken there by Felipe IV.

㉙ Plaza de la Paja

Map 4 D3. 🚇 La Latina. San Andrés: **Open** 9am–1pm, 6–8pm Mon–Sat, 10am–1pm Sun. Capilla del Obispo: 🕗 10am–12:30pm Tue, 4–5:30pm Thu.

Once the focus of medieval Madrid, the area around the Plaza de la Paja – literally Straw Square – is still atmospheric. Many interesting buildings are located around the square itself and the area is pleasant to walk around.

As you climb upwards from the Calle de Segovia, a glimpse left along Calle del Príncipe Anglona yields a view of the Mudéjar-style brick tower of the **Iglesia de San Pedro**, dating from the 14th century. Ahead is the **Capilla del Obispo** (Bishop's Chapel), which

first belonged to the adjoining Palacio Vargas. One of the few examples of Gothic architecture in Madrid, the chapel has an inner door made of walnut, decorated with reliefs depicting biblical scenes. The adjacent Baroque-style **Iglesia de San Andrés**, with its cherub-covered dome, can also be visited. Since it was partially destroyed during the Spanish Civil War, little remains of the original 12th-century church. It was frequented by the patron saint of Madrid, San Isidro, who was also buried here. His remains were moved to the Basílica de Nuestra Señora del Buen in the 18th century.

Nearby is a cluster of inter-linked squares, ending in the Plaza Puerta de Moros, a reminder of the Muslim community which once occupied the area. From here, a right turn leads to the domed bulk of San Francisco el Grande, an impressive landmark.

㉚ La Latina

Map 4 D4. 🚇 La Latina.

The district of La Latina, together with the adjacent Lavapiés, is considered to be the heart of *castizo* Madrid (*see p107*). This term describes the culture of the traditional working classes of Madrid – that of the true *Madrileño*.

La Latina runs along the city's southern hillside from the Plaza Puerta de Moros through the

streets where El Rastro flea market is held. To the east it merges with Lavapiés.

La Latina's steep streets are lined with tall, narrow houses, renovated to form an attractive neighbourhood. There are a number of trendy bars around the Plaza de la Cebada, which add to the charm of this part of Madrid. It is worth wandering through simply to savour its rich atmosphere and authenticity.

㉛ El Rastro

Calle de la Ribera de Curtidores. **Map** 4 E4. 🚇 La Latina, Embajadores. **Open** 10am–2pm Sun & public hols.

Madrid's celebrated flea market (*see p173*), established in the Middle Ages, has its hub in the Plaza de Cascorro and sprawls downhill towards the Río Manzanares. The main street is the Calle de la Ribera de Curtidores, or "Tanners' Riverbank", once the centre of the slaughterhouse and tanning industries.

Colourful ceramics at the Rastro flea market

Although some people claim that El Rastro has changed a great deal since its heyday during the 19th century, there are still plenty of *Madrileños*, as well as tourists, who shop here. They come in search of a bargain from the stalls which sell a huge range of wares – anything from new furniture to second-hand clothes. For crafts and antiques head to the Plaza de General Vara del Rey and the Galerías Piquer.

The Calle de Embajadores is the area's other main street. It runs down past the dusty Baroque façade of the **Iglesia de San Cayetano**, designed by José Churriguera and Pedro de Ribera. Its interior has been restored since fire destroyed it in the Civil War (*see p24*).

Further along the same street is the former Real Fábrica de Tabacos (Royal Tobacco Factory), a late 18th-century building that is now used by the Ministry of Culture as a venue for visual arts exhibitions.

The atmospheric Plaza de la Paja, once the heart of medieval Madrid

BOURBON MADRID

To the east of Old Madrid, there once lay an idyllic district of market gardens known as the Prado – the "Meadow". In the 16th century a monastery was built here. The Habsburgs extended it to form a palace, of which only fragments now remain; the palace gardens are now the popular Parque del Retiro *(see p81)*. The Bourbon monarchs, especially Carlos III, expanded the area in the 18th

century. Around the Paseo del Prado they built grand squares with fountains, a triumphal gateway and what was to become the Museo del Prado, one of the world's greatest art galleries. Since then, additions to the area have included the Museo Reina Sofía, a collection of Spanish and international modern art, and the Museo Thyssen-Bornemisza.

Sights at a Glance

Historic Buildings and Monuments

1. Puerta de Alcalá
2. Palacio de Linares
3. Palacio de Comunicaciones
5. Banco de España
7. Bolsa de Comercio
9. Hotel Ritz
11. Westin Palace
13. Círculo de Bellas Artes
15. Edificio Metrópolis
16. Congreso de los Diputados
17. Ateneo de Madrid
18. Teatro Español
23. Real Academia Española
27. Ministerio de Agricultura
28. Real Observatorio Astronómico de Madrid
30. Estación de Atocha
31. Palacio de Fernán Núñez

Museums and Galleries

6. Museo Naval
8. Museo Nacional de Artes Decorativas

12. *Museo Thyssen-Bornemisza pp74–7*
19. Casa de Lope de Vega
20. CaixaForum
21. *Museo del Prado pp82–5*
24. Casón de Buen Retiro
29. Museo Nacional de Antropología
32. *Museo Reina Sofía (MNCARS) pp88–91*

Churches

14. Iglesia de San José
22. Iglesia de San Jerónimo el Real

Streets, Squares and Parks

4. Plaza de Cibeles
10. Fuente de Neptuno
25. Parque del Retiro
26. Real Jardín Botánico

☐ Restaurants *pp166–7*

1. Bocaíto
2. Café del Botánico
3. Café del Círculo de Bellas Artes
4. Café Murillo
5. Casa González
6. Casa Manolo
7. El Mirador del Museo
8. Europa Decó
9. Palacio Cibeles
10. Paradis de Madrid
11. Pizzería Cervantes
12. Pulpería Maceira
13. Trattoria Sant'arcangelo
14. Zerain

See also Street Finder maps 7 & 8

◀ Manicured lawns and topiary in the Parque del Retiro

For keys to symbols *see back flap*

Street-by-Street: Paseo del Prado

In the late 18th century, before the museums, sumptuous palaces and lavish hotels of Bourbon Madrid took shape, the Paseo del Prado was laid out and soon became a fashionable spot for strolling. Today the main attractions of the wide, tree-lined Paseo are its museums and galleries. Most notable are the Museo del Prado (just south of the Plaza Cánovas del Castillo) and the Museo Thyssen-Bornemisza, both displaying world-famous art collections. Among the grand monuments built under Carlos III are the Puerta de Alcalá, the Fuente de Neptuno and the Fuente de Cibeles, all at the centre of busy roundabouts.

❹ ★ Plaza de Cibeles
A fountain with a statue of the Greco-Roman goddess of nature, Cybele, stands in this square.

Banco de España Metro

⓮ Iglesia de San José
Designed by Pedro Ribera, this Baroque church was built from 1730 to 1748.

❺ Banco de España
Spain's central reserve bank is housed in this massive building with three façades at the Plaza de Cibeles.

⓭ Círculo de Bellas Artes
This cultural foundation, established in 1880, offers a theatre, library, art exhibitions and a café overlooking Calle de Alcalá.

BARQUILLO

CALLE DE ALCALÁ

CALLE DEL MARQUES

CALLE DE LOS MADRAZO

DE CUBAS

ZORRILLA

0 metres 100
0 yards 100

⓬ ★ Museo Thyssen-Bornemisza
This excellent art collection occupies the Neo-Classical Villahermosa Palace, completed in 1806.

⓫ Westin Palace
A host of international artists, politicians and film stars have stayed at this elegant, centrally located hotel.

❿ Fuente de Neptuno
In the middle of Plaza Cánovas del Castillo stands this sculpted fountain of the god Neptune in his chariot.

PLAZA CÁNOVAS DEL CASTILLO

Museo del Prado

❶ ★ Puerta de Alcalá
Sculpted from granite, this former gateway into the city is especially beautiful when floodlit at night.

❸ Palacio de Comunicaciones
Madrid's city council is headquartered in this ornate building, often likened to a wedding cake.

Locator Map
See Street Finder maps 7 & 8

❷ Palacio de Linares
This grandly decorated late 19th-century palace now houses the Casa de América, an organization that promotes Latin American culture.

❽ Museo Nacional de Artes Decorativas
This museum, near the Retiro, was founded in 1912 as a showcase for the Spanish manufacturing industry and crafts.

❻ Museo Naval
Part of the Ministry of Defence, this museum contains a wealth of navigational instruments, maps, models of ships and reconstructions of cabins.

❼ Bolsa de Comercio
Madrid's stock exchange is housed in this attractive Neo-Classical building. Visitors can view events on the trading floor from a gallery.

❾ Hotel Ritz
With its *belle époque* interior, the Ritz is one of the most elegant hotels in all of Spain.

Key

— Suggested route

For keys to symbols *see back flap*

View through the central arch of the Puerta de Alcalá

❶ Puerta de Alcalá

Map 8 D1. 🔵 Retiro.

This ceremonial gateway is the grandest of the monuments erected by Carlos III (see p27) in his efforts to improve eastern Madrid. Designed by Francesco Sabatini, it replaced a smaller Baroque gateway which had been built by Felipe III (see p22) for his wife's entry into Madrid.

Construction of the gate was started in 1769 and lasted a total of nine years. It was built from granite in Neo-Classical style, with a lofty pediment and sculpted angels. It has five arches – three central and two outer rectangular ones.

Until the mid-19th century, the gateway marked the city's easternmost boundary. It now stands in the busy Plaza de la Independencia, and is best seen when floodlit at night.

❷ Palacio de Linares

Plaza de Cibeles 2. **Map** 8 D1.
Tel 91 595 48 00. 🔵 Banco de España.
Open Sat & Sun for guided tours only.
Closed some public hols. 🔵 🔵 11am,
noon & 1pm. Exhibition Room:
Open 11am–8pm Mon–Sun, 11am–3pm
Sun. **Closed** Aug & some public hols.
🔵 🔵 🔵 🔵 **casamerica.es**

In 1873 Amadeo I (see p27) rewarded the Madrid banker, José de Murga, for his financial support by granting him the title of Marqués de Linares. The newly designated aristocrat quickly set about building himself the most luxurious, palatial residence Madrid had ever known. The rooms inside the palace are an extravaganza of ornate Rococo decor, resplendent with gold plate, inlaid wood and marble floors, glittering chandeliers, nubile nymphs and allegorical murals. The most striking rooms are on the first floor. They include the gala dining room, ballroom, the Salón Chino (Oriental Room) and Byzantine-style chapel. In the garden is the Pabellón Romántico, a wooden, fairy-tale-style pavilion also known as the Casa de Muñecas (Dolls' House).

After the Marqués died, the family fortunes declined. Many furnishings and decorations were sold, and the rest disappeared during the Spanish Civil War (see p24). By 1977 the palace was almost derelict. However, it was saved by the Spanish government's decision to restore it for Madrid's year as European Capital of Culture in 1992. The main entrance to this French Baroque palace is on Plaza de Cibeles and access to the exhibition rooms is by a side entrance on Paseo de Recoletos. The building now houses the **Casa de América**, an organization which promotes Latin American art, literature and cinema.

Mailbox at the Palacio de Comunicaciones

❸ Palacio de Comunicaciones

Plaza de Cibeles. **Map** 7 C2. **Tel** 91
480 00 08. 🔵 Banco de España.
Open 10am–8pm Tue–Sun.
Closed 1 & 6 Jan, 1 May, 24, 25 & 31
Dec. 🔵 🔵 **centrocentro.org**

Occupying one corner of the Plaza de Cibeles, this impressive building was constructed to house the headquarters of Spain's postal service. Built between 1905 and 1917 by Antonio Palacios and Joaquin Otamendi, its appearance – white with tall pinnacles – is often likened to a wedding cake. In 2011, work was completed on a huge glass dome over the building's central courtyard. You can still see the old-fashioned brass letterboxes with the names of different Spanish cities and provinces that are embedded in the wall by the main entrance. The building now houses the offices of the Mayor of Madrid and the City Council, which also occupies another historical building in Plaza de la Villa. It also houses CentroCentro, a cultural centre. The restaurant and terrace on the top floor offer fabulous panoramic views of Madrid. On special occasions such as Christmas, the building is used as a backdrop for illuminations and projected images.

The height of Rococo extravagance in the Palacio de Linares ballroom

❹ Plaza de Cibeles

Map 7 C1. 🚇 Banco de España.

In addition to being one of Madrid's best-known landmarks, the Plaza de Cibeles is also one of the most beautiful. The **Fuente de Cibeles** stands in the middle of the busy traffic island at the junction of the Paseo del Prado and the Calle de Alcalá. This fine, sculpted fountain is named after Cybele, the Greco-Roman goddess of nature, and shows her sitting in her chariot, drawn by a pair of lions. Designed in the late 18th century by José Hermosilla and Ventura Rodríguez, it is considered a symbol of Madrid.

Four important buildings rise around the square, the most impressive being the **Palacio de Comunicaciones**, mockingly known as "Our Lady of Communications". On the northeast side is the **Palacio de Linares**, built in 1873 about the time of the second Bourbon restoration. In the northwest corner, surrounded by attractive gardens, is the army head-quarters, the **Cuartel General del Ejército de Tierra**, housed in the former Palacio de Buenavista. Commissioned by the Duchess of Alba in 1777, construction was twice delayed by fires.

Finally, occupying a whole block on the opposite corner, is the Venetian-Renaissance **Banco de España**, restored to its 19th-century magnificence.

❺ Banco de España

Calle de Alcalá 48. **Map** 7 C2. **Tel** 91 338 53 65. 🚇 Banco de España. **Open** by appt only – write to Servicio de Protocolo. 📧 🌐 bde.es

Viewing this vast building, with façades facing Paseo del Prado, Plaza de Cibeles and Calle de Alcalá, you might wonder which is the main entrance. In fact it is the one on the Paseo del Prado, used only for ceremonial occasions nowadays. The original bank dates from 1882–91 and occupied the corner of Cibeles, while new wings were added later. The Bank of Spain itself was founded in 1856.

The Fuente de Cibeles, with the Palacio de Linares in the background

The bank's vast main staircase, made of Carrara marble and overlooked by stained-glass windows with mythological and allegorical themes, leads to the Patio del Reloj, a glass-roofed central courtyard with the cashiers' windows. It is a striking example of Art Deco design. The library, which is open to researchers, is located in another large hall, the interior of which is made entirely of wrought-iron filigree, painted off-white. There is also an older, smaller library with glassed-in mahogany bookshelves.

The various meeting rooms and hallways are decorated with the bank's sizeable collection of tapestries, vases, antique furniture and paintings, including a first printing of Goya's series of etchings of bullfighting, the *Tauromaquia*. In the circular Goya room are eight further paintings by the Spanish master *(see p32)*, including portraits of Carlos IV and various governors of the Bank of Spain. In *Conde de Floridablanca in the Artist's Studio*, rather than looking out at the viewer, Goya is seen gazing at his companion.

Beneath the Patio del Reloj, 30 m (98 ft) below street level and off limits to visitors, is a chamber with an island-like structure ringed by a moat. On it is the vault containing the bank's gold. Prior to sophisti-cated security gadgetry, this chamber would immediately flood were there any threat of a bank robbery.

❻ Museo Naval

Paseo del Prado 5. **Map** 7 C2. **Tel** 91 523 85 16. 🚇 Banco de España. **Open** 10am–6:45pm Tue–Sun (Aug: till 3pm). **Closed** some public hols. 📧 🚻 ♿ 🌐 museonavalmadrid.com

Added to the Ministry of Defence building in 1977, the copper-tinted glass Naval Museum has 18 display halls charting Spain's centuries-old history of seafaring. As well as a large collection of scale models of ships throughout the ages, often dating from the same period as the ships them-selves, there are numerous figureheads, amphorae, globes, astrolabes, sex-tants, compasses and maps. Weapons used in Spain's con-quest of the New World *(see p20)* also feature

Astrolabe from the Museo Naval

here. One unusual exhibit is a map of the world dated 1500. It was drawn for Isabel and Fernando *(see p26)*, and features the Americas for the first time. There is also a piece of the tree trunk upon which Hernán Cortés is said to have rested after *La Noche Triste* (The Sad Night) in 1520, when he and his men fled from Montezuma's Aztec capital, Tenochtitlán.

View from the gallery – dealers at work in the grand Bolsa de Comercio

❼ Bolsa de Comercio

Plaza de la Lealtad 1. **Map** 7 C2.
Tel 91 709 50 00. 🚇 Banco de España.
Open noon Thu by appt (2 months in
advance). **Closed** Sat, Sun & public
hols. 🖾 🖉 by appointment, email:
exposicion@grupobme.es
🌐 **bolsamadrid.es**

The Madrid Stock Exchange was
established in 1831. It operated
in 11 different, generally
inadequate venues – it was
once housed in a convent –
before moving in 1893 to the
headquarters it now occupies.
Designed by Enrique María
Repullés y Vargas, the building
took more than six years to
construct, at a cost of around
three million pesetas. Nearly
one third of this went on the
concave, Neo-Classical façade
and main entrance, with its six
giant columns topped by
Corinthian capitals.

Dealers occupy the **Sala de
Contratación** (trading floor). This
large, vaulted space of 970 sq m
(10,400 sq ft) has an ornate Neo-
Baroque clock on a marble plinth
at its centre. Visitors can watch
the proceedings from the **Salón
de los Pasos Perdidos** (Hall of

the Lost Steps). This gallery is
often used for exhibitions on the
history of the institution.

❽ Museo Nacional de Artes Decorativas

Calle de Montalbán 12. **Map** 8 D2.
Tel 91 532 64 99. 🚇 Retiro, Banco
de España. **Open** 9:30am–3pm
Tue–Sat (also 5–8pm Thu), 10am–3pm
Sun & public hols. 🖾 (free Thu pm &
Sun). 🖉 Sun (except Jul & Aug).
🌐 **mnartesdecorativas.mcu.es**

Housed in an aristocratic
residence built in the 19th
century and near the Parque del
Retiro (see p81), the National
Museum of Decorative Arts
contains an interesting
collection of furniture and *objets
d'art*. The exhibits are mainly
from Spain and date back to
Phoenician times.

On show are excellent
ceramics from Talavera de la
Reina, a town famous for the
craft, and a collection of
jewellery and ornaments from
the Far East. Other exhibits on
display include a carefully
preserved 18th-century kitchen.

❾ Hotel Ritz

Plaza de la Lealtad 5. **Map** 7 C3.
Tel 91 701 67 67. 🚇 Banco de España.
🖾 ♿ 🌐 **mandarinoriental.com/
ritzmadrid**

A few minutes' walk from the
Prado (see pp82–5), this hotel
is said to be Spain's most
extravagant. It was commissioned in 1906, around the time
that Alfonso XIII (see p27) was
embarrassed by the lack of
luxury accommodation in the
city for his wedding guests.

At the start of the Civil War
(see p24), the hotel became a
hospital, and anarchist leader
Buenaventura Durruti died here
of his wounds in 1936.

The opulence of the Ritz is
reflected in its prices (see p155).
Each room is beautifully decorated in a different style, with
carpets made by hand at the
Real Fábrica de Tapices (see p114).

❿ Fuente de Neptuno

Map 7 C3. 🚇 Banco de España.

Dominating the Plaza Cánovas
del Castillo is the majestic Fuente
de Neptuno, a fountain with a
statue of Neptune in his chariot,
being pulled by two horses. The
statue was designed in 1777 by
Ventura Rodríguez as part of a
grand scheme by Carlos III (see
p24) to beautify eastern Madrid.

The plaza itself takes its name
from Antonio Cánovas del Castillo,
one of the leading statesmen in
19th-century Spain. He was later
assassinated in 1897.

The Fuente de Neptuno

The relaxed elegance of the Westin's glass-domed Rotunda Hall lounge

⓫ Westin Palace

Plaza de las Cortes 7. **Map** 7 B3.
Tel 91 360 80 00. Sevilla, Banco
de España & Atocha.
W westinpalacemadrid.com

The former palace of the Duque de Medinaceli was torn down to build this hotel, which opened in 1912. Alfonso XIII wanted his capital to have elegant hotels to match those in other European cities, and actively encouraged the project. Its life as an elegant hotel was interrupted only during the Civil War, when it housed a hospital and refuge for the homeless, as well as the Soviet Embassy.

For many years, the Westin and the Ritz were the only grand hotels in Madrid. However, while the Ritz was the exclusive reserve of its titled guests, none of whom would dare to venture from their rooms without a tie, the no less luxurious but more informal Westin was open to non-residents and was a lively meeting place for *Madrileños*. It was the first establishment in Madrid where ladies could take tea unaccompanied. It is still a favourite rendezvous, and the wood-panelled **Palace Bar** and **Rotonda Hall** lounge, with its huge glass dome roof, are Madrid landmarks.

Statesmen, spies, literati and film stars have all stayed at the Westin. Past guests include Henry Kissinger, Mata Hari, Ernest Hemingway, Orson Welles, David Bowie, Richard Attenborough, Michael Jackson and Salvador Dalí, who once drew lewd pictures on the walls of his hotel room. Unfortunately, an over-zealous maid scrubbed the walls clean the next day.

The hotel has a Royal Suite, solarium and fitness centre, as well as a wine cellar for tastings and sales.

⓬ Museo Thyssen-Bornemisza

See pp74–7.

Stairway at the Círculo de Bellas Artes

⓭ Círculo de Bellas Artes

Calle del Marqués de Casa Riera 2.
Map 7 B2. **Tel** 91 360 54 00. Banco
de España, Sevilla. **Open** 10am–9pm
(café closes 1am). **Closed** Aug.
by appt. Exhibitions: **Open** 11am–
2pm, 5–9pm Tue–Sat, 11am–2pm
Sun. **W** circulobellasartes.com

The Círculo de Bellas Artes is a cultural foundation established in 1880. Since 1926, it has been housed in this building designed by Antonio Palacios, architect of the Palacio de Comunicaciones *(see p70)*. The building has a vast ballroom, exhibition halls, a theatre, library and studios for use by artists and sculptors. As well as exhibitions, workshops and lectures, it hosts cultural and social events, such as the Carnival Masquerade Ball held every February.

Although the foundation is for members only, the token admission fee gives visitors access to parts of the building, including the café. Known as **La Pecera** (Fishbowl) for its large windows, it is a great place to observe life on the Calle de Alcalá. There is also a cinema and a great terrace with impressive views.

⓮ Iglesia de San José

Calle de Alcalá 43. **Map** 7 B1.
Tel 91 522 67 84. Banco de
España. **Open** 7am–1:30pm, 6:30–
8:30pm daily (Sat from 7:30am & Sun
from 9:15am).

This church was once part of a Carmelite convent founded in 1605. The convent was demolished in 1863 to build a theatre, and the church itself was rebuilt during the reign of Felipe V. When the Gran Vía *(see p52)* opened in 1908, the church was changed yet again. Adorning the façade, with its three arched entrances, is an attractive statue of the Virgen del Carmen. A number of the church's treasures are housed in the Prado *(see pp82–5)*, but a few interesting images remain on the Neo-Classical main altar and in the Baroque side chapels. Many are by French sculptor Robert Michel, who carved the Cibeles fountain's lions *(see p71)*. No. 41, next door, is still referred to as the **Casa del Párroco** (parish priest's house). On 4 April 1910, Alfonso XIII symbolically struck the church with a pickaxe to signal the start of demolition work which would make way for the Gran Vía.

⑫ Museo Thyssen-Bornemisza

This magnificent museum is based on the collection assembled by Baron Heinrich Thyssen-Bornemisza and his son, Hans Heinrich, the succeeding baron. In 1992 it was installed in Madrid's 18th-century Villahermosa Palace, and was sold to the nation the following year. From its beginnings in the 1920s, the collection sought to illustrate the history of Western art, from Italian and Flemish primitives through to Expressionism and Pop Art. It is regarded by many as the most important privately assembled art collection in the world and includes masterpieces by Titian, Goya, Van Gogh and Picasso. In spring 2004 a new extension opened, displaying 250 more paintings, mainly Impressionist works acquired by Baroness Carmen Thyssen-Bornemisza.

★ **Our Lady of the Dry Tree** (c.1465)
This tiny painted panel is by Bruges master Petrus Christus. The letter A hanging from the tree stands for "Ave Maria".

★ **Harlequin with a Mirror**
The figure of the harlequin was a frequent subject of Picasso's. The careful composition on this 1923 canvas, which is thought by some to represent the artist himself, is typical of Picasso's "Classical" period.

Gallery Guide
The galleries are arranged around a covered central courtyard, which rises the full height of the building. The top floor starts with early Italian art and goes through to the 17th century. The first floor continues the story with 17th-century Dutch works and ends with Expressionism. The ground floor is dedicated to 20th-century paintings.

Hotel Room (1931)
Edward Hopper's painting is a study of urban isolation. The solitude is made less static by the suitcases and the train timetable on the woman's knee.

Portrait of Baron Thyssen-Bornemisza
This informal portrait of the previous baron, against the background of a Watteau painting, was painted by Lucian Freud in 1981–2.

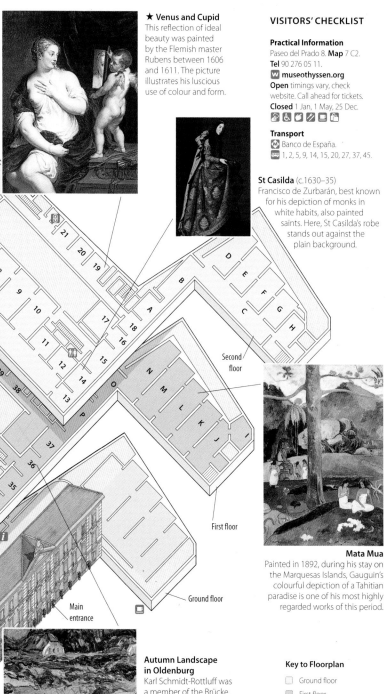

★ Venus and Cupid
This reflection of ideal beauty was painted by the Flemish master Rubens between 1606 and 1611. The picture illustrates his luscious use of colour and form.

VISITORS' CHECKLIST

Practical Information
Paseo del Prado 8. **Map** 7 C2.
Tel 90 276 05 11.
W museothyssen.org
Open timings vary, check website. Call ahead for tickets.
Closed 1 Jan, 1 May, 25 Dec.

Transport
Banco de España.
1, 2, 5, 9, 14, 15, 20, 27, 37, 45.

St Casilda (c.1630–35)
Francisco de Zurbarán, best known for his depiction of monks in white habits, also painted saints. Here, St Casilda's robe stands out against the plain background.

Second floor

First floor

Ground floor

Main entrance

Mata Mua
Painted in 1892, during his stay on the Marquesas Islands, Gauguin's colourful depiction of a Tahitian paradise is one of his most highly regarded works of this period.

Autumn Landscape in Oldenburg
Karl Schmidt-Rottluff was a member of the Brücke Expressionist group, founded in Dresden in 1905. He painted this north German landscape two years later.

Key to Floorplan

- ☐ Ground floor
- ▨ First floor
- ☐ Second floor
- ☐ Temporary exhibitions
- ☐ Non-exhibition space

Exploring the Museo Thyssen-Bornemisza

This collection provides a sweeping overview of Western art between the 14th and 20th centuries, touching on every school and trend in European art over the last 500 years. It is strong in areas where the Prado is weak, such as in Italian and Dutch primitives, 19th-century American painting, Impressionism and Expressionism. Portraiture from different periods is also well represented. The Carmen Thyssen Collection contains mainly landscapes, from 17th-century Dutch examples to Impressionist and Expressionist works.

Christ and the Samaritan Woman (1311) by Duccio

The Birth of the Renaissance

Early Italian art (room 1), while still influenced by medieval aesthetics and often overwhelmingly religious in subject matter, shows a gradual return to naturalism. Paintings become more three-dimensional and strive to tell a story, as in Duccio's *Christ and the Samaritan Woman* (1311).

The section on medieval art (room 2) illustrates how Italian influences combined with the Gothic style popular in Europe, such as Koerbecke's *Assumption of the Virgin* (c.1457).

Room 3 shows early Dutch art, including two jewels of the collection, Jan van Eyck's *The Annunciation* (c.1433–5) and Petrus Christus's *Our Lady of the Dry Tree* (c.1465). The stage is set for the aesthetic revolution of the Renaissance and a return to Classical forms, which began in Italy in the 1400s. The best example is Bramantino's *Resurrected Christ* (room 4).

Later, religion ceases to be the dominant theme, as seen in the outstanding series of early Renaissance portraits (room 5), including Holbein's detailed *Henry VIII* (c.1537).

Renaissance to Baroque

This section encompasses the height of the Renaissance, ending with Baroque art and 18th-century Italian painting. Outstanding examples of high Renaissance in Italy (room 7) include Carpaccio's *Young Knight in a Landscape* (1510) and Raphael's *Portrait of a Young Man* (c.1515).

Rooms 8–10 are dedicated to German and Dutch painters of the same period, including Dürer, with his *Jesus among the Doctors* (1506). Room 11 has works by Titian (*St Jerome in the Wilderness*, c.1575), Tintoretto and El Greco.

Room 12 begins with early Baroque, when artists started to break with the rigid Classical rules of the Renaissance and introduce elements of drama and pathos into their work. This new trend flourishes in the art in rooms 13–15, with examples from Italy, France and Spain, where the period corresponded with the

Young Knight in a Landscape (1510) by Vittore Carpaccio

Siglo de Oro (Golden Century) of the arts. Included here is Murillo's *Madonna with Child with St Rosalina of Palermo* (c.1670).

Italy's continuing influence on European art is recognized in rooms 16–18, devoted to 18th-century Italian art, in which landscapes make an appearance. This is illustrated by two views of the *Canal Grande in Venice*, one by Canaletto (c.1723–4) and a later one by Francesco Guardi.

Dutch and Flemish Painting

The remarkable series of Dutch and Flemish art is a strong point of the collection. Room 19 features 17th-century Flemish painting, with works by Jan

Esau Selling His Birthright (c.1627) by Hendrick ter Brugghen

Brueghel the Elder and Van Dyck, though the big attraction is *Venus and Cupid* (c.1606–11), one of four Rubens on display.

The growing distinction between Flemish and Dutch works can be seen by comparing the preceding works with the Dutch art in rooms 20–21. The theme here is the Italian influence on Dutch portraiture and painting, for example in *Esau Selling his Birthright* (c.1627) by Brugghen.

Some of the most interesting works are in rooms 22–26, where everyday scenes, landscapes and informal portraits reveal the unique quality of Dutch art. Excellent examples are Frans Hals's *Family Group in a Landscape* (c.1645–8) and Nicholas Maes's *The Naughty Drummer* (c.1655). Dutch still lifes from the period are well represented in room 27.

Waverly Oaks (1864) by Winslow Homer

Rococo to Realism

Rococo to Neo-Classicism is the theme of this section, indicating a rapid shift in tastes over a relatively brief period. Rococo took Europe by storm at the beginning of the 18th century. It is best represented here in room 28 by Antoine Watteau's *The Rest* (c.1709) and *Pierrot Content* (c.1712), and by François Boucher's *La Toilette* (1742). However, the increasingly exaggerated forms of Rococo were eventually rejected in favour of more restrained and elegant lines. Meanwhile,

different developments were taking shape across the ocean. Rooms 29–30 display 19th-century American painting. Landscape art fulfilled a need to express America's romantic spirit and pride in the land, as seen in the paintings of Thomas Cole. American artists were increasingly interested in depicting everyday scenes, such as idyllic fishing trips and strolls through the woods.

The coming of age of American art at the end of the century is represented by the paintings of Winslow Homer, especially *Waverly Oaks* (1864), James Whistler and John Singer Sargent.

In Europe, the 19th century saw the dawn of Romanticism (room 31), a transition best illustrated here through three works by Goya. The series also demonstrates a growing trend towards Realism, a shift that is plainly depicted in Corot's *The Parc des Lions at Port-Marly* (1872).

Modern Masters

The year 1863 was pivotal in the evolution of modern art. Artists whose work was rejected by Paris's art salon were displayed in a parallel Salon des Refusés. This show of "discarded art" marked the birth of Impressionism. Some of the most highly regarded exponents of the movement are represented in rooms 32–33, including Manet, Degas with *Swaying Dancer* (1877–9), Renoir and Sisley. Impressionism freed the artist and led to further developments, such as Post-Impressionism and Symbolism, which centred on the artist as an individual. Such is the case with Vincent van Gogh, represented here by *Les Vessenots in Auvers* (1890), Toulouse-Lautrec with *Gaston Bonnefoy* (1891), Cézanne with

Swaying Dancer (1877–9) by Degas

his *Portrait of a Farmer* (c.1905–6) and Gauguin, whose *Mata Mua* (c.1892), in room L, is now part of the Carmen Thyssen-Bornemisza Collection. A series of works in room 34, belonging to the Fauve school, demonstrates this short-lived movement based on bright colours and simplified forms.

A name that did endure was Expressionism, which started in Germany. This school drew on the artist's emotions, and sought to precipitate an emotion in the viewer. Its earliest practitioners were centred around the Dresden group, "The Bridge", founded in 1905. Among its members was Karl Schmidt-Rottluf, whose *Autumn Landscape in Oldenburg* (1907) is shown here. The Expressionist art in rooms 35–40 includes Edward Hopper's *Hotel Room* (1931).

Eight ground-floor rooms (41–48) deal with modern and contemporary art, divided into three themes – "Experimental Avant-Garde", "The Synthesis of Modern" and "Surrealism, Figurative Tradition and Pop Art". Among the gems are Picasso's *Harlequin with a Mirror* (1923), Mark Rothko's *Green on Maroon* (c.1961) and portraits by Lucian Freud.

Parisian-inspired cupola of the Edificio Metrópolis

15 Edificio Metrópolis

Calle de Alcalá 39. **Map** 7 B1.
🚇 Sevilla. **Closed** to the public.

Of unmistakable French inspiration, this building, jutting out like a ship's prow at the corner of Calle Alcalá and the Gran Vía *(see p52)*, is a Madrid landmark. Inaugurated in 1911, it was designed by Jules and Raymond Février for the Unión y el Fenix Español insurance company.

The restrained ground level is topped by ornate colonnaded upper floors, each pair of columns serving as a pedestal for allegorical statues representing Commerce, Agriculture, Industry and Mining. The rounded corner tower is crowned by a double-layered dome of dark slate with gilded ornaments. It used to hold the symbol of the Unión y el Fenix company – a bronze statue representing the mythological Phoenix and, astride it, a human figure with upraised arm representing Ganymede. In the early 1970s, the company sold the building to its present owners, the Metrópolis insurers. In a controversial move, they decided to take the statue – by then a familiar element of the Madrid skyline – to their ostentatious new headquarters on the Paseo de la Castellana. Eventually the statue was replaced by a new one, representing Winged Victory; the original Phoenix is in the garden of the Unión y el Fenix's modern building.

In front of the circular tower of the Edificio Metrópolis used to stand the "La Violetera", a small statue of a young woman selling violets. It recalls a character from a popular *zarzuela* (Spanish light opera), which later inspired the film *La Violetera*, starring Sara Montiel. The violet-sellers – Madrid's answer to Eliza Doolittle of *Pygmalion* – would sell their flowers to theatregoers on the Gran Vía after each performance. An inscription at the base of the statue bears the first two lines of the song *La Violetera*: "Como ave precursora de primavera, en Madrid aparece la violetera" ("The violet-seller appears in Madrid like a bird announcing spring"). The statue can now be seen in Las Vistillas Park.

Interior of the Café Comercial

La Tertulia – Literary Groups in Madrid

The Ateneo de Madrid was one of many homes for the unique Madrid institution of *la tertulia*. Groups of people with common interests gathered to discuss everything from politics or the arts to the finer points of bullfighting. Not a formal club, yet more than a casual conversation among friends, *tertulias* were a major source of news, ideas and gossip in the 19th century, and more than one political plot was hatched over cups of coffee. They were usually held at Madrid's 19th-century cafés. Those which occupied choice bits of real estate, such as the Pombo, El Oriental and the Paix, have since disappeared, but there are a few survivors. The best known are the Café Comercial on Glorieta de Bilbao and the Café Gijón *(see p96)* on Paseo de Recoletos.

16 Congreso de los Diputados

Plaza de las Cortes. **Map** 7 B2. **Tel** 91 390 65 25. 🚇 Sevilla. **Open** 9am–2:30pm Mon & Fri, 9am–2:30pm, 4–6:30pm Tue–Thu (Jul: 10am–12:30pm Sat). ✉ ♿ 🖥 congreso.es

This imposing yet attractive building is home to the Spanish parliament, the Cortes. Built in the mid-19th century, it is characterized by Classical columns, heavy pediments and bronze lions. It was here, in 1981, that Colonel Tejero of the Civil Guard held the deputies at gunpoint, as he tried to spark off a military coup *(see p25)*. His failure was seen as an indication that democracy was firmly established in Spain.

Bronze lion guarding the Cortes at the Congreso de los Diputados

17 Ateneo de Madrid

Calle del Prado 21. **Map** 7 B3. **Tel** 91 429 17 50. 🚇 Antón Martín, Sevilla. **Open** for guided tours by appt (Secretario Primero, C/ del Prado 21, Madrid 28014). Library: 9am–12:45am Mon–Sat, 9am–9:45pm Sun. **Closed** public hols. 🖥 ateneodemadrid.com

Formally founded in 1835, this learned association is similar to a gentlemen's club in atmosphere, with a grand stairway and panelled hall hung with portraits of famous fellows. Often closed down during periods of repression, it is still a mainstay of liberal thought in Spain. Many leading Socialists, writers and other intellectuals are members.

La Zarzuela – Spanish Light Opera

The *zarzuela*, a direct descendant of Italian light opera, started out as an amusement for kings, but was soon appropriated by the common people as Madrid's most characteristic performing art genre. The name is derived from the Palacio de La Zarzuela, current home of the Spanish royal family, outside Madrid. Zarzuelas were initially performed during the reign of Felipe IV, in the 17th century. With the ascendancy of the Bourbon kings *(see p21)*, who preferred traditional Italian opera, the *zarzuela* left the royal palaces and was taken up in the popular theatres of Madrid. It was here that it evolved into the light-hearted spectacle we know today, halfway between opera and musical comedy. Although no new *zarzuelas* have been written in decades, the genre has a tremendous following in Madrid, where there are regular performances and where record shops always have a section devoted to it. The best known title is *La Revoltosa*, a portrayal of the chemistry between the residents in a typical Madrid *corral de vecinos*, which were humble dwellings grouped around a central courtyard.

Calderón de La Barca, the famous 17th-century Spanish playwright, was one of the first great exponents of this type of opera. Others followed, most notably Tomás Breton (born 1850), who composed nearly 40 *zarzuelas*. His most famous is *La Verbena de la Paloma*.

The central theme of *zarzuelas* is life in *castizo* Madrid *(see p107)*, with its streetwise *majas* (women) and cocky *chulos* (men) dressed in traditional costumes. It combines singing, spoken dialogue and a variety of dances, such as the Madrid jig, the *chotis*.

By the middle of the 19th century, *zarzuela* was so popular that a theatre was specially built for performances. Today, the 1,200-seat Teatro de la Zarzuela *(see p182)* continues to stage *zarzuelas*, as do others. In summer, outdoor shows are held at Jardines de Sabatini *(see p119)*.

A colourful *zarzuela* performance by the Compañía de Zarzuela J Tamayo

Sunlit balconies of the magnificent Teatro Español

⓲ Teatro Español

Calle del Príncipe 25. **Map** 7 A3.
Tel 91 360 14 84. 🚇 Sol, Antón
Martín & Sevilla. **Open** for performances from 5pm Tue–Sun. 🚗 ♿
🔲 teatroespanol.es

Dominating the Plaza de Santa
Ana *(see p51)* is the Teatro
Español, one of the oldest and
most beautiful theatres in
Madrid. In the late 16th century
many of Spain's finest plays were
performed in the Corral del
Príncipe which originally stood
here. Replaced by the Teatro del
Príncipe in 1745, it underwent
extensive restoration in the mid-
19th century and was renamed
Teatro Español. Names of great
Spanish dramatists are engraved
on the façade, including that of
Federico García Lorca *(see p32)*.

⓳ Casa de Lope de Vega

Calle de Cervantes 11. **Map** 7 B3.
Tel 91 429 92 16. 🚇 Antón Martín.
Open 10am–6pm Tue–Sun only for
tours by appt. **Closed** some public
hols. 🎦 🔲 madrid.org

Félix Lope de Vega, a leading
Golden Age writer *(see p32)*,
moved into this sombre house
in 1610 and lived here until his
death in 1635. It was here that
he wrote over two-thirds of his
plays, thought to total almost
1,500. The house was first
opened to the public in 1935
after a meticulous restoration
project, using some of Lope de

Vega's own furniture, and gives
a great feeling of Castilian life in
the early 17th century. A dark
chapel with no external windows
occupies the centre, separated
from the writer's bedroom by
only a barred window. The small
garden at the rear, complete
with the original well, is planted
with the flowers and fruit trees
mentioned in the writer's plays.
    Across the street, stands the
17th-century Convento de las
Trinitarias, where the remains of
Miguel de Cervantes *(see p137)*
and Félix Lope de Vega lie.

⓴ CaixaForum

Paseo del Prado 36 (between Calle
Gobernador and Calle Almadén).
Map 7 C4. **Tel** 91 330 73 00.
🚇 Atocha. **Open** 10am–8pm daily.
Closed 1 & 6 Jan, 25 Dec. 📷 🍴 ♿
🎦 🎬 ♿ 🔲 lacaixa.es/obrasocial

CaixaForum is a cultural centre
with exhibitions of modern art
and photography, workshops,

Félix Lope de Vega

conferences and concerts. It was
built by Swiss architects Herzog
& de Meuron in 2007 in a former
electric power station. The top-
floor café and restaurant are
highly recommended. Adjoining
the building is an extraordinary
vertical garden.
    Located nearby is **La Fábric**, an
open space devoted to culture.
It has an art gallery that caters
to new collectors, a photography
bookshop and a café. .

㉑ Museo del Prado

See pp82–5.

㉒ Iglesia de San Jerónimo el Real

Calle de Moreto 4. **Map** 8 D3. **Tel** 91
420 30 78. 🚇 Banco de España, Atocha.
Open Mar–Oct: 10am–1pm, 5–8:30pm
Mon–Sat, 9:30am–2:30pm, 5:30–8:30pm
Sun. **Closed** Easter Sat. ♿

Built in the 16th century for
Isabel I *(see p26)*, but since
remodelled, San Jerónimo is
Madrid's royal church. From the
17th century it was virtually a
part of the Buen Retiro palace
which once stood here.
    Originally attached to the
Hieronymite monastery, which
today stands beside it in ruins,
the church was the location for
the marriage of Alfonso XIII *(see
p27)* and Victoria Eugenia von
Battenberg in 1906. The church
is still a popular venue for
society weddings. The cloisters
and part of the atrium form an
annex of the Prado's extension.

㉓ Real Academia Española

Calle Felipe IV 4. **Map** 8 D3. **Tel** 91 420
14 78. 🚇 Banco de España, Retiro.
Closed to the public. 🔲 rae.es

Spain's Royal Academy's motto
is "*Limpia, brilla y da esplendor*"
("Cleans, polishes and shines").
It describes the function of
the organization, which is to
preserve the purity of the
Spanish language. Founded in
1713, the academy only moved
to this Neo-Classical building in

1894. The elegant façade has a majestic entrance with Doric columns and a carved pediment. The members include scholars, writers and journalists – the post, which is for life, is unpaid – who occupy seats identified by a letter of the alphabet. They meet regularly to assess the acceptability of any new trends in the language.

㉔ Casón del Buen Retiro

Calle de Alfonso XII 28. **Map** 8 D3.
🚇 Retiro, Banco de España.
Open noon Sun (by appt; call the Museo del Prado, see p83)

The Casón del Buen Retiro is one of the remaining buildings of the 17th-century Palacio del Buen Retiro, designed by Alonso Carbonel. It was originally built in 1637 for Felipe IV on a stretch of land next to the Monastery of San Jerónimo. However, the structure of the building evolved over the years – it was remodelled in the 19th century, and two monumental façades were included. Now part of the Museo del Prado, the building houses the museum's library that has a collection of 70,000 books. On the ceiling in the main hall is *The Allegory of the Golden Fleece*, a magnificent painting by Luca Giordano.

Nearby is the Salón de Reinos (Hall of Kingdoms) that is currently undergoing extensive refurbishment to restore the

Façade of Salón de Reinos (Hall of Kingdoms)

interiors to their former glory. Most of the artworks at Salón de Reinos are now displayed in Museo del Prado, and the building itself may eventually become part of the museum. Despite this closure, the Salón de Reinos is worth visiting to admire its impressive façade.

㉕ Parque del Retiro

Map 8 E3. **Tel** 91 530 00 41. 🚇 Ibiza, Retiro, Atocha. Park: **Open** 6am–10pm (Apr–Sep: till midnight). ♿ Casa de Vacas: **Open** 11am–8pm Mon–Fri, until 9pm Jul & Aug.

Retiro Park, in Madrid's smart Jerónimos district, was once the setting for Felipe IV's palace (see p26), the Real Sitio del Buen Retiro. In the 17th century the park was the private playground

of the royal family, and only became fully open to the public in 1869. Today, it is a popular place for relaxing.

A short stroll from the park's northern entrance is the lake, where rowing boats can be hired. On one side, in front of a half-moon colonnade, a statue of Alfonso XII (see p27) rides high on a column. On the other, portrait painters and fortune-tellers ply their trade.

To the south of the lake are the Palacio de Velázquez and the Palacio de Cristal, both built by Ricardo Velázquez Bosco. His other work includes the grandiose Ministerio de Agricultura building (see p86).

The Palacio de Velázquez was intended as a pavilion to stage the National Exhibition of Mining, Metal, Ceramics, Glass and Mineral Water industries in 1884. Today it is used by Museo Reina Sofía for temporary exhibitions.

Nearby, the iron-and-glass Palacio de Cristal was modelled on the Crystal Palace built for London's Great Exhibition in 1851. Designed to stage an exhibition of tropical plants in the Philippines Exposition of 1887, the palace has become an exhibition space too. Its reflection in the lake remains one of the best known images of Madrid. The pathway that links the park to the Paseo del Prado is a pedestrian avenue lined with bookstalls.

In the Paseo de Colombia, the Casa de Vacas puts on theatre and exhibitions.

Monument of Alfonso XII (1901) facing the boating lake in the Parque del Retiro

㉑ Museo del Prado

The Prado Museum contains the world's greatest assembly of Spanish painting – especially works by Velázquez and Goya – ranging from the 12th to 19th centuries. It also houses impressive foreign collections, particularly of Italian and Flemish works. The Neo-Classical building was designed in 1785 by Juan de Villanueva on the orders of Carlos III, and it opened as a museum in 1819. The Spanish architect Rafael Moneo constructed a building, over the adjacent church's cloister, that was completed in 2007 and now hosts temporary exhibitions. The Casón del Buen Retiro *(see p81)*, the museum's library, can be visited on Sundays for guided tours – call for details.

★ **Velázquez Collection**
The Triumph of Bacchus (1629), Velázquez's first portrayal of a mythological subject, shows the god of wine (Bacchus) with a group of drunkards.

The Adoration of the Shepherds (1612–14) This dramatic work shows the elongated figures and swirling garments typical of El Greco's style. It was painted during his late Mannerist period for his own funerary chapel.

The Three Graces (c.1635) This was one of the last paintings by the Flemish master Rubens, and was part of the artist's personal collection. The three women dancing in a ring – the Graces – are the daughters of Zeus, and represent Love, Joy and Revelry.

The Garden of Earthly Delights (c.1505) Hieronymus Bosch (El Bosco in Spanish), one of Felipe II's favourite artists, is especially well represented in the Prado. This enigmatic painting depicts paradise and hell.

Ticket office

Goya entrance (upstairs)

Gallery Guide

The museum's permanent collection is chronologically arranged over three main floors. Classical sculpture and early Renaissance works are on the ground floor, Velázquez on the first floor and the extensive Goya collection across all three floors. The permanent collection is accessed via the Velázquez and Goya entrances. Visitors to the temporary exhibitions should use the Jerónimos entrance.

Second floor

First floor

Murillo entrance

Ground floor

Velázquez entrance

★ Goya Collection
In *The Clothed Maja* (c.1800–8) and *The Naked Maja* (before1800), Goya tackled the taboo subject of nudity, for which he was later accused of obscenity.

The Annunciation
Fra Angelico's work of c.1425–8 is a high point of Italy's Early Renaissance, as illustrated by the detailed architectural setting.

Key to Floorplan

☐ Spanish Painting
☐ Flemish and Dutch Painting
▨ Italian Painting
☐ French Painting
☐ German Painting
☐ British Painting
☐ Sculpture
☐ Non-exhibition space

Casón del Buen Retiro
CALLE DE MORETO
Jerónimos Building Underground link
Villanueva Building
PASEO DEL PRADO
Jerónimos entrance
CALLE DE FELIPE IV
Salón de Reinos

Changes at the Prado

The Jerónimos Building houses temporary exhibitions and Renaissance sculptures, as well as a shop, café, restaurant and auditorium. In the future the Salón de Reinos might become part of the Prado.

▨ Museum Buildings
☐ Closed for refurbishment

Exploring the Prado's Collection

The importance of the Prado is founded on its royal collections. The wealth of foreign art, including many of Europe's finest works, reflects the historical power of the Spanish crown. The Low Countries and parts of Italy were under Spanish domination for centuries. The 18th century was an era of French influence, following the Bourbon accession to the Spanish throne. The Prado is worthy of repeated visits, but if you go only once, see the Spanish works of the 17th century.

St Dominic of Silos Enthroned as Abbot (1474–7) by Bermejo

Saturn Devouring One of his Sons (1820–23) by Francisco de Goya

Spanish Painting

Right up to the 19th century, Spanish painting focused on religious and royal themes. Although the limited subject matter was in some ways a restriction, it also offered a sharp focus that seems to have suited Spanish painters.

Spain's early medieval art is represented somewhat sketchily in the Prado, but there are some examples, such as the anonymous mural paintings from the Holy Cross hermitage in Maderuelo, which show a Romanesque heaviness of line and forceful characterization.

Spanish Gothic art can be seen in the Prado in the works of Bartolomé Bermejo and Fernando Gallego. The sense of realism in their paintings was borrowed from Flemish masters of the time.

Renaissance features began to emerge in the works of painters such as Pedro de Berruguete, whose *Auto-de-fé* is both chilling and lively. *St Catherine*, by Fernando Yáñez de la Almedina, shows the influence of Leonardo da Vinci, for whom Yáñez probably worked while training in Italy.

What is often considered as a truly Spanish style – with its highly wrought emotion and deepening sombreness – first started to emerge in the 16th century in the paintings of the Mannerists. This is evident in Pedro Machuca's fierce *Descent from the Cross* and in the Madonnas of Luis de Morales, "the Divine". The elongation of the human figure in Morales' work is carried to a greater extreme by Domenikos Theotocopoulos, who is better known as El Greco *(see p145)*. Although many of his masterpieces remain in his adopted town of Toledo, the

Prado has an impressive collection, including *The Nobleman with his Hand on his Chest*.

The Golden Age of the 17th century was a productive time for Spanish art. José de Ribera, who lived in (Spanish) Naples, followed Caravaggio in combining realism of character with the techniques of *chiaroscuro* (use of light and dark) and tenebrism (large areas of dark colours, with a shaft of light). Another master who used this method was Francisco Ribalta, whose *Christ Embracing St Bernard* is here. Zurbarán, known for still lifes and portraits of saints and monks, is also represented in the Prado.

This period, however, is best represented by the work of Diego de Velázquez. As Spain's leading court painter from his late twenties until his death, he produced scenes of heightened realism, royal portraits and religious and mythological paintings. Examples of all of these are displayed in the Prado. Perhaps his greatest work is *Las Meninas (see p33)*.

Another great Spanish painter, Goya, revived Spanish art in the 18th century. He first specialized in cartoons for tapestries, then became a court painter. His work went on to embrace the horrors of war, as seen in *The 3rd of May (see p22)*, and culminated in a sombre series known as *The Black Paintings*.

Still Life with Four Vessels (c.1658–64) by Francisco de Zurbarán

Flemish and Dutch Painting

Spain's long connection with the Low Countries naturally resulted in an intense admiration for the so-called Flemish primitives. Many exceptional examples of Flemish and Dutch art now hang in the Prado. *St Barbara*, by Robert Campin, has a quirky intimacy, while Roger van der Weyden's *The Descent from the Cross* is an unquestioned masterpiece. Most notable of all, however, are Hieronymus Bosch's weird and eloquent inventions. The Prado has some of his major paintings, including the *Temptation of St Anthony* and *The Haywain*. Works from the 16th century include the *Triumph of Death* by Brueghel the Elder. There are nearly 100 canvases by the 17th-century Flemish painter Peter Paul Rubens, including *The Adoration of the Magi*. The most notable Dutch painting on display is Rembrandt's *Artemisia*, a portrait of the artist's wife. Other Flemish and Dutch artists featured at the Prado are Antonis Moor, Anton Van Dyck and Jacob Jordaens, considered one of the finest portrait painters of the 17th century.

Italian Painting

The Prado is the envy of many museums, not least for its vast collection of Italian paintings. Botticelli's dramatic wooden panels telling *The Story of Nastagio degli Onesti*, a vision of a knight forever condemned to hunt down and kill his

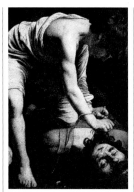

David Victorious over Goliath (c.1600) by Caravaggio

own beloved, were commissioned by two rich Florentine families and are a sinister high point.

Raphael contributes the superb *Christ Falls on the Way to Calvary* and the sentimental *The Holy Family of the Lamb*. *Christ Washing the Disciples' Feet*, an early work by Tintoretto, is a profound masterpiece and reveals the painter's brilliant handling of perspective.

Caravaggio had a profound impact on Spanish artists, who admired his characteristic handling of light, as seen in *David Victorious over Goliath*. Venetian masters Veronese and Titian are also very well represented. Titian served as court painter to Charles V, and few works express the drama of Habsburg rule so deeply as his sombre painting *The Emperor Charles V at Mühlberg*. Also on display are works by Giordano and Tiepolo, the master of Italian

Rococo, who painted *The Immaculate Conception* as part of a series intended for a church in Aranjuez.

French Painting

Marriages between French and Spanish royalty in the 17th century, culminating in the Bourbon accession to the throne in the 18th century, brought French art to Spain. The Prado has eight works attributed to Poussin, among them his serene *St Cecilia* and *Landscape with St Jerome*. The magnificent *Landscape with the Embarkation of St Paula Romana at Ostia* is the best work here by Claude Lorrain. Among the 18th-century artists featured are Antoine Watteau and Jean Ranc. *Felipe V* is the work of the royal portraitist Louis-Michel van Loo.

St Cecilia (c.1635) by the French artist Nicolas Poussin

German Painting

Although German art is not especially well represented in the Prado, there are several paintings by Albrecht Dürer, including his classical depictions of Adam and Eve. His lively *Self-Portrait* of 1498, painted at the age of 26, is undoubtedly the highlight of the small but valuable German collection in the museum. Lucas Cranach also figures, and works by the late 18th-century painter Anton Raffael Mengs include portraits of Carlos III.

The Descent from the Cross (c.1435) by Roger van der Weyden

㉖ Real Jardín Botánico

Plaza de Murillo 2. **Map** 8 D4.
Tel 91 420 30 17. Atocha.
Open 10am– dusk daily. **Closed** 1 Jan,
25 Dec. rjb.csic.es

South of the Prado *(see pp82–5)*,
and a suitable place to rest after
visiting the gallery, are the Royal
Botanic Gardens. The inspiration
of Carlos III *(see p22)*, they were
designed in 1781 by Gómez
Ortega, Juan de Villanueva,
architect of the Prado, and
Francesco Sabatini.

Interest in the plants of the
Philippines and South America
was taking hold in Spain at this
time, and the gardens offer a
large variety of trees, shrubs,
medicinal plants and herbs.

Statue of Bourbon King Carlos III in the
Real Jardín Botánico

㉗ Ministerio de Agricultura

Paseo de la Infanta Isabel 1. **Map** 8 D5.
Tel 91 468 93 60. Atocha. **Open** by
appt. mapa.es

This magnificent, imposing
building was originally the
home of the Ministry of
Development, whose remit was
to promote economic, industrial
and scientific growth in Spain in
the late 19th century. Today the
enormous edifice houses the
Ministry of Agriculture, and as
such is frequently the target of
protests by Spanish farmers and
olive oil producers. The building
itself is adorned with sculptures,

The elaborate but daunting face of Spain's
Ministerio de Agricultura

friezes and painted tiles and
brings together elements of both
Neo-Classical and Romantic styles.
It was constructed between 1884
and 1886 by Ricardo Velázquez
Bosco, architect of the Palacio
de Velázquez in the Parque del
Retiro *(see p81)*. The artist Ignacio
Zuloaga was later involved in
its design.

Gigantic Corinthian columns
line the exterior walls, with areas
of coloured bricks and decorative glazed tiles enhancing the
spaces between them. The
pediment above the columns is
decorated with the Spanish coat
of arms. Crowning the building
are allegorical sculptures created
by Agustín Querol. The three
central figures represent Glory
personified bestowing laurels
on Science and Art. On either
side are statues of Pegasus.
These were originally made of
marble, but were replaced by
bronze replicas when the stone
deteriorated. The original
statues are now at Plaza de
Legazpi, south of the city.

㉘ Real Observatorio Astronómico de Madrid

Calle de Alfonso XII 3. **Map** 8 E5.
Tel 91 597 95 64. Atocha.
Open weekends; booking essential
(call for appt). **Closed** public hols.
ign.es

When building began in 1790,
this was one of only four
observatories in Europe. The

Observatorio Astronómico was
designed by Juan de Villanueva
along Neo-Classical lines. The
vertical slit window was used
for telescopes, and the
colonnaded roof cupola for
weather observation.

There is one room open to
the public where 18th- and
19th-century telescopes, as
well as a Foucault pendulum,
are on display. You will need
to apply in writing to view the
larger telescopes and a collection
of English clocks, and to peer
through a telescope made in
1790 by Sir Frederick William
Herschel, the astronomer who
discovered Uranus.

Colonnaded roof cupola of the Real
Observatorio Astronómico de Madrid

㉙ Museo Nacional de Antropología

Calle de Alfonso XII 68. **Map** 8 D5.
Tel 91 530 64 18. Atocha. **Open**
9:30am–8pm Tue–Sat, 10am–3pm Sun.
Closed public hols. (free Sat afternoons & Sun). book in advance.
mnantropologia.mcu.es

Previously known as the Museo
Nacional de Etnología, this
three-floor museum, which is
built around a grand open hall,
was inaugurated by Alfonso XII
(see p27) in 1875.

Through the displays, the
anthropology and ethnology of
geographical groups of people
are studied. The ground floor
houses an important collection
from the Philippines. The
centrepiece is a 10 m- (33 ft-)
long dug-out canoe made from
a single tree trunk. There are
also some gruesome exhibits,
such as deformed skulls from

Peru and the Philippines, the mummy of a Guanche from Tenerife and the skeleton of Don Agustín Luengo y Capilla, a late 19th-century giant from Extremadura. He was 2.35 m (7 ft 4 in) tall and died aged 26.

The first floor is dedicated to Africa. As well as clothing, weapons, ceramics and utensils, there is a reproduction of a Bubi ritual hut from Equatorial Guinea, in which tribal members met the *boeloelo* (witch doctor). On the second floor is the American section, with exhibits on the lifestyles of indigenous groups.

⓿ Estación de Atocha

Plaza del Emperador Carlos V. **Map** 8 D5. **Tel** 90 232 03 20. ✪ Atocha RENFE. **Open** 5am–1am daily. ♿

Madrid's first rail service, from Atocha to Aranjuez, was inaugurated in 1851 by Isabel II *(see p27)*. Forty years later, the original station at Atocha was replaced by the present one. The older part of the station was one of the first big constructions in Madrid to be built from glass and wrought iron. Now, it houses a palm garden. Next to it is the modern AVE terminus, providing high-speed links to various towns including Toledo, Seville, Córdoba, Zaragoza, Valladolid,

Entrance of Madrid's Estación de Atocha, busy with travellers

Valencia and Barcelona *(see p204)*. Outside, a monument commemorates those who died in the terrorist attack of 2004, when 10 explosions occured on four trains at rush hour on 11 March.

⓿ Palacio de Fernán Núñez

Calle de Santa Isabel 44. **Map** 7 B4. **Tel** 91 151 10 02. ✪ Atocha. **Open** by appt. ✉ 🌐 **ffe.es/ fundacion/palacio.htm**

Also known as the Palacio de Cervellón, this building has a plain façade that gives scant indication of the riches within. Built for the Duke and Duchess of Fernán Núñez in 1847, the palace served as the family

home until 1936. It was requisitioned by the Republican militia at the start of the Civil War *(see p24)*; the lower part served as a bomb shelter while the upper floor was occupied by a Socialist Youth organization. Amazingly, when the palace was returned to the duke's family, they found that none of its treasures had been damaged or stolen.

In 1941, the palace was sold and became the headquarters of the Spanish State Railway. It now houses the Foundation of Spanish Railways, which organizes exhibitions here.

That the palace was built in two phases is clear. The large, restrained rooms in the first section contrast with the Rococo flourishes of the second. The older section has carpets from the Real Fábrica de Tapices *(see p114)*, as well as antique furniture, clocks and copies of paintings by Goya *(see p32)*. Attention, however, is inevitably drawn to the gold-plated ornamentation of the later section, especially the ballroom with its mirrors, chandeliers and cherubs playing musical instruments. Rooms in this part are often used for official receptions.

Near the palace is the cloistered Convento Santa Isabel with its octagonal dome. It was founded in 1595 by Felipe II.

The sumptuously decorated ballroom of the Palacio de Fernán Núñez

㉜ Museo Reina Sofía (MNCARS)

The highlight of this museum of 20th-century art is Picasso's *Guernica*. However, there are also other major works by influential artists, including Miró and Dalí. The collection is housed in Madrid's former General Hospital, built in the late 18th century. A major extension to the museum, designed by Jean Nouvel, was completed in 2005. Named after its architect, this stunning building greatly increased the museum's exhibition space and includes two temporary exhibition rooms, a library, café-restaurant, an art shop and auditoriums.

Portrait II (1938)
Joan Miró's huge work shows elements of Surrealism, but was painted more than 10 years after his true Surrealist period ended.

Nouvel building

206

Toki-Egin (Homenaje a San Juan de la Cruz) (1989–90)
In his abstract sculptures, Eduardo Chillida used a variety of materials, such as wood, iron and steel, to convey strength.

205

204

★ Woman in Blue (1901)
Picasso disowned this work after it won only an honourable mention in a national mpetition. Decades later it was located and acquired by the Spanish state.

2nd Floor

202

203

Gallery Guide

The collection, in the Sabatini Building, is arranged around an open courtyard. Collection 1, on the second floor, displays works dating from 1900 to 1945. There are rooms allocated to important movements such as Cubism and Surrealism. Collection 2, on the fourth floor, showcases works between 1945 and 1968, including Pop Art, Minimalism and more recent tendencies. Collection 3, from Revolt to Post-Modernism is located in the Nouvel building. Temporary exhibitions are located on the first and third floors and in the Nouvel building.

Key to Floorplan

☐ Exhibition space
☐ Non-exhibition space

Accident or Self-Portrait
Alfonso Ponce de León's disturbing work, painted in 1936, prefigured his death in a car crash later that same year.

VISITORS' CHECKLIST

Practical Information
Calle Santa Isabel 52. **Map** 7 C5.
Tel 91 774 10 00. **Open** 10am–9pm Mon & Wed–Sat, 10am–7pm Sun (not all exhibits will be open, so check the website). **Closed** 1 & 6 Jan, 1 & 15 May, 9 Nov, 24, 25, 31 Dec & public hols. 🎫 (free after 7pm Mon & Wed–Sat, after 3pm Sun). 🔲🧷🛗🎧🖥🏛🏛

Transport
Ⓜ Atocha. 🚌 6, 14, 19, 27, 45, 55, 86.

La Jorneta
Salvador Dalí was born in Figueres in Catalonia. He became a frequent visitor to the town of Cadaqués, on the Costa Brava, where he painted this landscape in the summer of 1923.

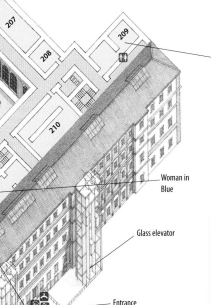

Woman in Blue

Glass elevator

Entrance

Visitors admiring *Guernica*

★ Guernica by Picasso

The most famous single work of the 20th century, this Civil War protest painting was commissioned by the Spanish Republican government in 1937 for the Spanish pavilion of the Paris World Fair. The artist found his inspiration in the mass air attack of the same year on the Basque town of Gernika-Lumo, by German pilots flying for the Nationalist air force. The painting hung in a New York gallery until 1981, reflecting the artist's wish that it should not return to Spain until democracy was re-established. It was moved here from the Prado in 1992.

★ La Tertulia del Café de Pombo (1920)
José Gutiérrez Solana depicts a gathering of intellectuals (*tertulia*) in a famous café in Madrid, which no longer exists.

Exploring the Museo Reina Sofía

The 20th century has undoubtedly been the most brilliant period in the history of Spanish art since the Golden Age of the 17th century. Many facets of the Spanish artistic genius are on show in the Museo Reina Sofía. Sculpture, paintings and even work by the Surrealist film-maker Luis Buñuel provide a skilfully arranged tour through an eventful century. Please note that the location of the artworks referred to below may be changing as a result of the extensive rearrangement taking place at the museum.

Guitar in Front of the Sea by Juan Gris (1925)

The Beginnings of Modern Spanish Art

Following the storm of creativity that culminated with Goya in the 19th century, Spanish painting went through an unremarkable period. A few artists, such as Sorolla, managed to break the mould, hinting at the dawn of a new era of artistic brilliance. An emerging middle class, particularly in places like the Basque country and Barcelona, gave rise to a generation of innovative artists whose works constitute the introduction to this collection. There are early 20th century landscapes by Zuloaga and Regoyos and representations of the female figure by artists such as Anglada-Camarasa, Nonell and Julio González. You will find the brooding, dark-coloured works of Gutiérrez Solana, whose favourite subjects are the fiestas and the people of his native Madrid. Influenced by the Spanish masters, especially Goya, his paintings include *La Tertulia del Café de Pombo* (1920) and the menacing *La Procesión de la Muerte* (1930).

There are also works by Blanchard, Delaunay and Lipchitz. Hinting at Cubism, they make a good introduction to the work of Juan Gris. Trained as a graphic designer, Gris moved to Paris in 1906 where, under the influence of Picasso, he produced *Portrait of Josette* (1916) and *Guitar in Front of the Sea* (1925). Also displayed are works in metal by Zaragoza-born sculptor Pablo Gargallo (1881–1934). Gargallo's most important piece is *The Great Prophet* (1933), a bronze casting more than 2 m (6 ft) high, which he completed shortly before his death.

Pablo Picasso

The works on display span five decades in the life of Pablo Picasso. Born in the Andalusian city of Málaga, Picasso embraced a wide variety of styles in the course of his long career, including Realism, Cubism and Surrealism. He defied classification, creating some of the most important works of art of the 20th century. The first image the visitor notices is the haunting *Woman in Blue* (1901) in room 201, one of Picasso's earliest works dating from his so-called "blue"

The Great Prophet by Pablo Gargallo (1933)

period. In Room 206 is the most-visited piece in the collection – the vast *Guernica* (1937). Aside from its unquestionable artistic merits, the canvas has a deep historical significance for Spaniards, recalling one of the most harrowing episodes of the Spanish Civil War *(see p24)*. The painting is complemented by a series of sketches and preliminary studies completed in the week following the bombing of the Basque town of Gernika-Lumo.

It is interesting to see many of the symbols Picasso chose for *Guernica* appearing in his earlier work, the *Minotauromaquia* (1935). This painting is of the fearsome Minotaur of Greek legend – a bull-headed devourer of human flesh.

Julio González

A friend and contemporary of Gargallo and Picasso, Julio González is known as the father of modern Spanish sculpture, chiefly because of

Minotauromaquia by Pablo Picasso (1935)

his pioneering use of iron as a raw material. Born in Barcelona, González began his career as a welder, learning to forge, cut, solder and bend the iron which had hitherto been considered an entirely industrial material. In the 1920s and 1930s he worked alongside Picasso and Gargallo in Paris, producing many three-dimensional pieces in the Cubist style. Look out for González' humorous self-portrait entitled *Tête dite "Lapin"* or *Head called "Rabbit"* (1930). In his work, you can also see many sketches that relate to the sculptures.

Girl at the Window by Salvador Dalí (1925)

Miró, Dalí and the Surrealists

Joan Miró turned his hand to many styles. His Surrealist experiments of the 1920s provide evidence of his love of the vivid colours and bold shapes of Catalan folk art. Similar elements remain in later pieces.

His fellow Catalan, Salvador Dalí, is especially well known as a member of the Surrealist movement – the style of art inspired by the work of Sigmund Freud, which depended on access to subconscious images without censorship by the rational mind. Other prominent Surrealists whose work is displayed here are Benjamín Palencia (*Bulls*, 1933), Oscar Domínguez and Luis Buñuel.

Dalí's Surrealist masterpiece, *The Great Masturbator* (1929) hangs in contrast to the realistic portrait, *Girl at the Window* (1925). Like many of his contemporaries, Dalí embraced widely differing styles of working in the course of his career. *The Great Masturbator* was painted after he visited Paris, and came into contact with the French Surrealists. His work starts to reflect all the unfettered obsessions and fetishes that

haunted this eccentric artist. Another product of this period are the films of Luis Buñuel whose 17-minute *Un Chien Andalou* (1929), a collaboration with Dalí, made a deep impression on the Surrealist movement.

Bulls by Benjamín Palencia (1933)

The Paris School

The turbulent history of Spain in the 20th century *(see pp23–5)* has resulted in a steady stream of talented Spanish artists leaving their native land. Many of them, including Picasso, Dalí, Juan Gris and Miró, passed through Paris, some staying for a few months, others staying for years. Artists of other nationalities also congregated in the French capital, mainly from Eastern Europe, Germany and the United States, including the German abstract painter Hans Hartung and the Russian Nicholas de Staël. All of these artists were part of the Paris

School and it is possible to see the mutual influence of this closely knit, yet constantly evolving, group of young artists. On display are works by a wide range of less well-known Paris School painters, including Daniel Vázquez Díaz and Francisco Bores.

Franco and Beyond

The Civil War (1936–9) had an enormous effect on the development of Spanish art. Under Franco, the state enforced rigid censorship; artists worked in an environment where communication with the outside world was sporadic and where their work did not benefit from official approval. They sought mutual support in groups such as El Paso and Grupo 57, whose members included Antonio Saura, Manuel Millares and Eduardo Chillida. Painting mainly in black and white, Saura used religious imagery, such as the twisted crucifix in *Scream No. 7* (1959). Chillida's work includes the use of forged iron.

The best-known member of the avant-garde association El Paso was Antoni Tàpies. Concerned with texture, he used a variety of materials, including oil paint mixed with crushed marble, to explore the magical qualities of everyday objects.

In the rooms of the fourth floor, the Museo Reina Sofía displays pieces of modern art from the 20th century. Works span the period from the end of World War II in 1945 through to 1968, and the development of different movements is marked. Artists on show include Robert Delaunay, Max Ernst, Francis Bacon and Georges Braque. Later works by Picasso and Miró can also be found here, as can pieces by sculptors Julio López-Hernández and Jorge Oteiza. In addition there are paintings on display by some noted contemporary American abstract artists including Ross Bleckner, Terry Winters and Mark Rothko.

AROUND LA CASTELLANA

The axis of modern Madrid is the tree-lined Paseo de la Castellana, a long, grand boulevard. A journey along it gives a glimpse of Madrid as Spain's commercial and administrative capital. The main north–south artery, it was first developed in the 19th century by the city's aristocracy with a string of summer palaces from Plaza de Colón northwards. The Museo Lázaro Galdiano, one of Madrid's best art museums, is housed in the former mansion of the financier José Lázaro Galdiano. To the east, La Castellana skirts the Barrio de Salamanca, an upmarket district of stylish boutiques and apartment blocks named after the 19th-century aristocrat who built it. To the southwest are Chueca and Malasaña, neighbourhoods offering a more authentic *Madrileño* atmosphere. The southern section of the boulevard is called Paseo de Recoletos. Nearby are the Museo Arqueológico Nacional, founded by Isabel II in 1867, and Café Gijón, an intellectuals' café founded in the early 20th century.

Sights at a Glance

Museums and Galleries
- 7 Museo de Cera
- 9 *Museo Arqueológico Nacional pp98–9*
- 12 Fundación Juan March
- 13 *Museo Lázaro Galdiano pp102–3*
- 14 Museo Sorolla
- 15 Museo de Arte Público
- 17 Museo del Romanticismo
- 18 Museo de Historia de Madrid

Churches
- 4 Iglesia de Santa Bárbara

Streets, Squares, Parks and Districts
- 2 Calle del Almirante
- 3 Plaza de Chueca
- 8 Plaza de Colón
- 10 Calle de Serrano
- 11 Salamanca
- 16 Calle de Zurbano
- 19 Malasaña

Historic Buildings
- 1 Café Gijón
- 5 Tribunal Supremo
- 6 Biblioteca Nacional de España
- 20 Cuartel del Conde Duque
- 21 Palacio de Liria

☐ Selected Restaurants *pp167–9*
1 A 2 Velas
2 Ainhoa
3 Bar Tomate
4 La Bicicleta Café
5 Bodega La Ardosa
6 Café Gijón
7 Casa Perico
8 Con 2 Fogones
9 Dionisos Chueca
10 El Cocinillas
11 Gumbo
12 Maricastaña
13 La Musa
14 Naif Madrid
15 Peggy Sue's American Diner
16 Quintana 30
17 Ramón Freixa Madrid
18 Restaurante Lúa
19 Sergi Arola
20 La Tape

See also Street Finder maps 2, 5 & 6

0 metres 250
0 yards 250

Street-by-Street: Paseo de Recoletos

Plaza de Colón is bordered by the fashionable designer shopping streets Calle de Serrano and Calle de Goya, the Museo Arqueológico Nacional, the Biblioteca Nacional (National Library) and Paseo de Recoletos, which is home to the classic Café Gijón. Between Calle del Almirante, another popular fashion street, and Calle de Génova is the Tribunal Supremo and the Iglesia de Santa Bárbara. Towards the Gran Vía are the narrow streets of Chueca with some interesting old taverns and eclectic bistros.

❹ Iglesia de Santa Bárbara
Both Bárbara de Braganza and her husband, Fernando VI *(see p23)*, are entombed in this fine Baroque church.

❺ Tribunal Supremo
Spain's supreme court of law is located in the former convent and school of the adjoining Iglesia de Santa Bárbara.

Calle de Barquillo contains the best shops in the city for music equipment, mobile phones and other electronic goods.

```
0 metres        100
0 yards         100
```

❸ Plaza de Chueca
The immaculate, exquisitely decorated Taberna de Ángel Sierra bar in the Plaza de Chueca has hardly changed since it was built in 1897.

❷ Calle del Almirante
Originally a street of basket shops, Calle del Almirante now boasts several of the city's own-label fashion shops.

❼ Museo de Cera
Madrid's wax museum has likenesses of many historical figures.

Locator Map
See Street Finder maps 2, 5 & 6

E DE GENOVA

PLAZA DE COLÓN

RAGANZA

PASEO DE RECOLETOS

CALLE RECOLETOS

CALLE DE SERRANO

❽ ★ Plaza de Colón
This large square is a monument to Christopher Columbus (Colón).

El Espejo is the most beautifully decorated *belle époque* bar and restaurant in the city.

❾ ★ Museo Arqueológico Nacional
This museum houses a collection of treasures from some of the world's ancient civilizations. The Biblioteca Nacional de España *(see p97)* is located in the same building.

❿ Calle de Serrano
Madrid's smartest shopping street is home to top Spanish designers.

❶ Café Gijón
For over a century, intellectuals have held discussion groups or *tertulias (see p78)* in this wood-panelled café.

Key

— Suggested route

❶ Café Gijón

Paseo de Recoletos 21. **Map** 5 C5.
Tel 91 521 54 25. 🚇 Banco de España.
Open 7:30am–1:30am Mon– Fri,
8am–2am Sat, 8am–1:30am Sun &
public hols. 🚻

Madrid's café life was one of
the most attractive features of
the city from the 19th century
right up to the outbreak of the
Civil War. Many intellectuals'
cafés once thrived (see p78), but
the Gijón is one of the few that
survives. It still attracts a lively
crowd of *literati*. Although it is
better known for its atmosphere
than its appearance, the café
has a striking interior with cream-
painted wrought-iron columns,
black-and-white table tops and
a lovely terrace.

❷ Calle del Almirante

Map 5 C5. 🚇 Banco de España,
Colón, Chueca.

Running between the Paseo
de Recoletos and Calle Barquillo,
this street is famous for its
own-label fashion shops. For
most of the 20th century it was
known as "Calle de Cesterías"
(basketwork street).

In earlier days there were five
cane shops where baskets, chairs
and other woven wares were sold.
There were also several taverns
where neighbours gathered
to pass the time. Such was the
fame of the street that the wives

of both Winston Churchill and
the Shah of Persia visited the
del Pozo cane shop.

During the transition to
democracy following Franco's
death in 1975, Calle del Almirante
gained a certain notoriety. Fewer
police patrolled the area, and street
crime rose. Two gay bars opened
in the street and male prostitutes
touted openly for business.

During this time Jesús del
Pozo – Antonio's brother and a
fashion designer – opened the
first boutique, now closed, selling outfits for society weddings
and events of his own design,
next to the family cane shop.
However, it was not until the
1980s, with the cultural movement of *La Movida* (see p106), that
the area became fashionable
and other clothes shops and a
number of chic furnishings and
decor outlets opened. Now Calle
del Almirante is a favourite haunt
of the wealthy and business people from neighbouring offices.

However, the street also retains
other original shops and cafés.
Cafetería Almirante, which serves
bocatas (sandwiches) for those
in a hurry, has been run by Juan
Encinas since 1972.

At No. 23 is the fascinating
Regalos Originales, a must-see
for browsers of antiques and
old curiosity shops.

❸ Plaza de Chueca

Map 5 B5. 🚇 Chueca.

The pedestrianized
Plaza de Chueca
sits between Calle
Augusto Figueroa
and Calle Gravina. It
was originally called
Plaza de San Gregorio
after a statue of the
saint that stood in
Calle San Gregorio, at
the main gate to the
manor house of the
Marqueses of Minaya.
In 1943 the square
was renamed after
Federico Chueca
(1846–1908), a
composer of
zarzuelas (see p79).

Lining the plaza are
small shops, bars and

Newsstand in the Plaza de Chueca

apartment buildings. On one
side of the square is the Taberna
de Ángel Sierra (see pp35 and
185), a *taberna* full of character
that was founded in 1897.

The neighbourhood around
the plaza is an intricate maze of
little streets, one of which,
Augusto Figueroa, is full of
wonderful, yet inexpensive, shoe
shops. Drop into the Mercado
de San Anton for gourmet tapas
and drinks at the rooftop bar.
Also called Chueca, by night it
is the main focus of Madrid's
gay community, with a good
selection of modish bars and
chic restaurants.

❹ Iglesia de Santa Bárbara

Calle General Castaños 2. **Map** 5 C5.
Tel 91 319 48 11. 🚇 Alonso Martínez,
Colón. **Open** 9am–1pm, 5–8pm
Mon–Fri (from 10am Sat & Sun).
🌐 **parroquiadesantabarbara.es**

No expense was spared on this
fine Baroque church, which was
built, along with an adjoining
convent (now the Tribunal
Supremo), for Bárbara de
Braganza, wife of Fernando VI.
To run the convent, which was
to include a school for daughters
of the nobility, Bárbara chose
Las Salesas Reales – an order
of nuns founded in 1610 by
St Francis de Sales and St Jane
Frances de Chantal in Annecy,
France. The church is sometimes
referred to as Las Salesas Reales.

François Carlier (1707–60),
whose father worked on the

The fashionable Calle del Almirante

gardens of La Granja de San Ildefonso *(see p133)*, was appointed architect. The first stone was laid in 1750 and, in 1757, the huge edifice was finished by builder Francisco de Moradillo. He added towers on the roof to Carlier's plans.

The main door is reached through pleasant gardens, added in 1930. The central medallion on the façade, by Doménico Olivieri, shows *The Visitation* of the pregnant Virgin to her cousin Elizabeth. The angels on either side hold the Cross and the two tablets of the Ten Commandments.

The extravagant interior decoration was assigned to Doménico Olivieri. To the right of the entrance is a painting of St Francis de Sales and St Jane de Chantal by Corrado Giaquinto. Opposite is *La Sagrada Familia* (The Holy Family), painted by Francesco Cignaroni.

To the right of the central aisle is the tomb of Fernando VI, adorned with tiers of angels crafted by Francisco Gutiérrez to a Neo-Classical design by Francesco Sabatini. Above the altar is a painting of Francisco Javier and Santa Bárbara. It is by Francisco de Mora, as is *La Visitación* above the high altar. The high altar is decorated with sculptures of San Fernando and Santa Bárbara. To the left is the 19th-century tomb of General O'Donnell by sculptor Jerónimo Suñol. Alongside it is the *Surrender of Seville* by Charles Joseph Flipart. The tomb of Bárbara de Braganza is to the right of the altar in a separate chapel.

❺ Tribunal Supremo

Plaza Villa de Paris. **Map** 5 C5. **Tel** 91 397 11 13. 🚇 Alonso Martínez, Colón. **Open** by appt (email visitas guiadas.ts@justicia.es). Open to the public one week in Nov.

Built by François Carlier in the 1750s as a convent and school for the adjoining Iglesia de Santa Bárbara, this stately Baroque building was run by the Las Salesas Reales nuns. It was built on the orders of Bárbara de

Elaborately decorated interior of the Iglesia de Santa Bárbara

Braganza, wife of Fernando VI. After her death, the nuns were allowed to remain in the convent until 1870, when the building was expropriated by the secular government to become the Palace of Justice. The building fell into disrepair, which was made worse by fires in 1907 and 1915. Fortunately, the Iglesia de Santa Bárbara was unaffected. Later restoration work was undertaken by Joaquín Rojí in 1991–5. In the 1990s, the building became the country's supreme court.

In front of the palace is the Plaza Villa de París, a large

Statue of Bárbara de Braganza in the Plaza Villa de Paris

French-style square. In the middle of it are statues of Fernando VI and Bárbara de Braganza. Across the square is the Audiencia Nacional (National Court). The surrounding roads are often lined with official cars and reporters.

❻ Biblioteca Nacional de España

Paseo de Recoletos 20–22. **Map** 6 D5. **Tel** 91 580 78 00. **Open** 9am–9pm Mon–Sat, 9am–2pm Sun. **Closed** public hols. ♿ 🖥 bne.es

The Biblioteca Nacional de España was founded in 1712 by King Philip V of Spain. It holds about 28 million publications, along with a large number of audiovisual records, maps and music scores. From the start, all printers have had to submit a copy of every book printed in Spain. Among the library's prized possessions is the first edition of *Don Quixote*, and two handwritten codes by Leonardo da Vinci.

The museum offers an overview of the library's history, along with a look at the evolution of writing, reading and other forms of media. There are regular exhibitions, talks and concerts, as well.

⓿ Museo Arqueológico Nacional

With hundreds of exhibits, ranging from prehistoric times to the 19th century, this palatial museum, in the smart district of Salamanca, is one of Madrid's best. It was founded by Isabel II in 1867 and contains many items uncovered during excavations all over Spain, as well as pieces from Egypt, ancient Greece and the Etruscan civilization. Highlights include items from the ancient civilization of El Argar in Andalusia, 7th-century gold votive crowns from Toledo province, Greek and Carthaginian coins, Roman mosaics and Islamic pottery. Following extensive renovations, the museum's courtyards have been covered with glass domes.

16th-century amphora from Talavera de la Reina, Toledo province

Ivory Canister
Commissioned by Al-Hakam II, Caliph of Córdoba, this delicate container from Zamora dates to 964 and is decorated with gazelles, peacocks and other birds.

Second floor

Mezzanine

★ Dama de Baza
This ancient Iberian bust (4th century BC) represents a woman from Baza, Granada. It has a niche at the back for the ashes of the dead.

Gold Bowls
These late Bronze Age bowls (13th–12th century BC) have beaten patterns. They were found in Axtroki in the Basque country, where they had been hidden, probably by a sun-worshipping cult.

Key

- ☐ Archeology and Heritage
- ☐ Prehistory
- ☐ Protohistory
- ☐ Roman Hispania
- ☐ The Medieval World
- ☐ The Modern Era
- ☐ History of the Museum
- ☐ Egypt and Nubia
- ☐ Greece
- ☐ Late Antiquity
- ☐ The History of Coins

Ritual Sword
This exceptional laminated, gold-handled sword from the Bronze Age Argar culture (19th–14th century BC) was discovered in Guadalajara *(see p137)*.

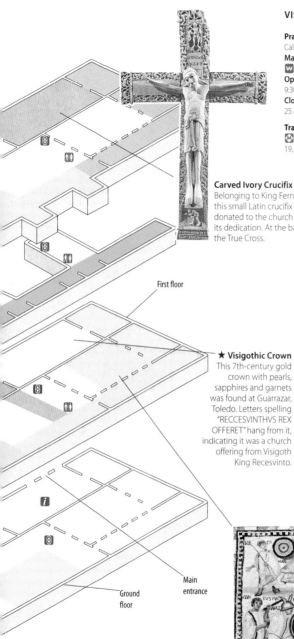

VISITORS' CHECKLIST

Practical Information
Calle de Serrano 13.
Map 6 D5. **Tel** 91 577 79 12.
W man.mcu.es
Open 9:30am–8pm Tue–Sat,
9:30am–3pm Sun.
Closed 1 & 6 Jan, 1 May, 24,
25 & 31 Dec. ♿🅿🎒📷📹

Transport
Ⓜ Serrano, Retiro. 🚌 1, 5, 9, 14,
19, 21, 27, 45, 51, 53, 74.

Carved Ivory Crucifix

Belonging to King Fernando I and Queen Sancha,
this small Latin crucifix was made in 1063 and
donated to the church of San Isidoro in León on
its dedication. At the back is a recess for a relic of
the True Cross.

First floor

★ Visigothic Crown

This 7th-century gold
crown with pearls,
sapphires and garnets
was found at Guarrazar,
Toledo. Letters spelling
"RECCESVINTHVS REX
OFFERET" hang from it,
indicating it was a church
offering from Visigoth
King Recesvinto.

Ground
floor

Main
entrance

★ Mosaic of Gladiators

This 3rd-century Roman mosaic depicts a
combat between gladiators Simmachius and
Maternus on the lower part while its upper
register shows the victory of Simmachius.

Gallery Guide

*The museum's displays date from prehistory
through to the 19th century and are in
chronological order, starting with prehistory on
the ground floor and finishing with the modern
era on the top floor. Temporary exhibitions are
regularly held in the basement.*

❼ Museo de Cera

Paseo de Recoletos 41. **Map** 6 D5.
Tel 91 319 93 30. Colón. **Open** 10am–
2:30pm, 4:30–8:30pm Mon–Fri, 10am–
8:30pm Sat, Sun & public hols.
W museoceramadrid.com

Madrid's Wax Museum, off Plaza
de Colón, houses some 450
wax dummies of well-known
Spanish and international
figures, mostly set in scenes.
A wax likeness of Miguel de
Cervantes, author of *Don
Quixote*, sits at his desk writing,
with windmills behind him.
Another scene imitates Goya's
famous painting, *The 3rd of
May*, depicting French reprisals
for the rebellions of 2 May
1808 in Madrid *(see p22)*. Also
shown is Christopher Columbus'
return from the New World.
Other scenes show navigators
and scientists, the Last
Supper and the history of the
Spanish colonies.

More recent figures include
cowboys from the Wild West,
pop stars, Hollywood actors,
athletes and the Pope. There is
also a café scene where visitors
to the museum are encouraged
to try to identify Spanish
intellectuals, past and present.
Those with children should bear
in mind that some of the scenes
are quite ghoulish. Particularly
gruesome is a bullfighting
scene with a horn piercing a
matador's eye.

Upstairs is *Multivision*, a
cinema where 27 projectors are
used simultaneously to show a
30-minute history of Spain.

Wax figure of Miguel de Cervantes in the
Museo de Cera

Modern monument to Christopher
Columbus, Plaza de Colón

❽ Plaza de Colón

Map 6 D5. Serrano, Colón.

This large square, one of
Madrid's focal points, is
dedicated to Christopher
Columbus (Colón in Spanish).
It is overlooked by 1970s
high-rise buildings, which
replaced the 19th-century
mansions that once stood
here. On the south side is a
palace housing the
National Library and
Archeological Museum
(see pp98–9). On the
north side, on the
corner of La Castellana,
the Post-Modern sky-
scraper of the Heron
Corporation towers
over the square.

The real feature of
the square, however, is
the pair of monuments
dedicated to Christopher
Columbus and his
discovery of the Americas.
The oldest, and prettiest,
is a Neo-Gothic spire
built in 1885, with
Columbus at its top,
pointing west. Carved
reliefs on the plinth
give highlights of his
discoveries. Across
the square is the
second, more modern
monument – a cluster
of four large concrete shapes
inscribed with quotations
relating to Columbus' historic
journey to America.

Statue of Columbus,
Plaza de Colón

Beneath the Plaza de Colón
is an extensive complex, the
Centro de Arte Fernán Gómez,
which includes the city's
municipal art centre, exhibition
halls, lecture rooms and a
theatre, renamed Fernán
Gómez after the famous actor.
Visitors can also find a tourist
information office here.

❾ Museo Arqueológico Nacional

See pp98–9.

❿ Calle de Serrano

Map 8 D1. Serrano.

Named after a 19th-century
politician, Madrid's smartest
shopping street runs north
from the triumphal Plaza de la
Independencia to the Plaza del
Ecuador, in the well-heeled
district of El Viso. The street is
lined with shops *(see p172)* –
many specializing in luxury
items – housed in old-
fashioned mansion-blocks.
Several of Spain's top
designers, including Adolfo
Domínguez and Roberto
Verino, have boutiques in
the middle of the street.
Towards the northern end
are the ABC Serrano mall *(see
p173)* and the Museo Lázaro
Galdiano *(see pp102–3)*.
A wide selection of luxury
goods shops can be found
on Calle de José Ortega y
Gasset, including branches
of the Italian shops
Valentino and Gucci, as
well as Chanel, Calvin
Klein and Escada. Lower
down Calle de Serrano,
towards Serrano Metro
station, are two
branches of El Corte
Inglés and the stylish
clothes and leather
goods shop Loewe.
On the Calle de
Claudio Coello, which
runs parallel with
Serrano, there are several
lavish antique shops, in
keeping with the area's
upmarket atmosphere.

Statue of Salamanca's founder, the Marqués de Salamanca

⓫ Salamanca

Map 6 E3. Velázquez, Serrano, Núñez de Balboa, Lista, Príncipe de Vergara, Goya, Diego de León.

Madrid's Salamanca district (Barrio de Salamanca) was developed in 1862–3 as an area for the bourgeoisie, and takes its name from its founder, José "Pepito" Salamanca, Marqués de Salamanca (1811–83). He was a lawyer who, by the age of 23, had already been elected as a deputy to the Cortes (Spanish parliament). The Marqués had a great flair for politics and business, and made his vast fortune from salt, railways and the building of Salamanca. He was also the founder of Banco de Isabel II, which was the forerunner of Banco de España (see p71).

The Marqués inaugurated his magnificent palace at Paseo de Recoletos 10 (now the BBVA Bank) in 1858, and by 1862 began developing his land behind it. The streets were planned to run north–south or east–west, and the area was to comprise apartment blocks, churches, schools, hospitals and theatres. He also built the first tramways in Madrid, connecting the Barrio de Salamanca with the centre of Madrid. A statue of the Marqués stands at the confluence of Ortega y Gasset and Príncipe de Vergara.

To this day the *barrio* consists mainly of six- to eight-floor apartment blocks, and is home to many well-to-do families. This is an area where just a hint of cool weather brings out the mink coats. Some of Madrid's best shops and markets can be found here, as well as a number of discreet restaurants. The *pijos* (rich spoiled children) gather at the *cervecerías* and bars around Calle de Goya and Calle de Alcalá.

The oldest church of the *barrio*, San Andrés de los Flamencos (Calle de Claudio Coello 99), built in 1884, now houses the Fundación Carlos de Amberes, a cultural centre maintaining links between Spain, Holland and Belgium. Behind the altar is a painting of *St Andrew* by Rubens. The unofficial parish church of Salamanca is the Iglesia de la Concepción (Calle de Goya 26), built between 1902 and 1914, with a notable white iron spire topped by a statue of the Virgin. At Calle de Hermosilla 45 is the charming Protestant Church of St George (1926).

The best-preserved of the area's Neo-Classical palaces is Palacio de Amboage (1918) by Joaquín Roji on the corner of Velázquez and Juan Bravo. It is now the Italian Embassy, and features a lovely garden.

Modern and fascinating is the architecture inside Platea, an avant-garde gourmet market in Plaza Colón. Different food stalls, offering a variety of products, can be found here. On the first floor, visit the restaurant, Arriba, and the cocktail bar, El Palcao, both arranged near the stage.

⓬ Fundación Juan March

Calle de Castelló 77. **Tel** 91 435 42 40. Núñez de Balboa. **Open** 11am–8pm Mon–Sat, 10am–2pm Sun & public. hols. (timings vary, call ahead). **march.es**

Established in 1955 with an endowment from financier Juan March, this cultural and scientific foundation is best known for its art exhibitions and concerts. The marble-and-glass headquarters, in Madrid's Barrio de Salamanca, opened in 1975. The foundation has published over 380 books and collections. It also owns the Museo de Arte Abstracto in Cuenca and a gallery of Spanish art in Palma de Mallorca. The ground floor houses a shop, as well as the main exhibition area. Works by Kandinsky, Picasso and Matisse have been shown here, alongside some of the collection of over 1,300 contemporary Spanish pieces. There is a 400-seat auditorium in the basement where free concerts are held.

Sculpture by Chillida, Fundación Juan March

The second-floor library has a collection of contemporary Spanish music, with listening desks. There is also a library on contemporary Spanish theatre and entertainment.

Hidden away from the public are the Juan March Institute for Study and Investigation – one of the world's top forums in the field of biology – and the Centre for Advanced Study in the Social Sciences.

Sculpture by Barrocol, by the main entrance to the Fundación Juan March

⑬ Museo Lázaro Galdiano

This Neo-Renaissance mansion houses nearly 3,000 items from the private collection of financier and editor José Lázaro Galdiano (1862–1947). The exhibits, ranging from the 6th century BC to the 20th century, include archeological finds, religious artifacts, Limoges enamels, Old Masters, medieval ivory, jewellery and silver. In 1903 Lázaro Galdiano married Argentine heiress Paula Florido and they built the mansion to celebrate – and to show off the growing collection. By the time Lázaro Galdiano died, some 13,000 items were brought together in Madrid.

Second floor

19

15

16

G2

Atrium

Portrait of a Lady
Joshua Reynolds painted this portrait in the late 18th century. Other British artists represented in the museum include Constable and Romney.

7

14

13

Marquetry Writing Desk
This elaborate, 16th-century German desk was among many exported to Spain by cabinet-makers in Augsburg and Nuremberg. Felipe II is known to have bought desks similar to this.

First floor

★ The Witches' Sabbath
(1798)
This painting by Francisco de Goya is based on a legend from Aragón, the artist's birthplace. It depicts a witches' Sabbath around the devil, who is represented by the scapegoat.

Gallery Guide

The ground floor houses one of the best European collections of silverware and jewellery, with items from the 3rd to the 19th century. The first floor contains Spanish paintings, including a room devoted to Goya. Highlights on the second floor include works by Bosch. The top floor has displays of textiles, ceramics, weapons, sculptures and enamels.

Main entrance

St John the Baptist
Surrounded by the lamb of spiritual life and other allegorical animals and birds, Hieronymus Bosch's contemplative *St John the Baptist* (c.1485–1510) reclines in an almost pastoral landscape punctuated by grotesque plants.

VISITORS' CHECKLIST

Practical Information
Calle de Serrano 122. **Map** 6 E1.
Tel 91 561 60 84. **W** flg.es
Open 10am–4:30pm Mon &
Wed–Sat, 10am–3pm Sun.
Closed Tue & public hols.
🎫 (free for the last hour).
📷 by appt. ♿🚻🅿🏛

Transport
Ⓜ Rubén Darío, Gregorio
Marañón. 🚌 7, 14, 16, 19, 27,
40, 150.

Inés de Zúñiga
This painting of the Countess of Monterrey was executed by Juan Carreño de Miranda in the late 17th century. She is dressed in a wide Spanish farthingale.

Ground floor

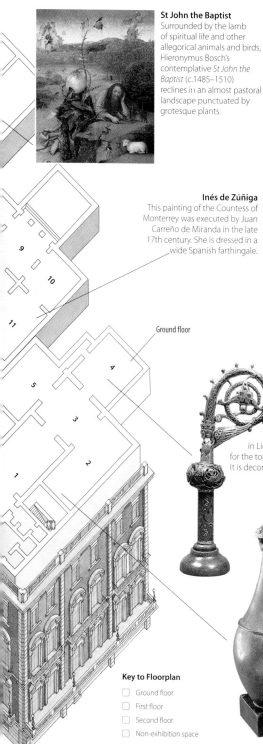

★ Crosier Head
This beautiful gilded and enamelled object was made in Limoges in the 13th century for the top of a bishop's staff (crosier). It is decorated with stylized plants.

★ Tartessic Ewer
One of the oldest and most interesting archeological items displayed in the Treasure Chamber of the museum is this Tartessic bronze jug, which has a fine feline head as its spout. It was made in the mid-6th century BC, in the Tartessic era.

Key to Floorplan
☐ Ground floor
☐ First floor
☐ Second floor
☐ Non-exhibition space

Former studio of Impressionist Joaquín Sorolla in the Museo Sorolla

⓮ Museo Sorolla

Paseo del General Martínez Campos 37. **Map** 5 C1. **Tel** 91 310 15 84. Ⓜ Rubén Darío, Iglesia, Gregorio Marañón. **Open** 9:30am–8pm Tue– Sat, 10am–3pm Sun. 🎫 (free Sat after 2pm & Sun). Ⓦ **museosorolla.mcu.es**

The studio-mansion of Valencian Impressionist painter Joaquín Sorolla is now a museum displaying his art, left virtually as it was when he died in 1923.

Although Sorolla is perhaps best known for his brilliantly lit Mediterranean beach scenes, the changing styles of his paintings are well represented here, with examples of his gentle portraiture and works depicting people from different parts of Spain. Also on display are objects amassed during the artist's lifetime, including tiles and ceramics. The house, built in 1910, is surrounded by an Andalusian-style garden, designed by Sorolla himself.

⓯ Museo de Arte Público

Paseo de la Castellana. **Map** 6 E2. Ⓜ Rubén Darío.

In the early 1970s J Antonio Fernández Ordóñez and Julio Martínez Calzón, the architects of the Calle Juan Bravo bridge, filled the space underneath it with abstract sculptures by 20th-century Spanish artists. The space on the east side of Paseo de la Castellana is dominated by *Sirena Varada, or Stranded Mermaid* (1972–3), a concrete sculpture hanging from four rods by

Eduardo Chillida, the noted Basque sculptor. Alberto Sánchez's *Toros Ibéricos* is another dramatic installation, and there is a penguin by Joan Miró. Other sculptors represented here are Andreu Alfaro, Julio González, Rafael Leoz, Gustavo Torner, José María Subirachs, Francisco Sobrino, Martín Chirino and Eusebio Sempere.

On the west side are two bronzes by Pablo Serrano. Visitors should take care when crossing the busy Paseo de la Castellana.

⓰ Calle de Zurbano

Paseo de la Castellana. **Map** 5 C3. Ⓜ Alonso Martínez, Rubén Darío.

This bustling street connects the trendy neighbourhoods of Chueca and Salesas to the business hub further north. There is much to discover here – from early 20th-century Revivalist buildings, charming shops and art galleries to bakeries, restaurants, hotels and beautiful mansions with verdant gardens.

⓱ Museo del Romanticismo

Calle de San Mateo 13. **Map** 5 A4. **Tel** 91 448 10 45. Ⓜ Tribunal, Alonso Martínez. **Open** 9:30am–8:30pm Tue–Sat (to 6:30pm Nov–Apr), 10am–3pm Sun & hols. 🎫 (free Sat pm & Sun am). **Closed** 1, 6 Jan, 1 May, 24, 25 & 31 Dec. 📷 by appt. Ⓦ **museoromanticismo.mcu.es**

This Neo-Classical mansion was designed by Manuel Martín in 1776 for the Marqués de

Matallana. By 1924 it had been turned into a museum by the Marqués de la Vega-Inclán, the founder of Spain's fine network of state-owned parador hotels *(see p150)*, who was an avid art collector. In 1921, the Marqués donated his 19th-century paintings, books and some furniture to form the nucleus of a museum. In 1927 the museum was acquired by the state, and reorganized to look like the home of a wealthy mid-19th century family, evoking the Romantic period.

The exhibits are housed in 26 rooms on the ground floor and first floor of the building. As well as a vast array of 19th-century objects, such as musical instruments, photographs, dolls and ornaments, there are many portraits by leading artists. They include *General Prim* by Esquivel, José de Madrazo's *Fernando VII* and *María Cristina* by Salvador Gutiérrez. Several works by Leonardo Alenza include the disturbing *Satire of a Romantic Suicide*.

In the ballroom is a Pleyel piano that belonged to Isabel II *(see p27)*. The ceiling is by Zacarías González Velázquez, and the carpet comes from the Real Fábrica de Tapices *(see p114)*.

The Museo del Romanticismo has a fine collection of works by the costumbristas – artists who painted scenes of everyday life in Andalusia and Madrid. Many of their works depict local festivals and traditions.

Earlier works on display in the museum include a painting of

Goya's *St Gregory the Great* in the chapel of the Museo del Romanticismo

St Gregory the Great by Goya *(see p32)* above the altar in the chapel in room 13.

The Mariano José de Larra Room is dedicated to this great satirical journalist and writer. Among his personal effects is the duelling pistol he used to kill himself, after being rejected by his lover.

⑱ Museo de Historia de Madrid

Calle de Fuencarral 78. **Map** 5 A4. **Tel** 91 701 18 63. 🚇 Tribunal. **Closed** for refurbishment (except one section open 9:30am–8pm Tue–Sun).
♿ 🚾 madrid.es/museodehistoria

The Museo de Historia de Madrid is worth visiting just for its majestic Baroque doorway by Pedro de Ribera, arguably the finest in Madrid. Housed in the former hospice of St Ferdinand, the museum was inaugurated in 1929. In the only room that is open during refurbishment, a series of maps shows how radically Madrid has been transformed. Among them is Pedro Texeira's 1656 map, thought to be the oldest of the city. There is also a meticulous model of Madrid, made in 1830 by León Gil de Palacio.

Modern exhibits include the reconstructed study of Ramón Gómez de la Serna, a key figure of the literary gatherings in the Café de Pombo *(see p89)*. In the garden is the *Fuente de la Fama* (Fountain of Fame), also by Ribera.

⑲ Malasaña

Map 2 E4. 🚇 Tribunal, Bilbao, San Bernardo.

Officially called Barrio de Maravillas, or District of Miracles, after a 17th-century church that once stood here, this area is more widely known as Malasaña. Thin streets slope down from Carranza and Fuencarral to its bohemian hub, the **Plaza del Dos de Mayo**. In 1808, *Madrileños* made an heroic last stand here against Napoleon's occupying troops at the gate of Monteleón

barracks. The arch in the square is all that is left of the barracks. In front of it is a memorial by Antonio Solá to artillery officers Daoiz and Velarde, who defended the barracks.

In the 1940s and 1950s the area deteriorated, but residents fiercely fended off demolition threats. It acquired its bohemian atmosphere in the 1960s, when hippies were lured into the district by cheap rents. Later it became the centre of *La Movida (see p106)*, the frenzied creative scene that began after the death of Franco.

Today Malasaña's streets combine the best of both worlds. Artists and writers have once again moved into the area, along with antique-sellers and yuppies. The charming streets have been cobbled, and boast pretty fountains and plenty of trees. At night, however, the streets are still thronged with people looking for a wild time.

Malasaña is rich in sites of historical and cultural interest. **Plaza de San Ildefonso**, one of many squares remodelled by José I (Joseph Bonaparte) *(see p22)*, has an attractive central fountain with serpents entwined around conch shells. Near the Neo-Classical **Iglesia de San Ildefonso**, built in 1827, one can still see the façade of the **Vaquería**, a

The main altar of Iglesia de San Plácido in Malasaña painted by Claudio Coello

dairy shop that opened in 1911 and closed in 2007. Decorative cows frame the door in Art Deco style.

In Calle de la Puebla, the 17th-century **Iglesia de San Antonio de los Alemanes** is remarkable for its elliptical interior, swathed in frescoes by Juan Carreño, Francisco de Ricci and Luca Giordano.

Close by is the 17th-century **Iglesia de San Plácido** with a cupola painted by Francisco Rizi and the work of Claudio Coello adorning the altars.

The **Iglesia de San Martín**, in Calle de San Roque, was built in 1648. The painting above the altar depicts St Martin of Tours giving half his cloak to a naked beggar.

Manuela Malasaña

The daughter of Juan Manuel Malasaña, a craftsman and hero of the 1808 uprising *(see p22)*, Manuela Malasaña died at the age of 16 in the struggle against Napoleon. She was a seamstress who, according to local legend, was caught carrying a pair of scissors by the French and was subsequently shot for possession of a concealed weapon. In 1961 Calle de Manuela Malasaña, which lies between Fuencarral and San Bernardo where the Monteleón artillery park had been, was named after this local heroine.

Ribera's sculptured door at the Cuartel del Conde Duque

⑳ Cuartel del Conde Duque

Calle del Conde Duque 9–11. **Map** 2 D4. **Tel** 91 722 05 73. Ⓜ Noviciado, San Bernardo. Cultural Centre: **Open** 10:30am–2pm, 5:30–9pm Tue–Sat, 10:30am–2pm Sun & public hols. ♿ Ⓦ **condeduquemadrid.es**

This enormous rectangular complex is named after Gaspar de Guzmán (1587–1645), Conde Duque de Olivares. As a minister of Felipe IV *(see p26)*, the count had a palace on this site. After his death, the palace was neglected and fell into ruin. Subsequently, the plot was divided into two distinct sections. On one section, the Palacio de Liria was built for the Duke of Alba. On the other, the barracks for Los Guardias de Corps were constructed between 1720 and 1754 by Pedro de Ribera, who adorned them with a Baroque façade. The three-storey barracks were in use for over a century but, in 1869, they suffered a major fire and eventually fell into a state of total dilapidation. A hundred years later, in 1969, Madrid's city hall made the decision to restore the old army barracks.

The building now houses the city's historical archives; the Museum of Contemporary Art; several council offices; a library; a cultural centre with four temporary exhibition rooms; and an auditorium

La Movida

With Franco's death in 1975 came a new period of personal and artistic liberty. A momentous ideological shift occurred among the people, a phenomenon known as *La Movida*, or "the action". At the time, it received the support of the mayor of Madrid, Tierno Galván, and saw flourishing creative expression in literature, photography, music, art, television and fashion. The movement also led to the rise and emergence of satirical film director Pedro Almodóvar.

Poster for Almodóvar's *Women on the Verge of a Nervous Breakdown*

within the old chapel, built in 1718 by de Ribera.

A theatre and rehearsal rooms were added to the complex after extensive renovation.

㉑ Palacio de Liria

Calle de la Princesa 20. **Map** 1 C4. **Tel** 91 547 53 02. Ⓜ Ventura Rodríguez. **Open** 10am, 11am & noon Fri (by appt); email: visitas@ fundacioncasadealba.com

The lavish but much-restored Palacio de Liria was completed by Ventura Rodríguez in 1780. It was once the home of the Alba family, and is still owned by the duke. The sumptuous rooms house an outstanding collection of art and Flemish tapestries. The walls are adorned with paintings by famous masters, among them Titian, Rubens and Rembrandt.

Spanish art itself is particularly well represented, and the Albas' collection includes a number of major works by Goya *(see p32)*. One such significant canvas is his 1795 portrait of the Duchess of Alba. Also featured are several interesting works by El Greco *(see p145)*, Zurbarán and Velázquez *(see p32)*.

Room adorned with paintings by Goya in the Palacio de Liria

Castizos of Madrid

The true working-class *Madrileños*, whose families have lived in the neighbourhoods of Old Madrid, Chamberí and Cuatro Caminos for many generations, are known as *castizos*. Around 1850, in their revolt against the bourgeoisie, who were basking in the Romantic and patriotic cultural revolution that followed the defeat of the French earlier in the 19th century, the *castizos* decided to reclaim their proud heritage. The Madrid equivalent of London's Cockneys, *los castizos Madrileños* not only revived their district fiestas, one of the world's best neighbourhood-bonding traditions, but also reinvented costumes to go with them and formed numerous associations that still thrive today. At any of the traditional Madrid fiestas or *romerías* (processions) you will see the *castizos*, or *majos* (dandies) as they are known, with their *manolas*, or partners, attired in what is now their smart, traditional uniform.

Typical *manola* costume consists of a flowery headscarf with at least one carnation in the front, an *alfombra* (literally translated as carpet), which is actually a huge embroidered shawl, or *mantón de Manila*, worn over the shoulders, and a *falda vestida* (long dress), sometimes with an apron.

Carnation on the headscarf

Black-and-white *parpusa* (hat)

White *barbosa* (shirt)

Black *alares* (trousers)

Alfombra – shawl with a long fringe

Colourful dress (*falda vestida*)

Men's clothes are referred to in *castizo* argot: black or black-and-white check *parpusa* (cap), a white *barbosa* (shirt), a black *chupín* (waistcoat), a black or black-and-white check *chupa* (jacket), a *safo* (white handkerchief), a *peluco* (pocket watch), a red carnation in the buttonhole, black or black-and-white check *alares* (trousers), *picantes* (socks) and shining *calcos* (shoes).

In May, the *castizos* are out in force during the Dos de Mayo fiesta. On 15 May is the Fiesta de San Isidro, with a *romería* from the Puerta de Toledo down to the Río Manzanares. The next major fiestas are on 13 June at San Antonio de la Florida; and 15 August, with the Fiesta de la Virgen de Paloma, a *castizo* favourite. *Castizo* processions include the Romería de San Blas on 3 February, and the Romería de San Eugenio on 14 November.

FURTHER AFIELD

Several of Madrid's best sights, including interesting but little-known museums, lie outside the city centre. The Museo de América displays artifacts from Spain's former colonies, while the Museo de Traje is dedicated to the development of fashion from the Middle Ages to the present day. There is a wealth of historic buildings outside the city centre, ranging from the Egyptian Templo de Debod and the Puerta de Toledo, a triumphal arch begun in 1813 on the

orders of José I (Joseph Bonaparte), to the old-style apartment building of La Corrala. There are a number of other attractions surrounding the centre of Madrid. To the north lies the modern commercial district of Azca, with skyscrapers, office blocks and upmarket shops. Perfect if you need to escape from the bustle of the city for a while, west of Old Madrid, across the Río Manzanares, is Madrid's vast, green recreation ground, the Casa de Campo.

Sights at a Glance

Historic Buildings
③ Sala del Canal de Isabel II
⑧ Real Fábrica de Tapices
⑪ La Corrala
⑫ Puerta de Toledo
⑬ Puente de Segovia and Río Manzanares
⑯ Templo de Debod
⑰ Estación de Príncipe Pío

Churches
⑮ Ermita de San Antonio de la Florida

Museums and Galleries
① Museo de América
② Museo del Traje
⑤ Museo de Ciencias Naturales
⑦ Museo Casa de la Moneda
⑨ Museo del Ferrocarril
⑩ Matadero Madrid

Squares, Parks and Districts
④ Azca
⑥ Plaza de Toros de Las Ventas
⑭ Casa de Campo
⑱ Parque el Capricho

Key
◻ Main sightseeing area
◻ Parks and open spaces
⸺ Highway/Motorway
⸺ Major road
⸺ Minor road

0 kilometres 1
0 miles 1

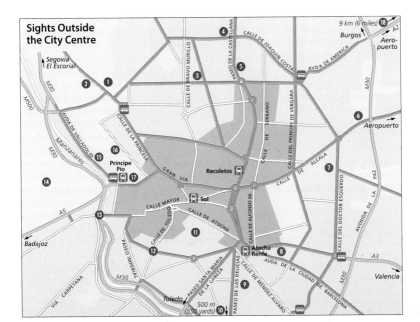

◀ Mudéjar arches and tilework on the exterior of the Plaza de Toros de Las Ventas

For keys to symbols *see back flap*

Old and new – the Mirador del Faro alongside the Museo de América

❶ Museo de América

Avenida de los Reyes Católicos 6.
Tel 91 549 26 41. 🚇 Moncloa.
Open 9:30am–8:30pm Tue–Sat (to 6:30pm Nov–Apr), 10am–3pm Sun & public hols. **Closed** some public hols. 🎫 (free on Sun). 🎧 by appt. ♿
🆆 **museodeamerica.mcu.es**

A unique collection of artifacts relating to Spain's colonization of the Americas is housed in this fine museum. Many of the exhibits, which range from prehistoric to more recent times, were brought to Europe by the early explorers of the New World *(see p20)*.

The collection is arranged on the first and second floors, and individual rooms have themes such as society, religion and communication. Exhibits document the Atlantic voyages made by the first explorers.

For many visitors, the highlight of the museum is the rare Mayan *Códice Tro-cortesiano* (AD 1250–1500) from Mexico. This is a type of parchment illustrated with hieroglyphics of scenes from everyday life.

Also worth seeing are the Treasure of the Quimbayas, a collection of pre-Columbian gold and silver objects from around AD 500–1000, and the collection of contemporary folk art from some of Spain's former American colonies.

❷ Museo del Traje

Avenida Juan de Herrera 2. **Tel** 91 550 47 00. 🚇 Moncloa, Ciudad Universitaria. 🚌 46, 82, 83, 132, 133, G.
🆆 **museodeltraje.mcu.es**

This fascinating museum is devoted to fashion, with outfits from the Middle Ages to those by contemporary designers. There are over 160,000 pieces in its collection, and since many of the items are fragile, the costumes are displayed on rotation. The museum also hosts special events, temporary exhibitions, courses and workshops, that are open to the public.

The current building was designed by Jaime López de Asiaín, and won the National Prize for Architecture in 1969. The building was inaugurated in 1975, when it first housed the Spanish Museum of Contemporary Art. This later became the Museo Reina Sofía, but once the museum relocated to central Madrid, Museo del Traje was founded.

Sala del Canal de Isabel II, a water tower turned exhibition centre

❸ Sala del Canal de Isabel II

Calle de Santa Engracia 125.
Tel 91 545 10 00. 🚇 Ríos Rosas.
Open 11am–2pm, 5–8:30pm Tue–Sat, 11am–2pm Sun & public hols.
Closed 1 Jan, Good Fri & 25 Dec. ♿
🆆 **madrid.org**

This renovated water tower is used to host photographic exhibitions but, on the whole, most visitors come to marvel at its complex construction. In the

late 19th century the water supply for Madrid was based on a project patronized by Isabel II *(see p27)* in 1851 and known as Canal de Isabel II, the name given to Madrid's water company. The first dam was built in the Lozoya valley, about 80 km (50 miles) north of Madrid in the Guadarrama mountains, and a duct carried the water south to a reservoir.

More reservoirs were built to cope with the capital's ever-increasing needs but, in 1903, the development of the high-lying suburbs of Chamberí and Cuatro Caminos dictated the need for a water tower to supply new pipes by gravity. Martín y Montalvo was the engineer enlisted to carry out the task. He designed a polygonal tower of brick and iron, 36 m (118 ft) high, surmounted by a 1,500-sq m (16,145-sq ft) tank resting on an iron ring. Work started in 1908, and by 1911 the water tower was finished at a cost of nearly 350,000 pesetas. It was in service until 1952.

The regional government of Madrid decided to restore the tower in 1985, taking out the water works but retaining the huge tank. Access to the exhibition floors within the tower has been made possible by hydraulically driven elevators (lifts) and steel staircases.

Bordering the tower are the busy Calle de Santa Engracia and the gardens and turf that form a roof over one of the major underground reservoirs of the Canal de Isabel II.

❹ Azca

🚇 Nuevos Ministerios, Santiago Bernabéu. Estadio Santiago Bernabéu: Avenida de Concha Espina 1. **Tel** 90 231 18 09. Tour & Museum: **Open** 10am–7pm Mon–Sat, 10:30am–6:30pm Sun. 🎧 🎫 only.
🆆 **realmadrid.com**

In 1969, work began on the development of this "mini-Manhattan" along the west side of the Paseo de la Castellana. It stretches from the **Nuevos Ministerios** complex in the south to the **Palacio de Congresos y Exposiciones** in the north. The idea was to create a modern commercial area away from the congested city centre. Today, some 30,000 people work here.

By day Azca is a mecca for shoppers. Department store El Corte Inglés (see p172) runs alongside Nuevos Ministerios station, and the Moda shopping mall is served by Santiago Bernabéu Metro. Across from the Plaza de Lima is the **Estadio Santiago Bernabéu**, home of Real Madrid Football Club, built in 1950.

Major companies operate in the tower blocks, alongside hotels, apartments, cinemas, restaurants and bars. The elderly are drawn by bingo halls, while the young throng the discos at the weekends.

In the centre of Azca is the multilevel pedestrian **Plaza Pablo Ruíz Picasso** with trees, benches, fountains and walkways. Azca is dominated by the aluminium-clad **Torre Picasso**, Madrid's tallest office building. Completed in 1989, it has 46 floors, bronzed windows and a heliport. It was designed by Minoru Yamasaki, architect of the twin towers of New York's World Trade Centre, which were destroyed in the terrorist attack of 2001.

The **Torre Europa** on Plaza de Lima is another notable building. Designed by Miguel de Oriol e Ybarra and completed in 1982, its exterior concrete supports incorporate a clock. As well as 28 floors of offices, it has three commercial floors below street level.

The rust-coloured **Banco Bilbao Vizcaya** on Azca's south corner was designed by Francisco Javier Sáenz de Oiza. Built in 1980, it stands over the underground rail line between Chamartín and Atocha.

Inside the modern Origins of Life section of Madrid's Museo de Ciencias Naturales

❺ Museo de Ciencias Naturales

Calle José Gutierrez Abascal 2. **Tel** 91 411 13 28. 🚇 Gregorio Marañón. **Open** 10am–5pm Tue–Fri, Sun & public hols, 10am–8pm Sat (Jul & Aug: 10am–3pm). **Closed** 1, 6 Jan, 1 May & 25 Dec. 📷 📹 by arrangement. ♿ 🌐 **mncn.csic.es**

This museum, built in 1887, contains 16,400 minerals, 220 meteorites, 30,000 birds and mammals and many more items in its archives. The entrance leads to the Biodiversity section. This is an ecological display of numerous examples of wildlife, from exotic birds to rare animals, insects and butterflies. Lions, tigers and deer stare out from the walls, while the shelves are heavy with bottled lizards, fish and snakes. An interactive computer display room provides valuable insight into the sounds and habitats of animals and birds.

In another part of the exhibition is information on the Atapuerca site near Burgos, north of Madrid, where Europe's earliest human remains (some 780,000 years old) were discovered in 1997. There is also a huge African elephant, shot by the Duke of Alba in the Sudan in 1916. The elephant's skin was sent back to Spain and reassembled.

The museum also houses displays on the origins of the earth and of life. The star of the show is the 1.8-million-year-old skeleton of *Megatherium americanum*, a bear-like creature from the late Cenozoic period found in Argentina in 1788. Nearby is a Glyptodon (giant armadillo), also from Argentina, along with a life-size reproduction of a Diplodocus dinosaur skeleton which was found in the United States.

The exhibition concludes with a glittering collection of minerals that includes metals and precious stones. There is also a large number of meteorite specimens.

The Industrial Engineers' School is also housed in the museum building, and behind are the headquarters of Spain's state scientific institute, CSIC. Opposite the entrances is a pleasant terrace bar which looks out over a small park with a fountain and a statue of Isabel I (see p26).

The Torre Europa rising above the commercial centre of Azca

Wall tiles at the Museo Taurino, Plaza de Toros de Las Ventas

❻ Plaza de Toros de Las Ventas

Calle de Alcalá 237. **Tel** 01 356 22 00.
Ventas. (by appt.) 10am–
7pm daily (Mar–Oct: till 4pm Sun).
Museo Taurino: **Tel** 91 725 18 57.
Open Mar–Oct: 9:30am–2:30pm
Mon–Fri, 10am–1pm Sun; Nov–Feb:
9:30am–2:30pm Mon–Fri.
W lasventastour.com

Whatever your opinion of
bullfighting, Las Ventas is
undoubtedly one of the most
beautiful bullrings in Spain.
Built in 1929 in Neo-Mudéjar
style, it replaced the city's
original bullring, which stood
near the Puerta de Alcalá

(*see p70*). Its
horseshoe arches
around the outer
galleries and
elaborate tilework
decoration make it
an attractive venue
for the *corridas*
(bullfights), held from
May to October. The
statues outside the
bullring are of two
Spanish bullfighters,
Antonio Bienvenida
and José Cubero.
Adjoining the
bullring is the
Museo Taurino.
This contains a varied
collection of bull-
fighting memorabilia,
including portraits
and sculptures of
famous matadors, as
well as the heads of several bulls
killed during fights at Las Ventas.
Visitors can examine bullfighters'
capes and *banderillas* – sharp
darts used to wound the bull.
The gory highlight of the
exhibition, for some people,
is the blood-drenched *traje de
luces* worn by Manolete during
his fateful bullfight at Linares
in Andalusia in 1947. Also on
display is a costume which
belonged to Juanita Cruz, a
female bullfighter of the 1930s
who was forced, in the face of
prejudice, to leave Spain. In
summer the bullring is used
as a venue for a season of
rock concerts.

❼ Museo Casa de la Moneda

Calle del Doctor Esquerdo 36. **Tel** 91
566 65 44. O'Donell. **Open** 10am–
5:30pm Tue–Fri, 10am–2pm Sat & Sun.
Closed 1 & 6 Jan, 1 May, Thu–Sun at
Easter, 24, 25 & 31 Dec.
W museocasadelamoneda.es

The Spanish Mint and stamp
factory is located in a vast
granite building. The museum,
in the north side of the building,
was founded in the 18th
century by Charles III's
Director of the Mint. It traces
the history of currency, from
early trading in salt, shells and
bracelets up to the euro – the
monetary unit of the European
Union – along 17 rooms that
hold around 200,000 pieces.
The collection was first made
open to the public in 1867.

Coins feature prominently,
with maps and photographs
complementing displays of
Greek and Roman coins. The
earliest coins have images of
mythical gods; the picture of
Cybele, mother of the gods,
on a Roman coin from 78 BC
is similar to the sculpture in
the Plaza de Cibeles (*see p71*).

As well as later Roman coins
endowed with more symbolic
images, there are Visigothic and
Moorish coins. Early Moorish
coins are inscribed in Latin
and later ones in Arabic.

There are also engravings
for currency notes, stamps,
medals and official documents.

Plaza de Toros de Las Ventas, Madrid's beautiful Neo-Mudéjar bullring

The Art of Bullfighting

Bullfighting is a sacrificial ritual in which men (and a few women) pit themselves against an animal bred for the ring. In this "authentic religious drama", as poet Federico García Lorca *(see p32)* described it, the spectator experiences the same intensity of fear and exaltation as the matador. There are three stages, or *tercios*, in the *corrida* (bullfight). The first two are aimed at progressively weakening the bull. In the third, the matador moves in for the kill. Despite opposition on the grounds of cruelty, bullfighting is still popular. For some Spaniards, talk of banning bullfighting is an assault on the essence of their being. For them, the *toreo*, the art of bullfighting, is a noble part of their heritage. However, fights today can be debased by practices designed to disadvantage the bull, in particular shaving its horns to make them blunt.

The toro bravo (fighting bull), bred for courage and aggression, enjoys a full life prior to its time in the ring. Bulls must be at least four years old before they can fight.

Manolete is regarded by most followers of bullfighting as one of Spain's greatest ever matadors. He was finally gored to death by the bull Islero at Linares, Jaén, in 1947.

The matador wears a **traje de luces** (suit of lights), a colourful silk outfit embroidered with gold or silver sequins.

Banderillas (barbed darts) are thrust into the bull's back muscles to weaken them.

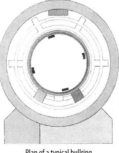

Joselito was a leading matador, famous for his purist style and his superb skill with the *capa* (red cape) and the *muleta* (matador's stick). He has now officially retired from the *ruedos* (bullring).

The Bullring

The *corrida* audience is seated in the *tendidos* (stalls) or in the *palcos* (balcony), where the *presidencia* (president's box) is situated. Opposite are the *puerta de cuadrillas*, through which the matador and team arrive, and the *arrastre de toros* (exit for bulls). Before entering the ring, the matadors wait in a *callejón* (corridor) behind *barreras* and *burladeros* (barriers). Horses are kept in the *patio de caballos* and the bulls in the *corrales*.

Plan of a typical bullring

Key
- ☐ Tendidos
- ☐ Palcos
- ☐ Presidencia
- ☐ Puerta de cuadrillas
- ☐ Arrastre de toros
- ☐ Callejón
- ☐ Barreras
- ☐ Burladeros
- ☐ Patio de caballos
- ☐ Corrales

❽ Real Fábrica de Tapices

Calle de Fuenterrabía 2. **Map** 8 F5. **Tel** 91 434 05 50. Menéndez Pelayo. 10am–2pm Mon–Fri. **Closed** public hols & Aug. **w** realfabricadetapices.com

Founded by Felipe V in 1721, the Royal Tapestry Factory is the only surviving factory opened by the Bourbons in the 18th century. In 1889 the factory was moved to this building, just south of the Parque del Retiro (see p81).

Visitors can see the making by hand of the carpets and tapestries, a process which has changed little since the factory was built. Goya (see p32) and his brother-in-law Francisco Bayeu drew cartoons on which the tapestries for the royal family were based. Some of the cartoons are on display here, in the museum; others are in the Prado (see pp82–5). Several tapestries can be seen at the Palacio de El Pardo (see p140) and at El Escorial (see pp128–31). Today the factory makes and repairs the beautiful carpets decorating the Hotel Ritz (see p72).

❾ Museo del Ferrocarril

Paseo de las Delicias 61. **Tel** 90 222 88 22. Delicias. **Open** 9:30am–3pm Tue–Fri, 10am–3pm Sat & Sun, weekend market once a month (check for timings). **Closed** 1 & 6 Jan, 1 May, Aug & 25 Dec. **w** museodelferrocarril.org

Although railways had existed in the country since 1848, it was only in 1880 that Madrid's first proper railway terminus opened – the station of Delicias. This was the main station for Portugal, and it remained in use until 1971.

In 1984 the station reopened as a railway museum. The majority of exhibits, in the form of trains, are located in the main terminus on tracks

Cafeteria of the Museo del Ferrocarril, set in a 1930s dining car

next to the original platforms. There are more than 30 locomotives – steam, diesel and electric – as well as rolling stock. Explanatory plaques give details and describe the routes of the locomotives. You can explore some of the carriages, including a 1930s dining car that now serves as the site's cafeteria.

One of the most interesting engines is "La Pucheta", a steam locomotive built in 1884 by Sharp Stewart in Britain. Its water supply was on top of the boiler, in a container that resembles a bowler hat.

A 1931 electric locomotive, built in Spain, earned itself the nickname "The Lioness" because of its weight – more than 150 tonnes. This was the heaviest engine ever used by the Spanish state railways (RENFE), and the longest, measuring approximately 25 m (82 ft). Also of special interest is a 1950s Talgo. These Spanish-designed express trains revolutionized railway transport in the country, and this model was in service until 1971. The train was light, with a very low centre of gravity, reduced height, and

1950s Talgo locomotive at the railway museum

an articulated system, all of which enabled it to travel much faster than conventional carriages.

The 1928 wooden-sided carriage, the ZZ-307 Coche Salon, was the most luxurious the West Railway Company had to offer. Peering through the windows, you can still see an elegantly laid table in the dining room, the sleeping compartments and a tiny galley.

One of the popular sights on show is the Mikado, a steam locomotive built in 1960, which has been cut away to reveal the mysteries of steam propulsion. This engine was in service until 1975, when the use of regular steam-hauled services came to an end in Spain. To one side of the station are four halls housing model train layouts, scale models of train stations and railway memorabilia, such as signals, lights, telegraphs and photographs.

❿ Matadero Madrid

Plaza de Legazpi 8. **Map** 4 F5. **Tel** 91 517 73 09. Legazpi. **Open** 9am–10pm daily (check website for activities). **w** mataderomadrid.org

At the turn of the 21st century, this former slaughterhouse inn was converted into a centre for contemporary art. A lively, creative space, the Matadero Madrid not only acts as a forum for dialogue between the arts, but also promotes interdisciplinary artistic experimentation.

This gorgeous structure was originally envisioned as a complex of pavilions, with the intention of functionality and simplicity. The architecture incorporates Neo-Mudéjar features, such as tiles with abstract designs. While the centre offers participatory artistic training, all forms of expression are valued and espoused. From the performing arts, cinema, theatre and music, to design, urban and landscape planning, architecture and literature, the centre is dedicated to design in all forms. There are projects related to industrial and graphic design as well.

Visitors can enjoy a meal, or simply unwind at any of the three eateries: La Cantina, the Theatre Café or the Matadero Terrace.

⑪ La Corrala

Calle del Mesón de Paredes, between Calle Tribulete & Calle del Sombrerete. **Map** 4 F5. 🚇 Lavapiés. **Closed** to public.

Corralas are timber-framed apartment blocks, or tenements, built during the 19th century mainly in poorer parts of the city, especially in the neighbourhood of Lavapiés. The buildings were arranged around an interior courtyard; balconies overlooked the courtyard and provided access to individual apartments.

La Corrala exemplifies this type of housing. Construction began in 1872, but as some of the building permits were not in order, only half of the building seems to exist. The courtyard, rather than being completely surrounded by the building, opens out on to a plaza. Its exposure means that there are good views of the building, and of all the laundry hanging from the balconies.

A *zarzuela* performance, using La Corrala as a backdrop

In 1977, La Corrala became a monument of historic interest, and later underwent complete restoration. In the past, *zarzuela* (light opera) performances *(see p79)* have been staged at the site, a fitting backdrop since *La Revoltosa*, the best-known *zarzuela*, is set in a corrala.

Nearby are several other *corralas* – one on the corner of Calle de Miguel Servet with Calle del Espino, one at Calle de Provisiones 12 and another at Calle de la Esperanza 11. Lavapiés, once the realm of *castizos (see p107)*, today reflects a multicultural country.

⑫ Puerta de Toledo

Glorieta de Puerta de Toledo. **Map** 4 D5. 🚇 Puerta de Toledo.

The construction of this triumphal arch began in 1813 on the orders of French-born Joseph Bonaparte, José I *(see p23)*. It was intended to commemorate his accession to the Spanish throne after the 1808 rout of Madrid. But in 1814, after a short-lived reign, José I fled Spain and was replaced by Fernando VII *(see p23)*. By the time the arch was completed in 1827, by the architect Antonio López Aguado, it had to be dedicated to Fernando VII.

The Puerta de Toledo is one of Madrid's two remaining city gates, and is topped by a group of sculptures that represent a personification of Spain. On either side of these are the allegorical figures of Genius and the Arts. All were carved in their entirety from Colmenar stone by Ramón Barba and Valeriano Salvatierra, and are flanked by sculptures based on military themes.

The majestic form of the Puerta de Toledo, one of Madrid's two remaining triumphal arches

⓭ Puente de Segovia and Río Manzanares

Calle de Segovia. 🚇 Puerta del Ángel.

Puente de Segovia, a grand granite bridge over the Río Manzanares, was commissioned by Felipe II (see p26) not long after he had decided to establish his court in Madrid. The bridge was to be a main entry point to Madrid and he chose Juan de Herrera, his favourite architect, to build it. Construction began in 1582. The bridge, with its nine arches topped with decorative bosses, was rebuilt in 1682.

Further downstream is the magnificent pedestrian bridge, **Puente de Toledo**, built between 1718 and 1732 for Felipe V (see p27). The architect was Pedro de Ribera.

A long stretch of the riverside has been landscaped with cycling and walking paths and is given the name Madrid Río.

The Manzanares, which is more of a stream than a river, never deserved such splendid bridges. It was the butt of many jokes; a German ambassador by the name of Rhebiner once said the river was the best in Europe because it had the advantage of being "navigable by horse and carriage". Alexandre Dumas (1802–70), author of The Three Musketeers, wrote of the Manzanares during his visit to Madrid that "however hard I looked for it, I could not find it".

The buttressed arches of Puente de Segovia over the Río Manzanares

The river now has several dams, and the introduced fish and ducks have been able to survive, proving that the water is fairly clean. Rising in the Sierra de Guadarrama and eventually joining the River Tagus, the river forms a link between Spain's capital and Lisbon, the capital of Portugal.

⓮ Casa de Campo

Avenida de Portugal. **Tel** 91 463 63 34. 🚇 Batán, Casa de Campo, Lago.

This former royal hunting ground of pine forests and scrubland extends over 17.5 sq km (6.7 sq miles) of southwestern Madrid. Its range of amenities and proximity to the centre make it a popular recreation area for Madrileños. Among its attractions are tennis courts, swimming pools, a boating lake, funfair – the **Parque de Atracciones** with over 50 rides – and the **Zoo-Aquarium**. In summer the park also stages concerts. One way to visit the park and take in the city's sights is to ride the **Teleférico** (cable car), which connects the Parque del Oeste with the Casa de Campo.

Tiger from the zoo at Casa de Campo

🎡 Parque de Atracciones
Tel 90 234 50 01. 🚇 Batán.
Open Sep–Easter: from noon Sat & Sun; Easter–Sep: from noon daily. Closing times vary from month to month; check locally. 🅿️
W parquedeatracc iones.es

🐠 Zoo-Aquarium
Tel 90 234 50 14. 🚇 Batán.
Open timings vary, check website. 🅿️ ♿
W zoomadrid.com

🚡 Teleférico
Paseo del Pintor Rosales.
Tel 90 234 50 20.
🚇 Argüelles. **Open** mid-Mar–Sep & 25 Dec: noon–dusk daily; Oct–mid-Mar: noon–dusk Sat, Sun & public hols. 🅿️ ♿
W teleferico.com

⓯ Ermita de San Antonio de la Florida

Glorieta San Antonio de la Florida 5. **Tel** 91 542 07 22. 🚇 Príncipe Pío. **Open** 9:30am–8pm Tue–Sun. **Closed** public hols. ✉️ ♿
W madrid.es/ermita

Goya enthusiasts should not miss this remarkable Neo-Classical church, built during the reign of Carlos IV (see p27). Standing on the site of two previous churches, the present building is dedicated to St Anthony and is named after the pastureland of La Florida, on which the original churches were built. It took Goya (see p32) just four months in 1798 to paint the cupola's immense fresco. It depicts St Anthony raising a murdered man from the dead so that he can prove innocent the saint's falsely accused father. Ordinary characters from late 18th-century Madrid are also featured in the painting. They include lowlife types and lively majas – shrewd but elegant women. The fresco is considered one of Goya's finest works. The artist lies buried under the dome of this church.

⓰ Templo de Debod

Calle Ferraz 1. **Map** 1 B5. **Tel** 91 366 74 15. 🚇 Plaza de España, Ventura Rodríguez. **Open** 9:30am–8pm Sat & Sun; Apr–Sep: 10am–2pm, 6–8pm Tue–Fri; Oct–Mar: 9:45am–1:45pm, 4:15–6:15pm Tue–Fri. **Closed** public hols. **W** madrid.es/templodebod

The authentic Egyptian temple of Debod was built in the 2nd century BC. It was given to Spain in 1968 by the Egyptian government as a tribute to Spanish engineers involved in rescuing ancient monuments from the floodwaters of the Aswan Dam on the River Nile. The temple's carvings depict Amen, a Theban god with a ram's head, symbolizing life

There are bars, restaurants, a cinema complex and a shopping centre. Another part of the station is a major transport interchange. Above the platforms is a splendid latticework canopy. Looking out along the tracks, you can see the Sierra de Guadarrama.

Egyptian temple of Debod, with two of its original gateways

and fertility, to whom the temple is dedicated.

Situated on high ground above the Río Manzanares, and surrounded by the landscaped gardens of the **Parque del Oeste**, the temple stands in a line with two of its original three gateways. From here there are sweeping views stretching as far as the Guadarrama mountains. The park is the site of the former Montaña barracks. In 1936, they were stormed by the people of Madrid in their hunger for weaponry. It was a desperate bid on their part to arm themselves against General Franco's encroaching army at the start of the Spanish Civil War *(see p24)*. It is also a place where many lost their lives to Napoleon in 1808.

Nearby is the **Paseo del Pintor Rosales**, popular for its pavement (sidewalk) cafés.

❼ Estación de Príncipe Pío

Paseo de la Florida 2. **Map** 3 A1.
Príncipe Pío. Shopping centre:
Open 10am–10pm daily.

Also known as Estación del Norte, this railway station was opened in 1880 to supply train services between Madrid and the north of Spain. Built by French engineers Biarez, Grasset and Mercier, iron from French and Belgian foundries was its main component. In 1915, the station's look was enhanced by Mudéjar-style pavilions designed by Demetrio Ribes. The entrance façade was added by architect Luis Martínez Ribes in 1926.

The interior of the main building of the former station has been transformed into a stunning modern space with a glass roof, but it still retains the character of the old station.

❽ Parque el Capricho

Paseo de la Alameda de Osuna s/n. **Tel** 91 588 01 14. Alameda de Osuna. **Open** Apr–Sep: 9am–9pm Sat; Oct–Mar: 9am–6:30pm Sat.

Created in the late 18th century under the Countess-Duchess of Benavente, this park is an outstanding example of landscape gardens in Spain. The construction reflects the theme of Romanticism. Blending Italian and French traditions beautifully, Parque el Capricho has an artificial river, a reed-covered boat-house known as the Casa de Cañas, a temple dedicated to Bacchus, a small fort and shrine, the Casa de la Vieja house and the unique El Abejero, a pavilion created to observe the activity of bees. Complementing these is the exquisite palace designed by Antonio and Martín López Aguado, where Francisco de Goya's paintings were once housed. Spring brings beautiful roses and lilacs to the groves, making it the perfect time for a visit.

The elegant main entrance to the Estación de Príncipe Pío

THREE GUIDED WALKS

Madrid is an excellent city for walkers: the contrast between the wide, majestic boulevards, grand squares and narrow backstreets make for a continually varied experience. Compared to many capitals, Madrid is not a large city and most of the main tourist attractions are fairly close to each other.

Each of the three central areas described in the *Area by Area* section of this book has a short walk marked on its *Street-by-Street* map. These walks have been designed to take you past many of the most interesting sights in that particular area. On the following five pages, however, are routes for three walks that take you through areas of Madrid not covered in detail elsewhere. These range from the remnants of Moorish

Madrid and vestiges of Spanish royalty in the Austrias district, to the capital's bustling gay district of Chueca, best undertaken at night to get the most out of the area *(see pp120–21)*, to the historic contrast between rich and poor in the Lavapiés and Letras districts *(see pp122–3)*. Along each of the walks suggestions are given for refreshment and dining stopping-off points to make each route a more leisurely experience.

Sociedad General de Autores near Chueca *(see p120)*

CHOOSING A WALK

The Three Walks
This map shows the location of the three guided walks in relation to the main sightseeing areas of Madrid.

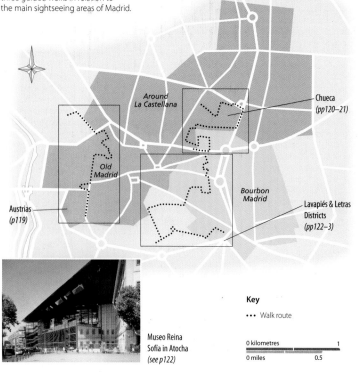

Around La Castellana

Chueca
(pp120–21)

Old Madrid

Bourbon Madrid

Austrias
(p119)

Lavapiés & Letras
Districts
(pp122–3)

Museo Reina
Sofía in Atocha
(see p122)

Key

••• Walk route

| 0 kilometres | | 1 |
| 0 miles | 0.5 | |

A 90-Minute Walk in the Austrias District

Old Madrid was mostly built on a plateau, and because of its superb vantage point the Moors built their alcázar (fortress) on the ridge. The magnificent Palacio Real now stands on the site. This walk follows the ridge and Calle de Bailén past monuments such as the Arab city walls, two cathedrals, the Royal Palace, a Habsburg convent and an incongruous Egyptian temple.

⑦ Café de Oriente in Plaza de Oriente

Basílica de San Francisco el Grande to Plaza de Oriente

Start at the Basílica de San Francisco el Grande ① in Plaza de San Francisco (see pp64–5), a few minutes' walk from La Latina station. St Francis of Assisi visited Madrid in 1217 and founded the order that built this 18th-century church, which features the largest dome in Madrid. Follow Calle de Bailén and just before the bridge on the left is the Ventorillo Café & Terraza de las Vistillas ② at Bailén 14. In summer many watch the sunset here with views across the Manzanares river to the Guadarrama mountains and the Casa de Campo (see p116). Nearby is the flamenco venue Corral de la Morería ③ at Calle de Morería 17.

Cross the viaduct over Calle de Segovia, continue up and turn left at the lights at the junction with Calle Mayor for the remains of a 9th-century Arab wall, the Muralla Árabe ④ (see p64). Back on Bailén, turn left to the Catedral de la Almudena ⑤, built between 1883 and 1993; Carlos V had proposed a cathedral here 475 years earlier (see p64). Alongside it is the

de la Encarnación to reach the Palacio del Senado ⑩. The 16th-century building was once a university and convent, but was rebuilt in 1814 as the Spanish parliament, later to become the senate (see p57). On your left is the La Mi Venta tapas bar ⑪. At the bottom of the street turn left and cross Calle de Bailen Street to enter the Jardines de Sabatini ⑫. Exit northwards to Cuesta de San Vicente and walk up to Plaza de España ⑬ and the monument to Cervantes (see p57). Leave by the northern corner into Calle de Ferraz towards the Museo Cerralbo ⑭, with its fine collection of paintings, furniture and porcelain (see p56).

Continue up Ferraz to the Templo de Debod ⑮, a 2nd-century BC Egyptian temple presented to Spain in 1968 (see p116). Return to Plaza de España for the nearest Metro.

visitors' entrance to the Palacio Real ⑥, built in 1764 on the site of a Moorish alcázar destroyed by fire (see pp58–61). Cross Bailén to the Plaza de Oriente (see p62). A good refreshment stop is the Café de Oriente ⑦ (see p164).

Plaza de Oriente to Plaza de España

At the top of the plaza is Teatro Real ⑧, the city's opera house (see p62). Turn left down Calle de Felipe V and left into Calle de Arrieta to reach the Monasterio de la Encarnación ⑨, whose severe exterior belies the riches within (see p57). Go along Calle

Tips for Walkers

Starting point: Basílica de San Francisco el Grande on Plaza de San Francisco.

Length: 2 km (1 mile).

Getting there: Arrive via the 148, 60 and 3 bus routes or La Latina Metro station.

Stopping-off points: The elegant Café de Oriente is worth a visit, with outdoor tables in summer, as is the old Madrileño taberna La Mi Venta, just after the Senate.

Key

••• Walk route

0 metres   400
0 yards   400

For keys to symbols see back flap

A 90-Minute Walk in and around Chueca

After the death of Franco in 1975 *(see p25)* Spain experienced a revolutionary transformation, which exploded in the *Movida* cultural movement of the early 1980s *(see p106)* when the innovative and the shocking were all the rage. The run-down Chueca area emerged as the new capital of hip fashion and was colonized by the gay community. Now all are welcome to its myriad of trendy shops, restaurants, tapas bars and discos packed into its maze of streets. To make the most of this walk, do it in early evening.

② Iglesia de Santa Bárbara

Plaza de Santa Bárbara to Plaza de Chueca

Start near Plaza de Santa Bárbara outside the Sociedad General de Autores de España on Calle de Fernando VI ①, one of the finest Art Nouveau buildings in Madrid *(see p37)*. The SGAE collects royalties of writers, one of whom was the composer Federico

Chueca (1846–1908), creator of many comic operas and *zarzuelas* and after whom this area of the city is named.

Walk down Calle de Fernando VI to the Iglesia de Santa Bárbara ② beside Plaza de Las Salesas, named after the Salesian order *(see p96)*. The church was built in the 18th century for Bárbara de Braganza and she is buried with her husband, Fernando VI, in the Baroque tombs here. Walk up to Plaza Villa de París ③. On one side is Spain's Tribunal Supremo ④, built between 1750–58 by Bárbara de Braganza as a school and monastery adjoining her church, but used as a court since 1870 *(see p97)*.

Leave the plaza by Calle de García Gutiérrez opposite the court and pass on your left the Audiencia Nacional ⑤. This

modern complex witnesses trials for terrorism and other major Spanish crimes. Turn right into Calle de Génova and walk down to Plaza de Colón ⑥ with its Christopher Columbus column *(see p100)*. The Jardines de Descubrimiento are dedicated to the discovery of America. On the right is the large 19th-century National Library with the Museo Arqueológico Nacional *(see pp98–9)* behind.

Turn right into Paseo de Recoletos and reach, on the right, the lovely *belle époque*-style bar and restaurant El Espejo ⑦. Across the road is its pavilion and

Tips for Walkers

Starting point: Sociedad General de Autores, Fernando VI 6.
Length: 2 km (1 mile).
Getting there: The start of this walk is on the 3, 21 and 37 bus routes or 200 m (220 yd) from Alonso Martínez Metro station.
Stopping-off points: Paseo de Recoletos is a long street with a central pedestrianized strip and is lined with restaurants and cafés, including the famous Café Gijón. Plaza de Chueca is also a good stopping-off point for a drink, especially in early evening. Calle de la Libertad and Gran Vía are also good places to find good-value bars and cafés where you can ease tired feet.

⑦ El Espejo restaurant pavilion

⑫ Taberna de Ángel Sierra on Plaza de Chueca

The entrance to the car park includes a huge red anti-AIDS ribbon cast in steel. Walk through the plaza and turn left down Calle de las Infantas. Not far is Liquid ⑰ at Barbieri 7, a minimalist techno bar popular with the gay set. Turn back to Calle de la Libertad, named after local nuns whose main task was to get Christians released from the Moors in the 11th century. Bocaíto ⑱ at Libertad 6 is a renowned tapas bar (see p166). Further up, also on the right, is Café Libertad 8 ⑲, a relaxed, bohemian bar with live music in the back room.

Turn right down Calle de San Marcos and then right again into Calle de Barquillo to reach Plaza del Rey on your right. Here the Casa de las Siete Chimeneas ⑳ is easy to see with its seven tall chimneys. Built in the 16th century, legend has it that a beautiful but wayward *señorita* lived here, "protected" by the king. The king was forced to arrange a marriage for her and gave her seven gold coins, signifying her seven deadly sins. She died a mysterious death in the mansion and her ghost is said to materialize at night between the seven chimneys. The building is now home to the Ministry of Culture.

Walk down Barquillo to Calle de Alcalá, turn right and continue until you reach the bar known as Museo Chicote ㉑ at Gran Vía 12. Sit back after your walk and enjoy a cocktail in its lovely Art Deco interior.

Continue down Calle del Almirante passing Calle de Barquillo and its trendy designer shops ⑩, and you will reach Plaza de Chueca ⑪. This is the nerve centre of the gay area with outdoor café tables in summer (see p96).

Plaza de Chueca to Gran Vía
Overlooking the plaza is Taberna de Ángel Sierra, an old *bodega* with lots of character ⑫. Leave the plaza opposite this bar, turn right into Calle de Augusto Figueroa, with its quality and outlet shoe shops. Drop into the Mercado de San Antón ⑬, a market with gourmet stalls and a terrace bar on the roof, and then turn left into Calle de San Bartolomé. The Restaurante El Armario at San Bartolomé 7 ⑭ has a good reputation, as does the intimate disco alongside, Why Not, at San Bartolomé 6 ⑮.

Walking straight on you reach Plaza de Vázquez de Mella ⑯.

Key

••• Walk route

0 metres 200
0 yards 200

summer terrace. Further down Paseo de Recoletos is the venerable Café Gijón ⑧. For more than a century intellectuals frequented here but now you are just as likely to see a banker or a fellow tourist (see p96). Just before Café Gijón is Calle del Almirante ⑨ with a host of fashion shops (see p96).

⑳ Entrance portal of the Casa de las Siete Chimeneas

For keys to symbols *see back flap*

A Two-Hour Walk in the Lavapiés & Letras Districts

Central Madrid is divided into *barrios* (districts) each with their own identity, and the contrasts you will encounter on this walk are fascinating. The cobbled streets of Lavapiés, the old Jewish Quarter, slope up towards the city centre, and the 19th-century *corralas* (tenements) here testify to the original working-class population. Today immigrants from Morocco, India and China inhabit the area, and Arab tearooms, Indian restaurants and Chinese stores abound. In contrast Letras is so called because many giants of Spanish literature lived here, close to theatres and other cultural centres.

⑩ Taberna Antonio Sánchez

and turn into Calle de Tribulete ⑤ with its Arab tearooms, Indian shops and the specialist comic shop El Coleccionista ⑥.

On the corner of Calle del Mesón de Paredes is La Corrala ⑦, one half of a typical 19th-century tenement block (*see p115*). Another *corrala* is nearby at Tribulete 25 ⑧. Retrace your steps passing Chinese-run clothes shops and the Biblioteca Escuelas Pías ⑨ and walk up Mesón de Paredes. At No. 13 is the Taberna Antonio Sánchez ⑩, named after a matador from 1870. His son also became a bullfighter, but after a

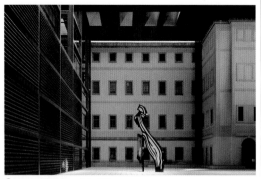

① New wing of the Museo Reina Sofía

The Lavapiés District

Start near the Atocha Metro station, at the Museo Reina Sofía ① which was opened to display Spanish art from 1900 to the present day (*see pp88–91*). You reach the modern Jean Nouvel-designed extension, opened in 2005, by turning left outside the museum and walking up Calle de Santa Isabel.

Tips for Walkers

Starting point: Museo Reina Sofía.
Length: 3 km (2 miles).
Getting there: The Atocha Metro station and bus routes 6, 10, 14, 19, 27, 34, 37 and 45 will take you to the starting point of this walk.
Warning: Petty crime is rife in Lavapiés so make sure you do this walk in daylight.
Stopping-off points: Calle de Tribulete is a good stop for a cup of Arab tea, or, for something more substantial, stop at the Taberna Antonio Sánchez on Mesón de Paredes.

On your right is Calle del Doctor Mata where Madrid's premier music school, the Real Conservatorio Superior de Música, is situated ②.

Turn left down Calle del Hospital then right up Calle de Argumosa towards Plaza de Lavapiés, the old Jewish area. On the left is the rebuilt Teatro Valle-Inclán ③. Crossing the plaza to Calle del Ave María, you reach the Barbieri café ④, an old haunt for artists and writers. Return to the plaza

Key

••• Walk route

0 metres 250
0 yards 250

serious goring he retired to run the bar and his victims and paintings adorn the walls.

Carry on up Mesón de Paredes and turn right into Calle de Soler y González which becomes Calle de la Cabeza. On the corner with Calle de Lavapiés is Bar Avapiés ⑪, once a medieval prison and

⑬ Cine Doré exterior

part of an ancient *corrala*. Further up, on the corner with Calle del Olivar is Casa Lastra ⑫, which has been serving Asturian cuisine for decades. Follow Cabeza to Calle de Rosa and ahead is the charming Cine Doré cinema building ⑬ at Calle de Santa Isabel 3, which opened in 1923, and is one of the National Film Archive sites.

here from 1610 to 1635 *(see p80)*. Turn right into Calle de San Agustín to reach the burial place of Cervantes ⑮ in the Convento de las Trinitarias. Turn left then left again to Plaza de Jesús; at No. 2 is Los Gatos tapas bar ⑯ with a collection of memorabilia. Nearby is the Basílica Jesús de Medinaceli ⑰ where kissing a 17th-century sculpture of Jesus is said to redeem one's sins. Walk up Duque de Medinaceli, pass the Hotel Palace ⑱ on your left *(see p73)* and enter Plaza de las Cortes ⑲. The Congreso de los Diputados ⑳ is flanked by bronze lions *(see p78)*.

Take Calle Fernanflor to Calle de Jovellanos to view the Teatro de la Zarzuela ㉑, where light operas are performed *(see p182)*. Turn right into Calle de los Madrazo, then left into Calle del Marqués de Casa Riera, and finish at the Círculo de Bellas Artes ㉒ art complex *(see 73)* near Banco de España Metro station.

The Letras District

Head to Plaza de Antón Martín and cross Calle de Atocha to reach the start of Calle del León. You are now in Letras where the authors of the Spanish Golden Age lived. On the corner of León and Calle de Cervantes is a plaque to show that Cervantes *(see p137)* lived in the house. Walk down Cervantes to the Casa de Lope de Vega ⑭. The playwright lived

⑯ Eclectic decor at Los Gatos tapas bar and restaurant

⑱ Elegant glass-domed lounge of the famous Hotel Palace

BEYOND MADRID

Spain's vast central plateau consists mainly of wheat fields and awesome expanses of sienna and ochre plains which exude an empty beauty. Yet it also has mountains, gorges, forests and lakes filled with wildlife, while the towns and cities are permeated with history, reflected in some stunning architecture – Toledo's Gothic cathedral, Segovia's alcázar and the 15th-century castle at Manzanares el Real.

It is surprising how quickly one can escape past Madrid's dormitory towns and industrial estates to the real countryside. There is plenty of superb scenery and good walking country in the sierras to the north – a refuge for city dwellers who go there to ski in winter or sail and windsurf during the torrid summers. The Sierra Norte offers a paradise for bird-watchers, especially around the Moorish town of Buitrago del Lozoya.

In the western foothills of these mountains stands El Escorial, the royal monastery-palace built by Felipe II, from which he ruled his empire. Close by is the Valle de los Caídos, the war monument erected by Franco. The smaller royal palace of El Pardo is on the outskirts of Madrid, and south of the city is the 18th-century Aranjuez summer palace, set in lush parkland.

Historic towns include Alcalá de Henares – the birthplace of Cervantes, Sigüenza, with its impressive castle-parador, and Chinchón, where local garlic, wine and anis are sold beneath the creaking wooden balconies of its medieval plaza. Segovia, from where Felipe II's predecessors ruled Castile, is packed at weekends as visitors sample the famous roast lamb and suckling pig and stop to admire its aqueduct – the largest Roman structure in Spain.

Toledo, which was the capital of Visigothic Spain, is an outstanding museum city. Its rich architectural and artistic heritage derives from a coalescence of Muslim, Christian and Jewish cultures with medieval and Renaissance ideas.

The picturesque Monasterio de El Parral in Segovia

◀ *The Glory of the Spanish Monarchy* by Luca Giordano, El Escorial

Exploring Beyond Madrid

Stretching along the northern horizon of the province of Madrid are the peaks of the Sierra de Guadarrama. Reaching 2,430 m (7,972 ft), they are often capped with snow until June. There are many hiking and even skiing opportunities in these mountains. Below, in the pine-scented southern folds of the Guadarrama, basks the monolithic monastery of El Escorial.

To the south lies the *meseta*, Spain's vast central plateau. Thanks to the mountains, rivers flow towards the arid plains, creating fertile valleys where olives grow. The historic towns of Castile nestle amid the rocky promontories. The River Jarama joins the Tagus *(Tajo)* near the 18th-century Royal Summer Palace and gardens in Aranjuez. Downstream it curls around ancient Toledo.

The 15th-century Casa de los Picos *(see p134)* in Segovia

Vast, fertile plain of the Spanish *meseta*

Sights at a Glance

1. El Escorial see pp128–31
2. Santa Cruz del Valle de los Caídos
3. Manzanares el Real
4. Sierra Centro de Guadarrama
5. Monasterio de Santa María de El Paular
6. La Granja de San Ildefonso
7. Segovia see pp134–5
8. Buitrago del Lozoya
9. Sierra Norte
10. Sigüenza
11. Guadalajara
12. Alcalá de Henares
13. Palacio de El Pardo
14. Museo del Aire
15. Chinchón
16. Palacio Real de Aranjuez
17. Illescas
18. Toledo see pp142–7

Exterior of Museo del Greco *(see p145)* in Toledo

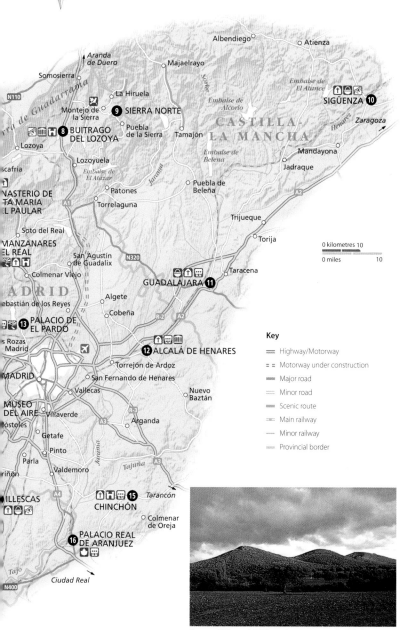

Getting Around

The best way to explore sites beyond Madrid is with a car and a good map reader. Six toll-free dual carriageways (the A1 to A6), four toll motorways (the R2, R3, R4 and R5) and the free motorway to Toledo (the A42) fan out from the city, linked by the M30 and M40 ring roads. Scheduled bus services can be slow. Railways serve the historic cities, with high-speed trains (AVE) to Toledo, Segovia and Cuenca.

Albendiego

Atienza

Aranda
de Duero

Majaelrayo

Somosierra

Embalse de
El Atance

N110

La Hiruela

SIGÜENZA **10**

Montejo de
la Sierra

9 SIERRA NORTE

Embalse de
Alcorlo

CASTILLA-
LA MANCHA

Lozoya

8 BUITRAGO
DEL LOZOYA

Puebla
de la Sierra

Tamajón

Zaragoza

Lozoyuela

Mandayona

scafría

Embalse de
El Atazar

Embalse de
Belena

Jadraque

NASTERIO DE
TA MARIA
L PAULAR

Patones

Puebla de
Beleña

Torrelaguna

A1

A2

Soto del Real

Trijueque

MANZANARES
EL REAL

San Agustín
de Guadalix

Torija

N320

0 kilometres 10

Colmenar Viejo

Taracena

0 miles   10

ADRID

GUADALAJARA **11**

ebastián de los Reyes

Algete

13 PALACIO DE
EL PARDO

Cobeña

R-2

A2

s Rozas
Madrid

Key

MADRID

12 ALCALÁ DE HENARES

Torrejón de Ardoz

Highway/Motorway

San Fernando de Henares

Motorway under construction

Vallecas

Nuevo
Baztán

Major road

MUSEO
DEL AIRE

Villaverde

R3

Minor road

óstoles

Arganda

Scenic route

Getafe

Main railway

Pinto

A3

Minor railway

Parla

Tajuña

Provincial border

Valdemoro

iñón

ILLESCAS

Tarancón

15
CHINCHÓN

A4

Colmenar
de Oreja

16 PALACIO REAL
DE ARANJUEZ

Tajo

Ciudad Real

N400

The tranquil Montes de Toledo, a mountain range south of Toledo

❶ El Escorial

Felipe II's imposing grey palace of San Lorenzo de El Escorial stands out against the foothills of the Sierra de Guadarrama to the northwest of Madrid. It was built between 1563 and 1584 in honour of St Lawrence, and its unornamented severity set a new architectural style which became one of the most influential in Spain. The interior was conceived as a mausoleum and contemplative retreat rather than a splendid residence. Its artistic wealth, which includes some of the most important works of art of the royal Habsburg collections, is concentrated in the museums, chapterhouses, church, royal pantheon and library. In contrast, the Royal Apartments reflect a more sober Flemish style.

★ Royal Pantheon
The funerary urns of Spanish monarchs line the marble mausoleum.

KEY

① **Patio de los Reyes**

② **The Alfonso XII College** was founded by monks in 1875 as a boarding school.

③ **Bourbon Palace**

④ **Architectural Museum**

⑤ **Sala de Batallas**

⑥ **The Basílica's** highlight is the lavish altarpiece. The chapel houses statues of Felipe II and Carlos I (Holy Roman Emperor Charles V) at prayer.

⑦ **The Royal Apartments**, on the second floor of the palace, consist of Felipe II's modestly decorated living quarters. His bedroom opens directly on to the high altar of the basilica.

⑧ **The Patio de los Evangelistas** is a temple by Herrera.

⑨ **Felipe II** commissioned the monastery in 1558. Since 1885, it has been run by Augustinian monks.

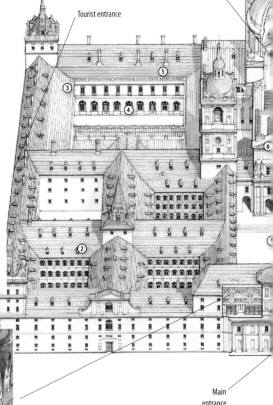

Tourist entrance

Main entrance

★ Library
This impressive library held Felipe II's personal collection. At its peak it boasted 40,000 volumes and an exceptional number of precious manuscripts. The long Print Room has beautiful 16th-century ceiling frescoes by Tibaldi.

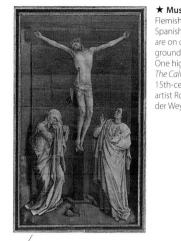

★ Museum of Art
Flemish, Italian and Spanish paintings are on display in this ground-floor museum. One highlight is *The Calvary*, by 15th-century Flemish artist Rogier van der Weyden.

VISITORS' CHECKLIST

Practical Information
Paseo de Juan de Borbón y Batemberg. **Tel** 91 890 59 04.
W patrimonionacional.es
Open 10am–8pm Tue–Sun (Oct–Mar: till 6pm). **Closed** 1 & 6 Jan, 1 May, 31 May, 10 Aug, 8 Sep, 24, 25 & 31 Dec. Free Wed & Thu 4–7pm (Oct–Mar: 3–6pm) for EU residents. 10am daily; 7pm Sat; 10am, 11am, noon, 1pm & 7pm (8pm in summer) Sun.

Transport
from Atocha, Sol or Chamartín.
661, 664 from Moncloa.

Chapterhouses
On display here is Carlos I's portable altar. The allegorical ceiling frescoes are grotesque in style.

The Glory of the Spanish Monarchy by Luca Giordano
This fresco above the main staircase depicts Carlos I, Felipe II and the building of the monastery.

The Building of El Escorial
When chief architect Juan Bautista de Toledo died in 1567 he was replaced by Juan de Herrera, royal inspector of monuments. The plain architectural style of El Escorial is called *desornamentado*, literally, "unadorned".

Exploring El Escorial

Felipe II built this palace as the final resting place of his revered father, Carlos I of Spain – Holy Roman Emperor Charles V – whom he succeeded in 1556. The gigantic building, with around 2,600 windows, was sited on the slopes of the Guadarrama and offered a stunning view that stretched away to the Spanish Empire. Felipe II, as King of Naples, Sicily, Milan, The Netherlands, Spain and the New World, used the finest talent available in the realm to decorate the austere monastery. The official tour goes through the Royal Apartments and Royal Pantheon in 45 minutes, leaving you to explore the rest by yourself.

Infanta Isabel Clara by Bartolomé González in the Royal Apartments

Royal Apartments

The Palacio de los Austrias, or Royal Apartments, are built around and adjoining the basilica. From her bed, the Infanta Isabel Clara (Felipe II's daughter) could see the high altar and the officiating priest. On the right wall are paintings of her and her sister Catalina by Bartolomé González (1564–1627); between them is a portrait of *Felipe II* by Sánchez Coello (1531–88).

The **Sala de Retratos** is full of portraits, beginning above the fireplace with *Carlos I* by Juan Pantoja de la Cruz (1553–1608) – a copy of the original painting by Titian lost in a fire in 1604. Moving anti-clockwise, the next portrait is of *Felipe II* by Antonio Moro (1519–76), then *Felipe III* by Pantoja de la Cruz, young *Felipe IV* by Bartolomé González and young *Carlos II* by Juan Carreño de Miranda (1614–85). In a corner

of the room, in a glass case, is the folding chair that Felipe II, afflicted by gout, used during the last years of his life.

At both ends of the **Salas de los Paseos** are magnificent German marquetry doors. Blue Talavera tiles cover the lower part of the walls, while the upper parts are decorated with 16th-century maps and paintings of famous Spanish military victories. Inlaid in the floor of this room and the next-door dining room are solar adjusters made in 1755 for setting clocks. In the king's chamber, the bed stands where Felipe II died in September 1598, with a view of the basilica's high altar. In his study is the last portrait of the king from Pantoja's studio.

Pantheons

Directly beneath the high altar of the basilica is the **Royal Pantheon**, where almost all Spanish monarchs since Carlos I are laid to rest. This pantheon, with Spanish black marble, red jasper and Italian gilt bronze decorations, was finished in

Altar in the Royal Pantheon, where most of the Spanish monarchs are laid to rest

1654. Kings lie on the left of the altar and queens on the right. The most recent addition to the pantheon is the mother of Juan Carlos I.

Of the eight other pantheons, one of the most notable is that of **Juan de Austria**, Felipe II's half-brother, who became a hero after defeating the Turks at the Battle of Lepanto. Also worth seeing is **La Tarta**, a white marble polygonal tomb that resembles a cake, where royal children are buried.

Chapterhouses

The Salas Capitulares, or Chapterhouses, in the monastery's southeast corner, contain wooden benches for the monastery's 100 monks. These four light and spacious rooms with their fine vaulted ceilings are decorated with numerous paintings.

Among the highlights are some by Titian (1490–1576), who painted many scenes for El Escorial. Here can be seen his *St Jerome at Prayer* and *The Last Supper*, the latter unfortunately trimmed to fit its place. Diego de Velázquez (1599–

Enamelled and gold-plated retable in the Chapterhouses

1660) is also represented, with *Joseph's Tunic* (1630), painted while the artist was in Italy.

A collection of paintings by Hieronymus Bosch (1450–1516), known as "El Bosco", is found here. A version of *The Haywain* – the original hangs in the Prado (*see p85*) – was executed by the Bosch school. This painting is said to originate from the Flemish proverb, "The world is like a hay-cart and everybody takes what he can". Felipe II kept it in his bedroom, along with Bosch's *The Garden of Earthly Delights*, also in the Prado. A copy of one panel is displayed here.

Nearby is the beautiful enamelled and gold-plated wooden retable of Carlos I, Holy Emperor Charles V. The king took this portable altar with him on military campaigns.

The Martyrdom of St Maurice and the Theban Legion by El Greco

The Museums

Within El Escorial are several small museums. The north façade entrance leads to St Maurice's Hall, home of *The Martyrdom of St Maurice and the Theban Legion* by El Greco (1541–1614). Nearby stairs lead down to the small **Architectural Museum**, which contains plans, models and engravings of the palace.

Upstairs, the **Museum of Art** covers mostly 16th- and 17th-century works. The first room is dedicated to Italian masters, while the next two contain Flemish art. Michel Coxcie (1499–1592), known as the "Flemish Rafael", is featured here. Most notable is *The Martyrdom of St Philip* triptych.

The long fourth room is dominated by the superb *Calvary* by Rogier van der Weyden (c.1400–64), and copies of the Flemish master's *Virgin* and *St John* by Juan Fernández Navarrete (c.1538–79), on either side.

In the fifth room is *St Jerome Doing Penance* by José de Ribera (1591–1652). In the last room are 16th- and 17th-century Spanish and Italian paintings.

The Library

Established by Felipe II, this was the first public library in Spain, and boasts a vaulted ceiling and a marble floor. In 1619 the king issued a decree that a copy of each new publication in his empire should be sent to him. At its zenith, it contained some 40,000 books and manuscripts, mainly from the 15th and 16th centuries.

The long **Print Room** has a marble floor and glorious vaulted ceiling. The ceiling frescoes by Pellegrino Tibaldi (1527–96) depict Philosophy, Grammar, Rhetoric, Dialectics, Music, Geometry, Astrology and Theology. The Doric wooden shelving was designed by Juan de Herrera (1530–97).

On each of the four main pillars hang portraits of the members of the royal House of Austria – Carlos I, Felipe II, Felipe III and Carlos II. On display are coins and Felipe II's pine Ptolemaic sphere (1582), which placed the earth in the centre of the universe.

The Basílica

Historically, only the aristocracy were permitted to enter the basilica, while the townspeople were confined to the vestibule at the entrance. The Monks' Choir above is still closed to the public.

The basilica contains 45 altars. Among its highlights are the exquisite statue of *Christ Crucified* (1562) in Carrara marble by Benvenuto Cellini. It is found in the chapel to the left of the entrance, with steps leading up to it. Either side of the altar, above the doors leading to the royal bedrooms in the Palacio de los Austrias, are fine gilded bronze cenotaphs of Carlos I and Felipe II worshipping with their families.

The enormous altarpiece was designed by Juan de Herrera with coloured marble, jasper, gilt-bronze sculptures and paintings. The central tabernacle, backlit by a window, took Italian silversmith Jacoppo da Trezzo (1515–89) seven years to craft. The paintings are by Federico Zuccaro (1542–1609) and Pellegrino Tibaldi, who also executed the fresco above. The wood for the cross (also used for Felipe II's coffin) came from a Spanish ship, the *Cinco Llagas* ("Five Wounds").

Palace of the Bourbons

In contrast to the simple rooms of the Palacio de los Austrias (Felipe II's royal apartments), the Bourbon apartments are sumptuously furnished. They were created by Carlos IV (reigned 1788–1808), and are hung with framed tapestries, some by Goya, from the Real Fábrica de Tapices *(see p114)*.

A china cabinet displays the dinner service which was part of the trousseau of Victoria Eugenia (Queen Victoria's granddaughter) when she married Alfonso XIII in 1906.

Dining room in the sumptuous Palacio de los Borbones (Palace of the Bourbons)

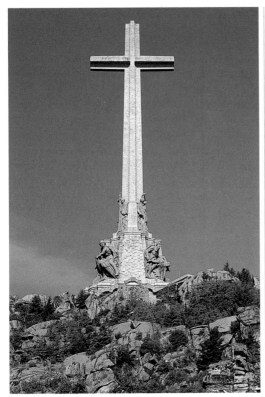

Gigantic cross at Valle de los Caídos, a symbol of Franco's dictatorship

❷ Santa Cruz del Valle de los Caídos

Madrid. North of El Escorial on M600.
Tel 91 890 54 11. 🚃 from El Escorial.
Open Apr–Sep: 10am–7pm; Oct–Mar: 10am–6pm (due to excavations being carried out, only the basilica is open to visitors. Entry to the basilica is free throughout the duration of the work).
🅦 patrimonionacional.es

General Franco had the Holy Cross of the Valley of the Fallen built as a memorial to those who died in the Spanish Civil War *(see p24)*. The vast cross is located some 13 km (8 miles) north of El Escorial *(see pp128–31)*, and can be seen for miles in every direction. Some Spaniards find its chilling a symbol of the dictatorship to be enjoyable, while for others its sheer size is rewarding.

The cross is 150m (490 ft) high and rises above a basilica carved 250 m (820 ft) deep into the rock by prisoners of war. A number of them died during the 20-year project.

Next to the basilica's high altar is the plain white tombstone of Franco and, opposite, that of José Antonio Primo de Rivera, founder of the Falange Española party. Another 40,000 coffins of soldiers from both sides in the Civil War lie here out of sight, including those of two unidentified victims.

❸ Manzanares el Real

Madrid. 🗠 9,000. 🚌 ℹ️ (91 853 00 09 / 63 917 96 02). 🕎 Tue & Fri. 🎉 Fiesta de Verano (early Aug), Cristo de la Nave (14 Sep).
🅦 manzanareselreal.org

From a distance, the skyline of Manzanares el Real is dominated by its 15th-century castle. Although the castle has some traditional military features, such as double machicolations and turrets, it was used mainly as a residential palace by the Dukes of Infantado. Below the castle is a 16th-century church, a Renaissance portico and fine capitals. Behind the town, bordering the foothills of the Sierra de Guadarrama, is **La Pedriza**, a mass of granite screes and ravines, popular with climbers, and part of a nature reserve.

Environs
Colmenar Viejo, 12 km (7.5 miles) to the southeast of Manzanares, has a superb Gothic-Mudéjar church.

❹ Sierra Centro de Guadarrama

Madrid. 🚃 Puerto de Navacerrada, Cercedilla. 🚌 Navacerrada, Cercedilla. ℹ️ Navacerrada (91 856 00 06).

The central section of the Sierra de Guadarrama was linked to Madrid by train in the 1920s. The pine-covered granite slopes are now dotted with holiday chalets. Villages such as **Navacerrada** and **Cercedilla** have grown into popular resorts for skiing, mountain biking, rock climbing, horse riding and

Breathtaking Navacerrada pass in the Sierra de Guadarrama

walking. The **Valle de Fuenfría**, a nature reserve of wild forests, is best reached via Cercedilla. It has a well-preserved stretch of Roman road, as well as picnic spots and marked walks.

Altarpiece in the Monasterio de Santa María de El Paular

❺ Monasterio de Santa María de El Paular

Southwest of Rascafría on M604. **Tel** 91 869 14 25. 🚌 Rascafría. 🕐 mid-April–Oct: noon, 1pm, 5pm Mon–Sat (and 6pm Sat), 1pm, 5pm, 6pm Sun; Nov–mid-April: noon, 1pm, 5pm Mon–Sat (and 4pm Sat), 1pm, 4pm, 5pm Sun. **Closed** Thu & some public hols. W **monasteriopaular.com**

Castile's first Carthusian monastery was founded in 1390 on the site of a medieval royal hunting lodge. Although it was built in the Gothic style, many Plateresque and Renaissance features were added later.

In 1836, when government minister Mendizábal ordered all church property to be given over to the state, the monastery was abandoned and fell into disrepair. In the 1950s the state decided to restore it. Today the complex, in a beautiful, tranquil setting, comprises a private hotel, a working Benedictine monastery and a church.

The church's delicate alabaster altarpiece dates from the 15th century and is thought to be the work of Flemish craftsmen. Its panels are decorated with scenes from the life of Jesus Christ. The sumptuous Baroque *camarín* (chamber), behind the altar, dates from 1718 and was designed by Francisco de Hurtado.

Every Sunday, the monks sing an hour-long Gregorian chant. It is worth asking them to show you the cloister's Mudéjar brick vaulting and double sundial, or Vicente Carducho's restored paintings. They are happy to do this if they are not busy.

The monastery is an excellent starting point from which to explore the pretty country towns of **Rascafría** and **Lozoya** in the Lozoya valley. To the southwest lies the **Lagunas de Peñalara** nature reserve.

❻ La Granja de San Ildefonso

Plaza de España 15, Segovia. **Tel** 921 47 00 19. 🚌 from Madrid or Segovia. **Open** 10am–8pm Tue–Sun (Oct–Mar: till 6pm). Gardens: **Open** 10am–6pm daily (till 9pm in summer). **Closed** 1, 6 & 23 Jan, 1 May, 24, 25 & 31 Dec. 🎟 (free Apr–Sep after 5pm & Oct–Mar after 3pm). 🕐 W **patrimonionacional.es**

This Royal Pleasure Palace stands on the site of a hunting lodge built by Enrique IV in the 15th century.

In 1720, Felipe V embarked on a project to build the palace and numerous artists and architects contributed to the rich furnishings and the splendid gardens. Some rooms were damaged by fire in 1918, but nearly 8 million euros have been spent restoring them.

There are countless salons decorated with *objets d'art* and Classical frescoes. From the ceilings hang huge chandeliers. The church is adorned in high Baroque style, and the Royal Mausoleum contains the tomb of Felipe V and his queen, Isabel de Farnesio.

The spectacular garden fountains portray Felipe V and his queen as Apollo and Diana. They run between May and July on Wednesdays and Saturdays at 5:30pm and on Sundays at 1pm.

Serenely beautiful royal gardens at La Granja de San Ildefonso

❼ Segovia

Segovia is the most spectacularly sited city in Spain. The old town is set high on a rocky spur and is surrounded by the Río Eresma and Río Clamores. From afar it looks like a ship, the medieval alcázar on its sharp crag forming the prow, the pinnacles of the Gothic cathedral rising up like masts, and the aqueduct trailing behind like a rudder. The view of the old town from the valley below at sunset is magical.

A relatively short journey from Madrid by car, bus or train, Segovia is readily accessible to visitors to the capital and well worth a look. Easy to negotiate on foot, it offers plenty to see and do for a day trip or an overnight stay. Weekends, particularly in summer, are the busiest time in Segovia.

The imposing Gothic cathedral of Segovia

Exploring Segovia

Segovia is dotted with many notable churches, including the 11th-century Romanesque **San Juan de los Caballeros**, with a fine sculptured portico; 13th-century **San Esteban** with a five-storey tower; and 11th-century **San Martín** with its arcades, capitals and gilded altarpiece. The **Iglesia de San Millán**, a Romanesque jewel in the newer part of town, has a Mozarabic tower and a 14th-century Gothic crucifix. The **Iglesia de la Vera Cruz**, outside the old town, is a 12-sided crusader's church (1208).

🏛 Cathedral

Plaza Mayor. **Tel** 921 46 22 05. **Open** 9:30am–5:30pm Mon–Sat (6:30pm Apr–Sep), 1:30–5:30pm Sun (6:30pm Apr–Sep). 🅿 (free Sat am) ♿

Dating from 1525, this massive Gothic structure replaced the old cathedral, which was destroyed in 1520. The old cloister, however, survived and was rebuilt on the new site. Architect Juan Gil de Hontañón devised the austere but elegant design. The pinnacles, flying buttresses, tower and dome form an impressive silhouette.

The interior is light and elegantly vaulted, with stained-glass windows. It has a high altar designed by Sabatini in 1768. Lining the nave and apse are 18 beautiful chapels, most enclosed by graceful ironwork grilles. The most interesting is the Chapel of the Pietà, which took its name from the beautiful sculpture by Juan de Juni. The cloister, whose pointed arches are divided by slender mullions and perforated tracery, is accessed through an outstanding Gothic arch by Juan Guas in the Chapel of Christ's Solace. The cloister leads to the chapterhouse museum, which houses 17th-century Brussels tapestries, paintings, sculptures, silver, furniture, books and coins.

🏛 Museo de Segovia

Casa del Sol, Calle Socorro 11. **Tel** 921 46 06 13. **Open** Jul–Sep: 10am–2pm, 4–7pm Tue–Sat, 10am–2pm Sun; Oct–Jun: 10am–2pm, 5–8pm Tue–Sat, 10am–2pm Sun. 🅿 (free Sat & Sun).

This archeological museum contains 15,000-year-old Stone Age engravings as well as tools, arms, pottery and metalwork through the centuries. There are Roman coins and inscriptions, wall fragments from Arab houses and a collection of belt buckles.

Also worth seeing are two huge Celtic stone bulls which were excavated in the Calle Mayor. It is thought they may have been divine protectors of people or livestock. In the nearby province of Avila, such icons are linked with burials.

🏛 Casa de los Picos

Just inside the city walls is the Casa de los Picos, a mansion whose 15th-century façade is adorned with diamond-shaped stones. The building houses an art gallery and school.

🏛 Aqueduct

In use until the late 19th century, this aqueduct was built at the end of the 1st century AD by the Romans, who turned ancient Segovia into an important military base. With this feat of engineering, water from the Río Frío flowed into the city, filtered through a series of tanks along the way.

The Roman aqueduct running through the old town

The Alcázar, like a fairy-tale castle rising above the cliff

🏰 Alcázar

Plaza de la Reina Victoria Eugenia. **Tel** 921 46 07 59. **Open** Oct–Mar: 10am–6pm; Apr–Sep: 10am–7pm. **Closed** public hols. 🖼 (free 3rd Tue of month for EU residents only). 🖼 🖼 🖼 alcazardesegovia.com

Although there has been a fortress on this site since the Middle Ages, the present castle is mostly a reconstruction following a fire in 1862. Its rooms are decorated with armour, paintings and furniture for a medieval atmosphere. There is also a weaponry museum.

The virtually impregnable castle had its heyday in the Middle Ages. The rectangular Juan II tower was completed during the reign of Enrique IV in the 15th century and named after his father. It is worth climbing to the top for

breathtaking views of Segovia and the Guadarrama mountains. In 1764 Carlos III founded the Royal School of Artillery. Two of its pupils, Daoiz and Velarde, became heroes in the 1808 uprising of *Madrileños* against the French *(see p22)*.

🏛 Palacio Episcopal

Plaza de San Esteban. **Tel** 921 46 30 01. **Open** 10am–2pm, 4:30–7pm daily

Built for the Salcedos family, the 16th-century Palacio Episcopal was later acquired by Bishop Murillo.

⛪ Monasterio de El Parral

Subida al Parral 2. **Tel** 921 43 12 98. **Open** 11am & 5pm Wed–Sun (booking is recommended).

Just north of the city walls, Segovia's largest monastery has four cloisters and a Plateresque altarpiece. It contains the

VISITORS' CHECKLIST

Practical Information
🗺 54,900. 🛈 Plaza del Azoguejo 1 (921 46 67 21). 🔄 Tue, Thu, Sat. 🎪 San Juan (24 Jun), San Pedro (29 Jun), San Frutos (25 Oct).

Transport
🚉 🚌

Plateresque tombs of its benefactor, the Marqués de Villena, and his wife, María.

⛪ Iglesia de los Carmelitas

Alameda de la Fuencisla. **Tel** 921 43 13 49. **Open** 4–7pm Mon, 10am–1:30pm, 4–7pm Tue–Sun (Jun–Sep: till 8pm).

In a secluded Eresma valley, St John of the Cross founded this convent in the 16th century and was Prior from 1588–91. The mystical poet was also co-founder, with Santa Teresa, of a barefooted *(descalzos)* order of Carmelites which ran to the strictest of disciplines.

The tree-lined Plaza Mayor

Segovia City Centre

① Iglesia de San Juan de los Caballeros
② Aqueduct
③ Casa de los Picos
④ Iglesia de San Martín
⑤ Palacio Episcopal
⑥ Iglesia de San Esteban
⑦ Cathedral
⑧ Museo de Segovia
⑨ Alcázar

0 metres   250
0 yards   250

For keys to symbols *see back flap*

Buitrago del Lozoya, standing next to the river

❽ Buitrago del Lozoya

Madrid. 🅰 3,100. 🚌 *i* Calle Tahona 19 (91 868 16 15). 🅰 Sat. 🎭 La Asunción y San Roque (15 Aug), Cristo de los Esclavos (15 Sep).

Picturesquely sited above a meander in the Río Lozoya is the walled town of Buitrago del Lozoya. Founded by the Romans, it was fortified by the Arabs, and became a bustling market town in medieval times. The 14th-century Gothic-Mudéjar castle is in ruins, although the gatehouse, arches and stretches of the original wall survive. Today, the castle is used as a venue for bullfights and a festival of theatre and music in the summer.

The old quarter, within the town's walls, retains its charming atmosphere. The 14th-century church of **Santa María del Castillo** has a Mudéjar tower and ceilings moved here from the old hospital. The **town hall**, or *ayuntamiento*, in the newer part of the town preserves a 16th-century processional cross. In the basement is the small **Museo Picasso**. The prints, drawings and ceramics on display were collected by the artist's friend and barber, Eugenio Arias, an inhabitant of the town.

🏛 **Museo Picasso**
Plaza de Picasso 1. **Tel** 91 868 00 56. **Closed** Mon, Sun pm. 🅦 madrid. org/museo_picasso

❾ Sierra Norte

Madrid. 🚌 Montejo de la Sierra. *i* Calle Real 39, Montejo (91 868 43 01). 🅦 sierranorte.com

The black slate hamlets of the Sierra Norte, which was once known as the Sierra Pobre ("Poor Sierra"), are located in the most rural part of the Comunidad de Madrid (Madrid province). At **Montejo de la Sierra**, the largest village in the area, an information centre organizes riding, rental of traditional houses and visits to the nature reserve of the **Hayedo de Montejo de la Sierra**. This is one of the southernmost beech woods in Europe and a relic of an era when climatic conditions were more suitable for the beech. From Montejo, you can drive on to picturesque hamlets such as **La Hiruela** or **Puebla de la Sierra**, both of which are set in lovely walking country.

The drier southern hills slope down to the **Embalse de Puentes Viejas**, a reservoir where summer chalets cluster around artificial beaches. On the eastern edge of the Sierra Norte lies **Patones**, which supposedly escaped invasion by the Moors and Napoleon due to its isolated location.

❿ Sigüenza

Guadalajara. 🅰 5,000. 🚌 🚃 *i* Calle Serrano Sanz 9 (949 34 70 07). 🅰 Sat. 🎭 San Juan (24 Jun), San Roque (15 Aug). 🅦 siguenza.es

Dominating the hillside town of Sigüenza is its impressive castle-parador. The **cathedral**, in the old town, was begun in the 12th century. It is

Semi-recumbent figure of El Doncel on his tomb in Sigüenza cathedral

Romanesque in style, with later additions, such as the Gothic-Plateresque cloisters. In one of the chapels is the Tomb of *El Doncel* (the young nobleman). It was built for Martín Vázquez de Arce, Isabel of Castile's pageboy *(see p26)*, who was killed in a battle against the Moors in Granada in 1486. The sacristy has a beautiful ceiling carved with flowers and cherubs, by Alonso de Covarrubias.

Intricate diamond stonework on the façade of the Palacio de los Duques del Infantado

⓫ Guadalajara

Guadalajara. 🚹 92,200. 🚊 🚌 🅹
Plaza Aviación Militar Española (949 88 70 99). 🛒 Tue, Sat. 🎉 Virgen de la Antigua (Sep). 🆆 **guadalajara.es**

Although Guadalajara's history is largely lost in the modern industrial city, traces of its past

splendour survive. It was founded as the Roman settlement of Arriaca, and then replaced by the Moorish settlement of Wad-al-Hajarah. In 1085 it was taken by Alfonso VI in the Christian Reconquest *(see p19)*, and rose to prominence in the 14th century.

The **Palacio de los Duques del Infantado**, built from the 14th to the 17th century by the powerful Mendoza dynasty, is an outstanding example of Gothic-Mudéjar architecture. The main façade and the two-storey patio are adorned with delicate carvings. Following Civil War bombing, the palace was restored. It now houses the Museo Provincial – the local art museum.

Among the town's churches is the **Iglesia de Santiago**, which has a Gothic-Plateresque chapel designed by Alonso de Covarrubias. In the 15th-century **Iglesia de San Francisco** was the family mausoleum of the Mendoza family, while the cathedral is built on the site of a mosque. The 13th-century **Iglesia de Santa María** has typical Mudéjar horseshoe arches and a bell tower.

🏛 Palacio de los Duques del Infantado
Plaza de los Caidos 13. **Tel** 949 21 33 01. Museum: **Open** Tue–Sun (Sun am only). Palace: **Open** daily.

Façade of Colegio de San Ildefonso in Alcalá de Henares

⓬ Alcalá de Henares

Madrid. 🚹 205,000. 🚊 🚌
🅹 Callejón Santa María (918 89 26 94). 🛒 Mon & Wed. 🎉 Feria de Alcalá (late Aug). 🆆 **turismoalcala.es**

At the heart of a modern industrial town is one of Spain's most renowned university quarters. Founded in 1499 by Cardinal Cisneros, Alcalá's **university** became one of the foremost places of learning in 16th-century Europe, famous for its language teaching. The university was transferred to Madrid in 1836. Although most of the original 40 colleges have since been destroyed, the most historic one, the much-restored Renaissance **Colegio de San Ildefonso**, survives. It has a Plateresque façade (1543) by Rodrigo Gil de Hontañón. Former students include Lope de Vega *(see p32)*. In 1517 the university produced Europe's first polyglot bible, which had parallel texts in Latin, Greek, Hebrew and Chaldean.

Alcalá's other sights are the cathedral, the **Casa-Museo de Cervantes**, birthplace of the author and now an intriguing museum, and the restored 19th-century Neo-Moorish **Palacio de Laredo**.

🏛 Casa-Museo de Cervantes
Calle Mayor 48. **Tel** 918 89 96 54. **Open** Tue–Sun. **Closed** public hols. 🆆 **museo-casa-natal-cervantes.org**

🏛 Palacio de Laredo
Paseo de la Estación 18. **Tel** 918 80 28 83. **Open** Tue–Sun. 📷

Miguel de Cervantes

Miguel de Cervantes Saavedra, Spain's greatest literary figure *(see p32)*, was born in Alcalá de Henares in 1547. After fighting in the naval Battle of Lepanto (1571), he was held captive by the Turks for more than five years. In 1605, when he was almost 60 years old, the first of two parts of his comic masterpiece *Don Quixote* was published to popular acclaim. Cervantes continued writing novels and plays until his death in Madrid on 23 April 1616, the same day that Shakespeare died.

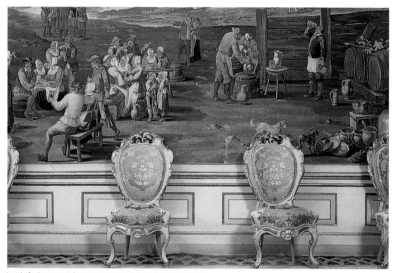

Lavish, finely woven 18th-century tapestry inside the Palacio de El Pardo

⑬ Palacio de El Pardo

El Pardo, northwest of Madrid on A6. **Tel** 91 376 15 00. 601 from Moncloa. **Open** Apr–Sep: 10am–8pm; Oct–Mar: 10am–6pm. **Closed** during royal visits and public hols. free from 3pm Wed & Thu for EU residents (Apr–Sep: from 5pm).
w patrimonionacional.es

This royal hunting lodge and palace, set in parkland, includes General Franco among its former residents. A tour takes in the palace's original Habsburg wing and identical 18th-century extension by Francesco Sabatini.

The Bourbon interior is decorated with frescoes, gilt mouldings and tapestries, many of which were woven at the Real Fábrica de Tapices (see p114). Today the palace is used to entertain heads of state and royalty. Surrounding the palace is an enormous oak forest, where you can eat at a restaurant or enjoy a picnic.

⑭ Museo del Aire

A5, km 10.5. **Tel** 91 509 16 90. 518, 521, 522, 523 from Estación de Príncipe Pío. **Open** 10am–2pm Tue–Sun. **Closed** 1 & 6 Jan, Easter, Aug, 12 Oct, 10, 24, 25 & 31 Dec.
w museodelaire.com

Among the many magnificent flying machines on display at the museum of Spanish aviation, the star exhibit is the Breguet-XIX *Jesús del Gran Poder*, which made the first Spanish transatlantic flight in 1929. Others include the 1911 Vilanova-Acedo, one of the first planes made in Spain, and the Henkel 111 German war-plane, the only one ever made. Also on display is La Cierva – half-plane, half-helicopter.

Some of the planes are linked with famous people. For example, in 1936 General Franco flew from the Canary Islands to Tetuán to start the Spanish Civil War in the De Havilland *Dragon Rapide*; Juan Carlos I flew a Bell 47G solo; Felipe VI made his first solo flight in a T-Mentor; and in the Trener Master, Tomás Castaños won the 1964 World Aerobatic Championships.

Prototypes of various Spanish aircraft include the Saeta, Super Saeta and the Casa C–101 Aviojet. The F–104 Starfighter, notorious for its tendency to crash, is one in which Spanish pilots flew a record 10,000 hours without accidents.

On the runway you may see the bulbous Boeing *Guppy*, which flies part of the fuselage (made nearby) of the Airbus to its assembly plant in France.

In addition to aircraft, the museum covers the lives of famous aviators, and features displays of Air Force regalia, flight plans and models. There are also films, videos, photographs and paintings.

Early Lufthansa aircraft at the Museo del Aire

◀ Colourful buildings of medieval Toledo at sunset

⓯ Chinchón

Madrid. 🏛 6,300. 🚌 ℹ️ Plaza Mayor
6 (91 893 53 23). 🅰 Sat. 🎭 Semana
Santa (Easter Week), San Roque (12–18
Aug). 🔲 ciudad-chinchon.com

Chinchón is arguably Madrid
province's most picturesque
town. The 15th- to 16th-century,
typically Castilian, porticoed
Plaza Mayor has a splendidly
theatrical air. It comes alive for
the Easter passion play (see p38)
and during the August
bullfights. The 16th-century
church, above the square, has
an altar painting by Goya (see
p32), whose brother was a
priest here. Just off the square
an 18th-century Augustinian
monastery has been converted
into a parador with a peaceful
patio garden. There is a ruined
15th-century castle on a hill to
the west of town. It is closed
to the public but, from the
outside, there are good views
of Chinchón and the
surrounding countryside.

Madrileños often come to the
town at weekends to sample
the superb chorizo and locally
produced *anís (see p159)* in the
town's many taverns.

⓰ Palacio Real de Aranjuez

Plaza de Parejas, Aranjuez. **Tel** 91
891 07 40. 🚉 🚌 **Open** Apr–Sep:
10am–8pm Tue–Sun; Oct–Mar:
10am–6pm; gardens 8am–dusk
daily, by appt for Casa del Labrador.
Closed some public hols. 🎟 free
from 3pm Wed & Thu for EU residents
(Apr–Sep: from 5pm).
🗂 ♿ 🔲 patrimonionacional.es

The Royal Summer Palace and
gardens of Aranjuez grew up
around a medieval hunting
lodge standing beside a natural
weir, the meeting point of the
Tagus and Jarama rivers.

Today's palace was built by
Fernando VI and in the 18th
century Carlos III added two
wings. An earlier Habsburg
palace, commissioned by Felipe
II, once stood on this site and
was destroyed by fire. A guided
tour takes you through
numerous Baroque rooms,
including the Chinese Porcelain

Chinchón's unique porticoed Plaza Mayor, occasionally used for bullfights

Room, the Hall of Mirrors and
the Smoking Room, modelled
on the Alhambra in Granada.
It is worth visiting Aranjuez for
the pleasure of walking in the
3 sq km (1 sq mile) of shady
gardens which inspired Joaquín
Rodrigo's *Concierto de Aranjuez.*
The Parterre Garden and Island
Garden survive from the original
16th-century palace.

The 18th-century Prince's
Garden is decorated with
fountains and trees from the
Americas. The Casa de Marinos
(Sailors' House) is a small
museum housing boats once
used by the royal family.

At the far end of the garden
stands the Casa del Labrador
(Labourer's Cottage), a richly
decorated royal pavilion built
by Carlos IV (see p22).

Pleasant grounds at the Palacio Real de Aranjuez

In summer, a 19th-century
steam train, built to take
strawberries to the market in
Madrid, runs between here
and the capital.

⓱ Illescas

Toledo. 🏛 25,000. 🚉 🚌 ℹ️ Plaza
del Mercado 14 (925 51 10 51). 🅰 Thu.
🎭 Fiesta de Milagro (11 Mar), Virgen
de la Caridad (31 Aug). 🔲 illescas.es

The town of Illescas was the
summer venue for the court of
Felipe II (see p21). While there is
little to see of the old town, it
does have two interesting
churches. The **Parroquial de la
Asunción**, built between the
13th and 16th centuries, is
easily identified by its Mudéjar
tower, one of the best examples
of its kind in the
region. Nearby is the
16th-century church
of the **Hospital de
Nuestra Señora de
la Caridad**, which
boasts an important
art collection. The
church owns five
works by El Greco
(see p145), the most
famous being *The
Virgin Dictating to
Saint Ildefonso.* In
its Chapel of Relics
there is a portrait of
Francisco Pacheco
de Toledo by Pantoja
de la Cruz and, in the
sacristy, there is an
original *Ecce Homo*
by Luis de Morales.

🏛 Hospital de
Nuestra Señora de
la Caridad
Calle Cardenal Cisneros 2.
Tel 925 54 00 35.
Open Mon–Sat. 🎟 ♿

⓲ Street-by-Street: Toledo

Picturesquely sited on a hill above the River Tagus is the historic centre of Toledo. Behind the old walls lies much evidence of the city's rich history. The Romans built a fortress on the site of the present-day Alcázar. The Visigoths made Toledo their capital in the 6th century AD, and left behind several churches. In the Middle Ages, Toledo was a melting pot of Christian, Muslim and Jewish cultures, and it was during this period that the city's most outstanding monument – its cathedral – was built. In the 16th century the painter El Greco came to live in Toledo, and today the city is home to many of his works.

The Iglesia de San Román, of Visigothic origin, now contains a museum relating the city's past under the Visigoths.

Puerta de Valmardón

To escalator

CARDENAL LORENZANA

CALLE DE SAN ROMÁN

CALLE DE ALFONSO X

CALLE D

★ Iglesia de Santo Tomé
This church, with a beautiful Mudéjar tower, houses El Greco's *The Burial of the Count of Orgaz.*

CALLE DE ALFONSO XII

CALLE DE LA TRINIDAD

CALLE

Sinagoga de Santa María la Blanca; Monasterio de San Juan de los Reyes

Sinagoga del Tránsito; Museo del Greco

Plaza del Ayuntamiento

Archbishop's Palace

Taller del Moro
Once used as a workshop by craftsmen building the cathedral, this Mudéjar palace now houses a museum of Mudéjar ceramics and tiles.

0 metres		100
0 yards		100

The Puerta del Sol has a double Moorish arch and two towers.

Ermita del Cristo de la Luz
This small mosque, the city's only remaining Muslim building, dates from around AD 1000.

The Plaza de Zocodover is named after the market which was held here in Moorish times. It is still the city's main square, with many cafés and shops.

Tourist information; Estación de Autobuses & RENFE

ALFILERITOS

PLAZA DE ZOCODOVER

CALLE DEL COMERCIO

CUESTA DE CARLOS V

SIXTO RAMÓN PARRO

CARDENAL CISNEROS

VISITORS' CHECKLIST

Practical Information
84,000.
toledo-turismo.com
Plaza del Consistorio 1 (925 25 40 30). Tue. Corpus Christi (May/Jun), Virgen del Sagrario, (15 Aug). Iglesia de San Román: **Open** Tue–Sun am. Taller del Moro: **Open** Tue–Sun.

Transport
Paseo de la Rosa (925 22 30 99). Avenida de Castilla-La Mancha 3 (925 21 58 50).

★ **Museo de Santa Cruz**
The city's main fine arts collection includes this 15th-century zodiac tapestry from Flanders, with well-preserved rich colours.

Key
— Suggested route

★ **Cathedral**
Built on the site of a Visigothic cathedral and a mosque, this impressive structure is one of the largest cathedrals in Christendom (see pp146–7). The Flamboyant Gothic high altar reredos (1504) is the work of several artists.

Alcázar
Inside the fortress, a statue of Carlos V portrays him triumphant over a Moor. An army museum is also housed here.

Toledo cathedral rising above the rooftops of the medieval part of the city

Exploring Toledo

Toledo is easily reached from Madrid by rail, bus or car, and is then best explored on foot. To visit all the main sights you need at least two days, but it is possible to walk around the medieval and Jewish quarters in a long morning. To avoid the heavy crowds, go midweek and stay for a night, when the city is at its most atmospheric.

🏰 Alcázar

Calle Unión s/n. **Tel** 925 23 88 00. **Open** 11am–5pm daily (except Wed). **Closed** 1 & 6 Jan, 1 May, 24, 25 & 31 Dec. (free Sun). Library: **Tel** 925 25 66 80. **Open** 9am–9pm Mon–Fri, 9am–2pm Sat.

The fortified palace of Carlos I (Holy Roman Emperor Charles V) stands on the site of former Roman, Visigothic and Muslim fortresses. Its severe square profile suffered fire damage before being nearly destroyed in 1936 when the Nationalists survived a 70-day siege by the Republicans. Restoration followed the original plans and the building now houses an army museum, the Museo del Ejército. The **library** contains the Borbón-Lorenzana collection with more than 100,000 books dating from the 16th to the 19th century and 1,000 manuscripts from the 11th to the 19th century.

🏛 Museo de Santa Cruz

Calle Miguel de Cervantes 3. **Tel** 925 22 10 36. **Open** 10am–7pm Mon–Sat, (till 2:30pm Sun). **Closed** 1, 6 & 23 Jan, 1 May, 24, 25 & 31 Dec.

This museum is housed in a 16th-century hospital founded by Cardinal Mendoza. The building has some outstanding Renaissance features, including the main doorway, staircase and cloister. The four wings, in the shape of a Greek cross, are dedicated to the fine arts. The collection is strong in medieval and Renaissance works of art. There are also paintings by El Greco, including one of his last, *The Assumption* (1613), still in its original altarpiece. Displays include two typical Toledan crafts: armour and damascene swords, made by inlaying

The Assumption (1613) by El Greco in the Museo de Santa Cruz

blackened steel with gold wire. Damascene work, including swords, plates and jewellery, is still made in the city. The basement displays archeological finds from the area.

🏛 Iglesia de Santo Tomé

Plaza del Conde 4. **Tel** 925 25 60 98. **Open** mid-Mar–mid-Oct: 10am–6:45pm daily (mid-Oct–mid-Mar: till 5:45pm). **Closed** some public hols.

Visitors come to Santo Tomé mainly to admire El Greco's masterpiece, *The Burial of the Count of Orgaz*. An important patron of the church, the Count paid for much of the 14th-century building that stands today. The painting, commissioned in his memory by a parish priest, depicts the miraculous appearance of St Augustine and St Stephen at his burial to raise his body to heaven. It has never been moved from the setting for which it was painted, nor restored. Nevertheless, it is remarkable for its contrast of colours. In the foreground, allegedly, are the artist and his son (both looking out) as well as Cervantes. The church is thought to date back to the 12th century, and its tower is one of the best examples of Mudéjar architecture in the city.

Nearby is the **Pastelería Santo Tomé**, a good place to buy locally made marzipan.

⬛ Sinagoga de Santa María la Blanca

Calle de los Reyes Católicos 4. **Tel** 925 22 72 57. **Open** 10am–6:45pm daily (Nov–May: till 5:45pm). **Closed** 1 Jan, 25 Dec. ♿ ♿

The oldest and largest of the city's eight original synagogues, this monument dates back to the 13th century. In 1405 it was taken over as a church by the military-religious Order of Calatrava. Restoration has returned it almost to its original beauty – finely carved stone capitals and wall panels stand out against plain white arches and plasterwork. In 1391 a massacre of Jews took place here, a turning point after years of religious tolerance in the city.

Mudéjar arches in the Sinagoga de Santa María la Blanca

⬛ Museo Sefardí

Calle de Samuel Leví 2. **Tel** 925 22 36 65. **Open** 9:30am–7:30pm Tue–Sat (Nov–Mar: till 6pm), 10am–3pm Sun. ♿ (free Sat pm & Sun am). **Closed** 1 Jan, 1 May, 10 Jun, 24, 25 & 31 Dec. 🌐 **museosefardi.mcu.es**

The most elaborate Mudéjar interior in the city is hidden behind the humble façade of this former synagogue, built in the 14th century by Samuel Ha-Leví, the Jewish treasurer to Pedro the Cruel. The frieze of the lofty prayer hall harmoniously fuses Islamic, Gothic and Hebrew motifs below a coffered ceiling.

Adjoining the synagogue is a museum of Sephardi (Spanish Jewish) culture. The manuscripts, costumes and sacred objects on display date from both before and after the Jews' expulsion from Spain at the end of the 15th century.

Ornate ceiling in the Monasterio de San Juan de los Reyes

⬆ Monasterio de San Juan de los Reyes

Calle de los Reyes Católicos 17. **Tel** 925 22 38 02. **Open** 10am–6:45pm daily (Nov–May: till 5:45pm). ♿ **Closed** 1 Jan, 25 Dec. ♿ (ground floor only). 🌐 **sanjuandelosreyes.org**

A wonderful mixture of architectural styles, this monastery was commissioned by the Catholic Monarchs in honour of their victory over the Portuguese at the battle of Toro (near Salamanca) in 1476. It was intended to be their burial place, but they were actually laid to rest in Granada. Largely the work of Juan Guas, the church's main Isabelline structure was completed in 1492. Although badly damaged by Napoleon's troops in 1808 *(see p22)*, it has been restored to its original splendour. It retains superb features such as a Gothic cloister (1510) with a beautiful Mudéjar ceiling. Near the church is a stretch of the Jewish quarter's original wall.

El Greco

Born in Crete in 1541, El Greco ("the Greek") came to Toledo in 1577 to paint the altarpiece in the convent of Santo Domingo el Antiguo. Enchanted by the city, he stayed here, painting religious portraits and altarpieces for other churches. Although El Greco was trained in Italy and influenced by masters such as Tintoretto, his works are closely identified with the city where he settled. He died in Toledo in 1614.

⬛ Museo del Greco

Paseo del Tránsito. **Tel** 92 522 36 65. **Open** 9:30am–7:30pm Tue–Sat (Oct–Mar: till 6pm), 10am–3pm Sun & hols. ♿ (free Sat pm & Sun am). ♿

Although after much debate it has now been established that El Greco did not actually live in this house in the Jewish quarter, it has been turned into a museum containing a collection of his works. Canvases on display include *View of Toledo*, a detailed depiction of the city at the time, and the superb series *Christ and the Apostles*. Underneath the museum is a chapel with a fine Mudéjar ceiling and a collection of art by painters of the Toledan School, such as Luis Tristán.

⬆ Iglesia de Santiago del Arrabal

Calle Real de Arrabal. **Open** only during Mass.

This is one of Toledo's most beautiful Mudéjar monuments. It can easily be identified by its tower, reminiscent of a minaret, which is said to date back to the 12th-century Reconquest *(see p19)*. The church, which was built slightly later, has a beautiful woodwork ceiling. The ornate Mudéjar pulpit and Plateresque altarpiece stand out against the plain interior.

⬛ Puerta Antigua de Bisagra

When Alfonso VI conquered Toledo in 1085, he entered it through this gateway, alongside El Cid. It is the only gateway in the city to have kept its original 10th-century military architecture. The huge towers are topped by a 12th-century Arab gatehouse.

Domenikos Theotocopoulos, better known as El Greco

Toledo Cathedral

The splendour of Toledo's massive cathedral reflects its history as the spiritual heart of the Spanish church and the seat of the Primate of all Spain. Still today, the Mozarabic Mass, which dates back to Visigothic times, is said here. The present cathedral was built on the site of a 7th-century church. Work began in 1226 and spanned three centuries, until the completion of the last vaults in 1493. This long period of construction explains the cathedral's mixture of styles: pure French Gothic – complete with flying buttresses – on the exterior and Spanish decorative styles, such as Mudéjar and Plateresque work, in the interior.

Sacristy
El Greco's *The Denuding of Christ*, above the marble altar, was painted especially for the cathedral. Also here are works by Titian, Van Dyck and Goya.

View of Toledo Cathedral
Dominating the city skyline is the Gothic tower at the west end of the nave. The best view of the cathedral, and the city, is from the parador (see p155).

★ Monstrance
The 16th-century Gothic silver and gold monstrance is over 3 m (10 ft) high. It is carried through the streets during the Corpus Christi celebrations (see p38).

KEY

① **The Puerta del Mollete**, on the west façade, is the main entrance to the cathedral. From this door, *mollete* (soft bread) was distributed to the poor.

② **The Cloister**, on two floors, was built in the 14th century on the site of the old Jewish market.

③ **The belfry** in the tower contains a heavy bell known as *La Gorda* ("the Fat One").

④ **Capilla de Santiago**

⑤ **The Capilla de San Ildefonso** contains the superb Plateresque tomb of Cardinal Alonso Carrillo de Albornoz.

⑥ **Puerta de los Leones**

⑦ **The Capilla Mozárabe** has a beautiful Renaissance ironwork grille, carved by Juan Francés in 1524.

⑧ **The Puerta del Perdón**, or Door of Mercy, has a tympanum decorated with religious characters.

★ Transparente
This Baroque altarpiece of marble, jasper and bronze, by Narciso Tomé, is illuminated by an ornate skylight. It stands out from the mainly Gothic interior.

VISITORS' CHECKLIST

Practical Information
Plaza del Ayuntamiento.
Tel 925 22 22 41.
W catedralprimada.es
Open 10am–6:30pm Mon–Sat, 2–6:30pm Sun. ↑ timings vary, check website for details. Choir, Treasury, Sacristy, Chapterhouse: **Open** 10am–6:30pm Mon–Sat, 2–6:30pm Sun. **Closed** 1 Jan & 25 Dec. 🕌 📷 📹 ♿

Chapterhouse
Above beautiful 16th-century frescoes by Juan de Borgoña is this spectacular, multicoloured Mudéjar ceiling.

★ High Altar Reredos
The polychrome reredos, one of the most beautiful in Spain, depicts scenes from Christ's life.

Puerta Llana (entrance)

★ Choir
The carvings on the wooden lower stalls depict scenes of the fall of Granada. The alabaster upper ones show figures from the Old Testament.

TRAVELLERS' NEEDS

WHERE TO STAY

When Alfonso XIII *(see p23)* was married in 1906, he was embarrassed that his city, unlike other European capitals, did not have elegant hotels to accommodate his wedding guests. He personally instigated the building of the luxurious Ritz and Palace, which are still two of the best hotels in Europe. Today, the city provides an abundance of comfortable lodgings, be they simple *pensiones*, pleasant three-star hotels in converted town houses, or palatial five-star establishments.

Stately façade of the ME Madrid hotel *(see p155)* from the Plaza de Santa Ana

Where to Look

Central Madrid has plenty of hotels, in every price category, close to the major sights. Some areas, such as Gran Vía and around Puerta del Sol, can be very noisy, both day and night, so soundproofing is a big consideration. If you are driving, parking in central Madrid is difficult, and a hotel with parking facilities is essential. If it is tranquillity you want, and you do not mind having to take a taxi or the Metro to go sightseeing, there are some good hotels in the residential districts of Salamanca (east) or Chamberí (north). A few modern luxury hotels, aimed mainly at business travellers, are located along the Paseo de la Castellana, and on the eastern side of the M30 ring road, convenient for those needing easy access to the airport.

Grading and Facilities

Spanish hotels are rated from one to five stars. The top category is Gran Lujo (GL), indicated by five stars. Although the star-rating gives a rough indication of standards and prices, it is not an exact science. Three-star hotels, for example, can include anything from charmless grey establishments in need of repair, to real gems with friendly staff and interesting decor. Both four- and five-star hotels should have a good range of extra facilities, and they will be fairly smart. Very few Madrid hotels have gardens or swimming pools.

One- and two-star hotels offer basic facilities; most have individual bathrooms. The better ones will have friendly staff, high standards of cleanliness and airconditioning, which is essential in summer.

Hostal-residencias (HR) are hotels without a meal service; otherwise, they are the same as other hotels. Accommodation with basic facilities is also offered in *hostales* (Hs) and *pensiones* (P) at much lower prices than hotels. The two types are essentially the same.

A double room for one person (*habitación doble uso individual*), which will cost slightly more than a single room, is an option for single travellers needing more space.

Some hotels have their own parking area. Those without often have an arrangement with neighbouring public car parks. There is an additional charge for this service, and it can be quite expensive.

Paradors

Paradors are the deservedly famous state-run hotels in Spain. The best of them are located in converted historic buildings, and many are worth a visit in their own right. Madrid itself has none, but some of the most picturesque paradors are

Sleek and elegant interiors at Hotel Urban *(see p155)*

◄ Outdoor seating at a café in Plaza Mayor

One of Madrid's many inexpensive *hostales* scattered around the centre

within striking distance of the city, one in Toledo *(see p155)* and one in the World Heritage town of Segovia.

How to Book

Prior booking is advisable. This can be done through hotel websites, online travel agencies or traditional travel agents. If you have any special requirements, such as a twin or double bed, interior room or one facing the street, make these known when booking Some hotels demand a credit card number or deposit to guarantee a booking. When checking in, you will be asked for ID (a national identity card or passport) and to sign a registration form.

Payment and Discounts

Practically all hotels take major credit cards, but not personal cheques. Rates are increased by 10 per cent value-added tax (IVA). Madrid hotels often offer discounts on weekend stays and in August. Companies can usually get a corporate rate – *precio de empresa* – which may mean a reduction of up to a third.

Special Needs

On the whole, Spain is not wheelchair friendly, but newer hotels have ramps, wide elevators (lifts) and certain rooms adapted for disabled people. Enquire with the hotel beforehand, and be specific about your needs; a receptionist might think a ramp up the

front steps makes the hotel "wheelchair accessible".

A maximum of 30 per cent of the rooms in any one hotel can be smoking rooms.

Self Catering

Apartment rentals have become increasingly popular, with a wealth of options available. These range from aparthotels with serviced units to private apartments in all price categories. The tourist office has a limited list of apartments: you'll find more by trawling the internet.

Children

Children are welcome in most Madrid hotels, whatever the category. For small children, a cot or an extra bed will be put in the parents' room, often at no additional cost. But, as a rule, hotels provide few facilities for children, and only some of the more expensive offer babysitting – in Spain children tend to go everywhere with their parents.

Hostels

The Spanish *hostal* is not a hostel, but a modest hotel. Madrid has a city-run youth hostel in the city centre (see www.ajmadrid. es) which is regularly filled with school groups, but there are scores of privately run youth hostels offering budget lodgings to backpackers. Useful websites include www.hostelworld.com and www.hostelbookers.com.

Recommended Hotels

The hotels listed in this guide cover the best boutique, family, guesthouse, historic and luxury accommodation types in Madrid. Each has earned a good reputation for hospitality and charm. The boutique category features hotels with chic, stylish decor that cater to a range of budgets. Hotels described as family are especially suited for visitors travelling with children, and offer suitable facilities, such as multiple beds. Guesthouses include family-run pensions and traditional inns that preserve plenty of old-fashioned charm. Historic hotels feature beautiful period furnishings and luxury hotels promise an extravagant experience.

The DK Choice label means the hotel is remarkably outstanding. It may enjoy a beautiful setting, have spectacular views, be a historically important landmark building, offer outstanding service or a romantic atmosphere, be particularly charming, or have a great spa or a noteworthy sustainable outlook. Whatever the reason, it is a guarantee of an especially memorable stay.

Outdoor lounge in the garden-courtyard at the Único hotel *(see p152)*

Where to Stay

Boutique Hotels

Old Madrid

Hotel Mayerling €
Calle del Conde de Ramanones 6
Tel *91 420 15 80*   **Map** 4 F3
🆆 mayerlinghotel.com
Former textile warehouse, now a great budget bet with minimalist rooms and lots of add-ons.

Hotel Liabeny €€
Calle de la Salud 3
Tel *91 531 90 00*   **Map** 4 F1
🆆 liabeny.es
A great central choice, with classically decorated rooms, plus sauna, restaurant and gym.

Posada del Dragón €€
Cava Baja 14
Tel *91 119 14 24*   **Map** 4 D3
🆆 posadadeldragon.com
Super-stylish in a beautifully restored historic inn, with a great tapas bar and restaurant.

Praktik Metropol €€
Calle de la Montera 47
Tel *91 521 29 35*   **Map** 4 F1
🆆 hotelpraktikmetropol.com
Old and new unite at this designer hotel. Choose rooms with balconies to enjoy views.

Room Mate Mario €€
Calle de Campomanes 4
Tel *91 548 85 48*   **Map** 4 D1
🆆 room-matehotels.com
White minimalism and chic design at this friendly hotel near the opera house.

Room Mate Óscar €€
Plaza Vázquez de Mella 12
Tel *91 701 11 73*   **Map** 7 A1
🆆 room-matehotels.com
A designer budget hotel with a popular rooftop pool where summer parties are held.

Bourbon Madrid

Hospes Madrid €€
Plaza de la Independencia 3
Tel *91 432 29 11*   **Map** 8 D1
🆆 hospes.es
Exquisite rooms in soothing tones. Lots of extras, including a fabulous spa and restaurant.

Hotel One Shot 23 €€
Calle del Prado 23
Tel *91 420 40 01*   **Map** 7 B3
🆆 oneshothotels.com
Near the lively Plaza Santa Ana, this hotel has chic, colourful decor with contemporary art. Amenities include bike rental.

Hotel Regina €€
Calle de Alcalá 19
Tel *91 521 47 25*   **Map** 7 A2
🆆 hotelreginamadrid.com
Bright spacious rooms are offered at the Hotel Regina. Choose between standard traditional or superior designer suites with terrace.

De Las Letras €€
Gran Vía 11
Tel *91 523 79 80*   **Map** 7 A1
🆆 hoteldelasletras.com
Elegant hotel with rooms dedicated to famous writers. There is a rooftop bar.

Room Mate Alicia €€
Calle del Prado 2
Tel *91 389 85 48*   **Map** 7 A3
🆆 room-matehotels.com
Bold, playful, contemporary design and a fantastic location overlooking Plaza Santa Ana.

Around La Castellana

Meliá INNSIDE Luchana 22 €€
Calle de Luchana 22
Tel *91 292 29 40*   **Map** 5 A3
🆆 melia.com
This hotel, housed in a Neoclassical building, has sleek, minimalist rooms with splashes of colour and all mod cons, including iPod bases and Wi-Fi.

Only You Hotel & Lounge Madrid €€€
Calle de Barquillo 21
Tel *91 005 22 22*   **Map** 5 B5
🆆 onlyyouhotels.com
The quirky, stylish interiors at this hotel were designed by Lázaro Rosa Violán and have a colonial-style feel. Excellent staff.

DK Choice

Único €€€
Calle de Claudio Coello 67
Tel *91 781 01 73*   **Map** 6 E3
🆆 unicohotelmadrid.com
In Madrid's main fashion district; elegant rooms, glorious marble-mosaic floors and a fabulous Michelin-starred restaurant. The staff organizes everything from opera tickets to shopping tours.

Further Afield

Clement Barajas Hotel €
Avenida General 43
Tel *91 746 03 30*
🆆 clementhoteles.com
Near the airport, with comfortable rooms, free parking and a complimentary airport shuttle service.

DormirDcine €
Calle del Príncipe de Vergara 87
Tel *91 411 08 09*
🆆 dormirdcine.com
A fun option, with rooms themed around different movies, from *Mary Poppins* to *A Clockwork Orange*.

Artrip Hotel €€
Calle Valencia 11
Tel *91 539 32 82*   **Map** 7 A5
🆆 artriphotel.com
Lovely, modern, art-filled hotel that preserves detailing of the original c.1900 building.

Beyond Madrid

ALCALÁ DE HENARES:
Evenia Alcalá Boutique Hotel €€
Calle Cardenal Cisneros 22
Tel *918 83 02 95*
🆆 eveniahotels.com
A modern hotel behind a 16th-century façade. Elegant rooms surround a tiled courtyard.

CHINCHÓN: Condesa de Chinchón €€
Calle de los Huertos 26
Tel *91 893 54 00*
🆆 condesadechinchon.com
Beautiful hotel with period-style decor and attractive rooms. Excellent restaurant.

SIGÜENZA: Casa el Castillo €
Calle Vigiles 9
Tel *94 939 16 13*
🆆 casadelcastillo.com
Atmospheric and friendly hotel close to the castle. Four lovely rooms, all with balconies.

Tastefully decorated dining room at the Único hotel

Family

Old Madrid

Exe Suites 33 €
Calle de Leganitos 33
Tel *91 758 38 50*   **Map** 2 D5
ⓦ exesuites33.com
An ideal base near the Plaza de España. Spacious rooms, including family rooms for three, good amenities and friendly staff.

Hostal Gala €
Costanilla de los Angeles 15
Tel *91 541 96 92*   **Map** 4 E1
ⓦ hostalgala.com
Stylish rooms and apartments that boast extras such as power showers and high-quality mattresses.

DK Choice

Hotel Petit Palace Ducal €
Calle de Hortaleza 3
Tel *91 521 10 43*   **Map** 7 A1
ⓦ hotelpetitpalaceducal chueca.com
Set in a handsomely converted 19th-century mansion, this chic hotel offers family rooms for up to five guests. All kinds of goodies available for kids – younger children get a small gift on arrival, while older kids will enjoy using the complimentary iPads, Wi-Fi and bike rentals.

Hotel Emperador €€
Gran Vía 53
Tel *91 547 28 00*   **Map** 4 D1
ⓦ emperadorhotel.com
A splendid *fin-de-siècle* building houses this elegant hotel, which features a fantastic rooftop pool. Babysitting can be arranged.

Hotel Santo Domingo €€
Plaza Santo Domingo 13
Tel *91 547 98 00*   **Map** 4 D1
ⓦ hotelsantodomingo.com
Close to the main shopping district, this hotel has urban decor and a charming rooftop pool.

Las Meninas €€
Calle de Campomanes 7
Tel *91 541 28 05*   **Map** 4 D1
ⓦ hotelmeninas.com
This hotel has contemporary rooms with wooden floors and spacious options for four, with family-size bathrooms.

Petit Palace La Posada del Peine €€
Calle de Postas 17
Tel *91 523 81 51*   **Map** 4 E2
ⓦ hpetitpalaceposadadelpeine.com
Dating back to the early 16th century, this is the oldest hotel in Spain. The ultramodern rooms,

Minimialist interiors at Hostal Gala

which include family-size options, offer all amenities. Guests have free access to iPads and bikes.

Bourbon Madrid

Lapepa Chic B&B €
Plaza de las Cortes 4
Tel *648 47 47 42*   **Map** 7 B2
ⓦ lapepa-bnb.com
Friendly B&B near the Prado, with sunny, modern rooms and a handy kitchen corner.

Catalonia Atocha €€
Calle de Atocha 81
Tel *91 420 37 70*   **Map** 7 B4
ⓦ hoteles-catalonia.com
Modern hotel with friendly staff and a Jacuzzi on the rooftop terrace. Bright, spacious rooms, including triples, and free cots.

Hotel Husa Paseo del Arte €€
Calle de Atocha 123
Tel *91 298 48 00*   **Map** 7 C4
ⓦ hotelhusapaseodelarte.com
Perfectly situated between the Museo del Prado and the Museo Reina Sofía, this hotel has family suites that consist of connected twin and double rooms.

Radisson Blu Madrid Prado €€€
Calle de Moratín 52
Tel *91 524 26 26*   **Map** 7 C3
ⓦ radissonblu.com
This luxurious, family-friendly hotel is situated across the street from the Museo del Prado and offers chic rooms. Great services, including a spa.

Villa Real €€€
Plaza de las Cortes 10
Tel *91 420 37 67*   **Map** 7 B2
ⓦ derbyhoteles.com
Owned by a celebrated art collector, this hotel's interiors have a mix of modern designs and antiques. There are split-level family suites for four, each with a private terrace.

Further Afield

Hotel Acta Madfor €€
Paseo de la Florida 13
Tel *91 547 14 00*
ⓦ hotel-madfor.com
Airy, spacious rooms. Offers free cots and baby baths, and is located near popular shopping and entertainment destinations.

Beyond Madrid

TOLEDO: Casa de la Mezquita €
Cuesta de las Carmelitas Descalzos 5
Tel *606 94 81 37*
ⓦ alojatoledo.com
In the heart of Toledo, with magnificent views, this friendly hotel offers apartments that can accommodate up to six guests. The hotel is ideal for families or groups.

Guesthouses

Old Madrid

DK Choice

Abracadabra B&B €
Calle de Bailen 39
Tel *656 85 97 84*   **Map** 3 C3
ⓦ abracadabrabandb.com
Guests are made to feel like family at this friendly B&B located near the Royal Palace. The warm and welcoming rooms are filled with a collection of esoteric objects gathered from around the world by the well-travelled owners. Hearty breakfasts.

Hospedaje A. Romero €
Gran Vía 64
Tel *91 559 76 61*   **Map** 2 D5
ⓦ hospedajeromero.com
Traditional guesthouse with simple, comfortable rooms, run by a charming family. Offers a view of Madrid's "Broadway".

For more information on types of hotels *see page 151*

Hostal Acapulco €
Calle de la Salud 13 (4th Floor),
Plaza del Carmen
Tel *91 531 19 45* **Map** 4 F1
Ⓦ hostalacapulco.com
This friendly, family-run
guesthouse offers pristine,
traditionally decorated rooms.

Hostal Art €
Calle del Conde de Romanones 9
(2nd Floor)
Tel *91 420 11 44* **Map** 4 F3
Ⓦ artmadridhostal.com
Pretty, well-equipped rooms and
friendly staff. The hotel is close to
several major sights. Free walking
tours offered.

Hostal Ivor €
Calle del Arenal 24
Tel *91 548 04 03* **Map** 4 E2
Ⓦ hostalivor.com
The pleasant rooms at this hostal
are basic, but have handy extras
such as a mini-fridge, Wi-Fi and
air conditioning.

Hostal Patria €
Calle Mayor 10
Tel *91 366 21 87* **Map** 4 E2
Ⓦ hostalpatria.com
This centrally located hotel has
well-equipped rooms that are
traditionally decorated; some
have pretty balconies.

Oriente Hostal €
Calle del Arenal 23 (1st Floor)
Tel *91 548 03 14* **Map** 4 D2
Ⓦ hostaloriente.es
Delightfully old-fashioned
guesthouse by the Royal Palace,
with immaculate rooms.

Bourbon Madrid

Hostal Adriá Santa Ana €
Calle Núñez de Arce 15 (3rd Floor)
Tel *91 521 13 39* **Map** 7 A3
Ⓦ hostaladriasantaana.com
Charming rooms, some with
original details such as beamed
ceilings. Near the Puerta del Sol.

Hostal Adriano €
Calle de la Cruz 26
Tel *91 521 56 12* **Map** 4 F3
Ⓦ hostaladriano.com
Centrally located, just off the Puerta
del Sol. Bright, attractive rooms,
some of which boast balconies.

Hostal Armesto €
Calle de San Agustín 6
Tel *91 429 90 31* **Map** 7 B3
Ⓦ hostalarmesto.com
Friendly, personal attention and
well-equipped rooms make for a
comfortable stay.

Hostal Barrera €
Calle de Atocha 96 (2nd Floor)
Tel *91 527 53 81* **Map** 7 B4
Ⓦ hostalbarrera.com
Long-established, family-run
hostel offering individually
decorated rooms.

Hostal Gonzalo €
Calle de Cervantes 34
Tel *91 429 27 14* **Map** 7 B3
Ⓦ hostalgonzalo.com
An old-fashioned guesthouse
with simple, cheerful rooms, a
great location and helpful staff.

Hostal Prado €
Calle Núñez de Arce 15
Tel *91 532 90 90* **Map** 7 A3
In the heart of a popular nightlife
district. Only a few quirky rooms
with modern art and bold colours.

JC Rooms Santa Ana €
Calle de la Cruz 8
Tel *91 531 44 03* **Map** 7 A2
Ⓦ jchoteles-santaana.com
A bright and breezy modern
hotel. Each well-equipped room
is dedicated to a Spanish city.

Hotel Miau €€
Calle del Príncipe 26
Tel *91 369 71 20* **Map** 7 A3
Ⓦ hotelmiau.com
Elegant, airy rooms, some
overlooking Plaza Santa Ana.
Also a lively little tapas bar.

Around La Castellana

Hostal Benamar €
Calle de San Mateo 20 2D
Tel *91 308 00 92* **Map** 5 A4
Ⓦ hostalbenamar.es
Nothing is too much trouble
for the friendly owner of this
welcoming guesthouse.

Hostal Pizarro €
Calle de Pizarro 14
Tel *91 531 91 58* **Map** 2 E5
Ⓦ hostalpizarro.eu
Bright rooms that feature extras
like king-size beds, mini-fridges
and air conditioning.

Hostal Santo Domingo €
Calle de la Luna 6 (2nd Floor)
Tel *91 531 32 90* **Map** 2 E5
Ⓦ hostalsantodomingo.es
An inviting ambience, stylish,
comfortable rooms and a long
list of amenities.

Beyond Madrid

ARANJUEZ: Hostal Castilla €
Carr. de Andalucia 98
Tel *91 891 26 27*
Ⓦ hostalesaranjuez.com
A classic, old-school hostel,
offering basic rooms arranged
around a charming patio.

NAVACERRADA: El Torreón €€
Calle la Tejera 16
Tel *91 842 85 24*
Ⓦ eltorreondenavacerrada.com
This charming mountain inn has
a great restaurant and a terrace
with lovely views.

Historic Hotels
Old Madrid

Hotel Plaza Mayor €
Calle de Atocha 2
Tel *91 360 06 06* **Map** 4 E3
Ⓦ h-plazamayor.com
Beautiful renovation of a 19th-
century building. The rooms
are cheerful and modern.

Hotel Atlántico €€
Gran Vía 38
Tel *91 522 64 80* **Map** 4 E1
Ⓦ bestwesternhotelatlantico.com
Graceful old structure, elegantly
transformed to contemporary
hospitality standards.

Posada del León de Oro €€
Calle de la Cava Baja 12
Tel *91 119 14 94* **Map** 4 D3
Ⓦ posadadelleondeoro.com
Renovated 19th-century inn and
restaurant, with smart, individually
decorated rooms arranged
around a traditional courtyard.

Attractive room at Hotel Plaza Mayor

Key to Price Guide *see page 152*

Bourbon Madrid

Catalonia Las Cortes €€
Calle del Prado 6
Tel *91 389 60 51* **Map** 7 A3
W hoteles-catalonia.com
A stone's throw from the Prado,
this is a handsomely renovated
18th-century mansion.

Hotel Intur Palacio San Martín €€
Plaza San Martín 5
Tel *91 701 50 00* **Map** 4 E1
W hotelpalaciosanmartin.es
This 15th-century coaching inn
has comfortable rooms arranged
around a glassed-over courtyard.
Some rooms have balconies that
overlook the square.

Around La Castellana

Adler €€
Calle de Velázquez 33
Tel *91 426 32 20* **Map** 6 F4
W adlermadrid.com
Set in a 19th-century palace near
the Retiro Park, this hotel pairs tra-
ditional luxury with chic interiors.

Further Afield

La Quinta de los Cedros €€€
Calle Allendesalazar 4
Tel *91 515 22 00*
W quintadeloscedros.com
A romantic spot outside Madrid,
in a charming Italianate mansion
with a restaurant.

Beyond Madrid

ÁVILA: Hotel Puerta de la Santa €
C/Empedrada 1
Tel *920 25 35 01*
W hotelpuertadelasanta.com
Next to the Church of Santa
Teresa, this hotel has modern
interiors behind a historic façade.

DK Choice

**SAN LORENZO DE EL
ESCORIAL: Hotel Posada
Don Jaime** €
Calle San Anton 24
Tel *61 930 89 36*
P posadadonjaime.es
This historic house, a few
minutes from El Escorial, is now
a small hotel with eight rooms,
some of which have Jacuzzis and
hydro-massage showers. There is
a plunge pool in the garden.

SEGOVIA: Hotel Don Felipe €
Calle de Daoiz 7
Tel *921 46 60 95*
W hoteldonfelipe.es
A converted historic mansion,
with modern facilities and a
peaceful garden.

Luxury Hotels

Old Madrid

The Principal €€€
Calle del Marqués de Valdeiglesias 1
Tel *91 521 87 43* **Map** 7 B1
W theprincipalmadridhotel.com
Set in a 19th-century mansion
overlooking the Gran Vía. Lovely
rooms, a spa and stunning views
from the rooftop terrace.

Bourbon Madrid

AC Palacio del Retiro €€€
Calle de Alfonso XII 14
Tel *91 523 74 60* **Map** 8 D2
W ac-hoteles.com
A gorgeous hotel in a renovated
19th-century mansion. The
attractive rooms all have the
original flooring.

DK Choice

Hotel Ritz €€€
Plaza de la Lealtad 5
Tel *91 701 67 67* **Map** 7 C3
W mandarinoriental.com
A *belle époque*-style gem set in
gardens right next to the Prado.
It boasts an opulently gilded
interior and the air of another
century (the hotel still imposes
a dress code after 11am). The
super service includes a splendid
bar where luminaries like Dalí
and Lorca once held court.

Hotel Urban €€€
Carrera de San Jerónimo 34
Tel *91 787 77 70* **Map** 7 A2
W derbyhotels.com
Ultra-fashionable hotel, with
sumptuous rooms and a choice
of bars and restaurants.

ME Madrid €€€
Plaza Santa Ana 14
Tel *91 701 60 00* **Map** 7 A3
W memadrid.com
This fashion pack favourite has
stunning rooms and suites, a
rooftop bar and a restaurant.

NH Palacio de Tepa €€€
Calle de San Sebastián 2
Tel *91 389 64 90* **Map** 7 A3
W nh-hotels.com
In a graceful 18th-century
building. Elegant rooms, good
service and a host of amenities.

Westin Palace €€€
Plaza de las Cortes 7
Tel *91 360 80 00* **Map** 7 B2
W westinpalacemadrid.com
Grand old-world charm, with
liveried doormen, marble and
glittering chandeliers. Fantastic
restaurants with diverse cuisines.

Exterior of the restaurant at Hotel Puerta
de la Santa, Ávila

Around La Castellana

Gran Mélia Fenix €€€
Calle de Hermosilla 2, Plaza de Colon
Tel *91 431 67 00* **Map** 6 D4
W gran-melia-fenix.com
One of the city's grandest hotels,
with a stunning loby, plush
rooms, a huge range of services
and old-world charm.

Hotel Orfila €€€
Calle de Orfila 6
Tel *91 702 77 70* **Map** 5 C4
W hotelorfila.com
Lavish, antique-furnished rooms
in a 19th-century mansion. The
hotel has a charming courtyard
and an elegant tea room.

Further Afield

Eurostars Madrid Tower €€€
Paseo de la Castellana 259
Tel *91 334 27 00*
W eurostarsmadridtower.com
A soaring hotel with great
facilities for business travellers.
Fabulous 360-degree views,
and a spa and fitness club.

**Hotel Silken Puerta
de América** €€€
Avenida de América 41
Tel *91 744 54 00*
W hoteles-silken.com
Each floor at this sleek hotel
was designed by a celebrity
architect, from Norman Foster
to Zaha Hadid.

Beyond Madrid

TOLEDO: Parador del Toledo €€
Cerro del Emperador
Tel *925 22 18 50*
W parador.es
Located close to the city centre,
this traditional building, with
wooden beams and railings,
offers panoramic views of the
city. Delightful rooms, a pool
and a terrace bar.

For more information on types of hotels *see page 151*

WHERE TO EAT AND DRINK

Even if Madrid didn't have its wealth of fabulous museums, palaces and monuments, it would be worth coming here just to experience its abundance of restaurants, cafés and bars. Regional food from all over Spain is served in picturesque *tabernas (see pp34–5)*, including some of the oldest in Europe, modest *casas de comidas* (local restaurants) and some of the continent's most elegant and creative culinary establishments. The restaurants reviewed in this chapter have been selected from the best that Madrid has to offer across all price ranges.

Sleek interior at El Abrazo de Vergara *(see p165)*

At lunchtime *Madrileños* adjourn to a bar for a *tapa* – an appetizer served with beer or a *vino* (glass of wine). This is followed by the midday *comida* or *almuerzo* (lunch), often eaten at a restaurant.

A late-afternoon *merienda* (tea) of sandwiches or pastries with coffee, tea or juice tides *Madrileños* over until the time comes for a second round of tapas at a bar in the evening, returning home for the *cena* (dinner) or enjoying another meal at a restaurant.

Restaurants and Bars

Lunchtime and the *sobremesa* – the casual conversation that follows the meal – are sacred in this city. There are hundreds of places to eat, from simple bistros that offer home cooking and daily menus at low prices, to some of Europe's most stylish establishments.

Some of the most famous restaurants are run by Basques, the acknowledged gastronomic masters of Spain. Every other Spanish region is represented as well, and Madrid also has restaurants serving international food. Most restaurants close on Sunday evenings. Many close Saturday lunchtime too, and a large number close for the whole of August.

Fast Food

In addition to home-grown bars serving tapas, Madrid has branches of most of the international franchises offering American-style hamburgers. Successful Spanish chains include Pans & Co (sandwiches) and Telepizza (pizzas, sandwiches and salads).

Eating Hours

Madrid is notorious for its late meal times, with lunch around 2–3pm and dinner around 10–11pm. *Madrileños* usually have two breakfasts (*desayunos*). The first may be a perfunctory coffee at home. The second, around 10 or 11am, is often eaten in a bar or a café. It might consist of coffee with *churros* – sticks of fried batter for dunking, – a thick slice of *tortilla* (potato omelette) or a sandwich (*bocadillo*). Most hotels offer either a continental breakfast or a breakfast buffet.

Reading the Menu

The Spanish phrase *menú del día* refers to the attractively priced daily fixed menu. Some gourmet restaurants also offer a *menú de degustación* – a sampler menu which might include several small portions of the house specialities.

On a set day of the week some restaurants may serve an elaborate, traditional dish such as *fabada* (bean stew) or *cocido Madrileño*, the classic hearty local dish *(see p159)*.

The Spanish word for menu is *la carta*. It starts with *sopas* (soups), *entremeses*

A scrumptious dish served at El Estragón *(see p165)*

An enticing place to rest – a terrace bar on Paseo de Recoletos

(hors d'oeuvres), *ensaladas* (salad), *huevos y tortillas* (eggs and omelettes) and *verduras y legumbres* (vegetable dishes). The *plato principal* (main course) may be *pescados y mariscos* (fish and shellfish) or *carnes y aves* (meat and poultry). Dessert is *postre*.

Prices and Tipping

Many Spanish restaurants offer a *menú del día*, a comparatively inexpensive daily fixed-price menu comprising two courses and a dessert. Some restaurants do not reveal their daily menu unless it is requested.

Certain dishes, especially seafood, might not be priced on the menu but labelled as *según peso* (according to weight) or *según mercado* (according to the market price that day). It is a good idea to ask for an estimate. Ten per cent value-added tax (IVA) is added to *la cuenta* (the bill), if the prices on the menu do not include it already, and tips in cash are customary – around five per cent of the bill. Almost all restaurants take credit cards, though MasterCard and Visa are the most commonly used.

Booking

As a rule, booking is essential in Madrid, especially at midday. Phoning a few hours ahead will usually secure a table. At the most popular or fashionable restaurants, however, you should reserve a table one or more days in advance.

Etiquette and Smoking

Apart from inexpensive and tourist restaurants, smart-casual dress is best in most places, and smart dress should be worn in more exclusive establishments. Smoking is prohibited indoors in all bars and restaurants.

Children

Children are welcome in most restaurants, even the more exclusive, during the day, but they do not receive the royal treatment they get in other parts of Spain, nor are children's menus or high chairs likely to be offered. Children might feel happiest in an informal restaurant, especially if it has an outdoor terrace.

Wheelchair Access

Facilities for disabled people are rare in Spanish restaurants and it is always worth phoning in advance (or asking the hotel staff to phone) to enquire about their provision.

Wine Choices

Your waiter might offer you an *aperitivo* (aperitif), in which case an excellent choice would be a sherry accompanied perhaps by olives or a *tapa*. Wine is usually served with the main course. Spain has a formidable selection of wines (*see pp162–3*). Although there is a significant mark-up in restaurants, they can still be reasonably priced, especially *vino de la casa* (house wine).

Vegetarians

Madrid has a growing number of vegetarian eateries, many of which have vegan options. If you eat eggs, the *tortillas* and *revueltos* (scrambled eggs) are a great choice. Try tapas with asparagus and artichokes. To be sure dishes aren't garnished with anything non-vegetarian, ask for the ingredients.

Recommended Restaurants

The listings cover a vast variety of eateries, including classic tapas bars which have barely changed in decades, the simple *casas de comidas* preparing a tasty set lunch menu, fashionable cafés for coffee and cakes, stylish gastro-bars serving sophisticated tapas, and refined restaurants for fine dining. Whether you're looking for traditional *Madrileño* favourites in an old, tiled tavern, market-fresh cooking by up-and-coming young chefs, or a spectacular *menú de degustación* (tasting menu) at an award-winning restaurant, we've provided plenty of choice. Places described as modern Spanish offer contemporary versions of traditional classics, while those defined as Traditional Spanish serve more conventional fare, such as stews and fish dishes.

The DK Choice label highlights an outstanding establishment. It may serve especially memorable meals with local specialities, be located in beautiful surrounds or a historically important landmark building, or provide a romantic atmosphere.

Modern, sophisticated decor at the Restaurante Lúa (*see p169*)

The Flavours of Madrid

Madrid offers a dazzling array of eateries, ranging from stylish award-winning restaurants and sleek café-bars to time-worn taverns. People from every corner of Spain have long been drawn to the city and typical *Madrileño* cuisine reflects this, by fusing cooking styles from all across the country. Visitors can take a culinary tour of the nation's varied regions, sampling Mediterranean rice dishes and Andalusian tapas alongside fish prepared in the Galician style. Surprisingly for a landlocked city, Madrid is noted for its seafood, which arrives daily from the ports. Juicy prawns and tender octopus are among the highlights.

Chorizo

A display of cured hams outside a restaurant in Plaza Mayor

Soups and Stews

Hearty soups and stews feature prominently on restaurant menus in Madrid. They make the perfect antidote to the city's long and bitterly cold winters, although seasonal *cazuelas* (stews) and *sopa de ajo*, a simple garlic soup, are served at almost any time of the year. A classic *Madrileño* dish is *cocido*, a slow-cooked casserole of pork, chicken, spicy sausage, black pudding, chunky vegetables and chickpeas. It is usually eaten in three stages: first the broth, then the vegetables, and finally the tender meat. Around Easter, look out for the traditional *potaje de garbanzos y espinacas* (chickpea and spinach soup), which is flavoured with salted cod.

Roasts

Central Spain is famous for its *asadores* (roast houses), where hefty slabs of meat – simply grilled over charcoal (*a la parrilla*) or baked in brick ovens (*al horno de leña*) – are served. Pork (*cerdo*) or lamb (*cordero*) are the most common meats, but you may also find kid (*cabrito*), rabbit (*conejo*) and chicken (*gallina* or *pollo*).

Black beans

Pinto beans

White (butter) beans

Chickpeas

Red (kidney) beans

Armuña lentils

Selection of pulses commonly used in *Madrileño* cooking

Local Dishes and Specialities

Madrid's sturdy stews and soups, often enriched with lentils and chickpeas, are a menu favourite during Madrid's freezing winters. In late spring and summer, sweet local strawberries and juicy melons feature strongly, offering refreshment in the scorching heat. Numerous *asadores* (roast houses) and *mesones* (taverns) serve roast lamb, pork, kid or game in season. *Madrileños* are usually happy to eat almost any part of an animal and offal – tripe, brains, kidneys – and pig's trotters are widely served. A classic dish is *callos a la Madrileña* (tripe and spicy sausage, flavoured with paprika). Remember also that *Madrileños* keep late hours so, unless you want to eat alone, do not go for dinner before 9pm and expect lunch to start around 2pm.

Garlic

Sopa de Ajo This warming garlic soup is thickened with breadcrumbs. An egg and a little paprika are often added.

Outdoor dining at El Madroño restaurant, Plaza de la Puerta Cerrada

In season, game will also be on the menu, particularly partridge (*perdiz*), pigeon (*pichón*) and perhaps even wild boar (*jabalí*).

Tapas

The *tapeo*, a bar crawl from tapas bar to tapas bar, is an established part of life in Madrid. The city is crammed with tapas bars, from the prettily tiled old taverns to the legion of new bars serving elaborate gourmet snacks. Classic tapas include *croquetas* (croquettes, usually filled with ham or cod), *tortilla de patatas* (a thick potato omelette), *patatas bravas* (fried potato chunks with a spicy sauce), *boquerones en vinagre* (marinated fresh anchovies) and platters of *embutidos* (cured meats) or *quesos* (cheeses). The *Madrileños* love

pickled and conserved foods, especially shellfish such as *mejillones* (mussels) and *berberechos* (cockles), all perfectly paired with a glass of chilled sherry or *vermut* (vermouth).

The classic *Madrileño* breakfast: hot *churros* with a cup of chocolate

Desserts and Pastries

Madrileños like to start the day with a breakfast of *porras* or *churros*, sugary fried dough strips, or an *ensaimada*, a brioche-style pastry originally from Mallorca, served with a cup of hot chocolate. As in most of Spain, each local festival has a special sweet treat. For Easter, *torrijas*, eggy pastries flavoured with lemon and cinnamon, are served. At the Fiestas de San Isidro in summer, you can tuck into chocolate-coated *churros*, and at Halloween enjoy *buñuelos*, puffs of choux pastry filled with a thick custard or chocolate sauce.

WHAT TO DRINK

Wine (vino) Madrid's own robust reds are a great match for the city's stews and roasts.

Cava This Spanish equivalent of champagne is the favoured celebratory drink in Madrid.

Beer (cerveza) *Mahou*, a slightly malty lager, makes a cooling drink in summer.

Anís de Chinchón An aniseed-flavoured liqueur, it comes sweet (*dulce*) or dry (*seco*).

Vermouth (Vermut) This classic *Madrileño* aperitif is good chilled with tapas.

Soft drinks As well as Coca-Cola and 7-Up, Bitter Kas, a dark red brew similar in taste to Campari, is very popular.

Tortilla de Patatas This thick omelette, stuffed with slices of potato, is popular served as tapas and for picnic lunches.

Cocido Madrileño Various meats, vegetables and chickpeas are cooked together to create this rich, hearty stew.

Buñuelos de Viento Puffs of choux pastry are stuffed with a sweet filling, usually a thick chocolate or vanilla cream.

Choosing Tapas

Tapas, sometimes called *pinchos*, are small snacks that originated in Andalusia in the 19th century to accompany sherry. Stemming from a bartender's practice of covering a glass with a saucer or *tapa* (cover) to keep out flies, the custom progressed to a chunk of cheese or bread being used, and then to a few olives being placed on a platter to accompany a drink. Once free of charge, tapas are usually paid for nowadays, and a selection makes a delicious light meal. Choose from a range of appetizing varieties, from cold meats to elaborately prepared hot dishes of meat, seafood or vegetables.

Mixed green olives

Patatas bravas is a piquant dish of fried potatoes spiced with a chilli and paprika sauce.

Albóndigas (meatballs) are a hearty *tapa*, often served with a spicy tomato sauce.

Almendras fritas are fried, salted almonds.

Banderillas are canapes skewered on toothpicks. The entire canape should be eaten at once.

Calamares fritos are squid rings and tentacles which have been dusted with flour before being deep fried in olive oil. They are usually served garnished with a piece of lemon.

Jamón serrano is salt-cured ham dried in mountain *(serrano)* air.

ON THE TAPAS BAR

Alitas de pollo Chicken wings

Almejas Clams

Berberechos Cockles

Berenjenas horneadas Roasted aubergines (eggplant)

Boquerones Anchovies

Boquerones al natural Fresh anchovies in garlic and olive oil

Buñuelos de bacalao Salt cod fritters

Butifarra Catalonian sausage

Calabacín rebozado Battered courgettes (zucchini)

Calamares a la romana Fried squid rings

Callos Tripe

Chistorra Spicy sausage

Chopitos Cuttlefish fried in batter

Chorizo al vino Chorizo sausage cooked in red wine

Chorizo diablo Chorizo served flamed with brandy

Cogollos fritos Lettuce fried in oil with garlic

Costillas Spare ribs

Criadillas Bulls' testicles

Croquetas Croquettes

Empanada Pastry filled with tomato, onion and meat or fish

Ensaladilla rusa Potatoes, carrots, red peppers, peas, olives, boiled egg, tuna and mayonnaise

Foie gras Liver pâté

Gambas al pil-pil Spicy, garlicky fried king prawns (shrimp)

Huevos de codorniz Hard-boiled quails' eggs

Jamón serrano Ham made from leg of pork, seasoned and air-dried

Tapas Bars

Even a small village in Spain will have at least one bar where the locals go to enjoy drinks, tapas and conversation. On Sundays and holidays, favourite places are packed with whole families enjoying the fare. In large cities like Madrid it is customary to move from bar to bar, sampling the specialities of each. A *tapa* is a single serving, whereas a *ración* is two or three. Tapas are usually eaten standing or perching on a stool at the bar rather that sitting at a table, for which a surcharge is usually made.

Diners make their choice at a busy tapas bar

Chorizo, a popular sausage flavoured with paprika and garlic, may be eaten cold or fried and served hot.

Salpicón de mariscos is a luxurious cold salad of assorted fresh seafood in a zesty vinaigrette.

Gambas a la plancha is a simple but flavourful dish of grilled prawns (shrimp).

Tortilla Española is the ubiquitous Spanish omelette of onion and potato bound with egg.

Queso Manchego is a sheep's-milk cheese from La Mancha.

Pollo al ajillo consists of small pieces of chicken (often wings) sautéed and then simmered with a garlic-flavoured sauce.

Judías blancas Butterbeans stewed with pork and vegetables

Lacón a la gallega Boiled and smoked ham slices with paprika

Longaniza roja Spicy red pork sausage from Aragón (*longaniza blanca* is paler and less spicy.)

Magro Pork in a paprika and tomato sauce

Manitas de cerdo Pig's trotters

Mejillones Mussels

Merluza a la romana Hake fried in a light batter

Morcilla Black (blood) pudding

Muslitos del mar Crabmeat croquette on a crab claw skewer

Orejas de cerdo Pig's ear

Paella Rice dish made with meat, fish and/or vegetables

Pan de ajo Garlic bread

Patatas a lo pobre Potato chunks sautéed with onions and red and green peppers

Patatas alioli Potato chunks in a garlic mayonnaise

Pescaditos Small fried fish

Pimientos rellenos Stuffed peppers

Pinchito Kebab on a skewer

Pisto Thick ratatouille of diced tomato, onion and courgette

Pulpitos Baby octopus

Rabo de toro Oxtail

Sepia Cuttlefish

Sesos Brains, usually lamb or calf

Surtido de ibéricos Assortment of cured hams

Tortilla riojana Ham, sausage and red pepper omelette

Tostas Bread with various toppings such as tuna or brie

What to Drink in Madrid

Spain is one of the world's largest wine-producing countries and many fine wines are made here, in addition to the famous sherries of southern Spain and the *cavas* (sparkling wines) of Catalonia. Beer is produced throughout Spain, and Madrid's *cervecerías* (beer bars) are especially adept at pulling a refreshing half pint. Some offer *sidra* (apple cider) from northern Spain. The full range of non-alcoholic drinks is available, including mineral water. Spanish coffee is rich and strong and, to round off a meal, many restaurants offer traditional liqueurs such as brandy and *anís*.

Customers enjoying a premeal drink at an outdoor terrace bar

Hot chocolate

A plate of *churros* (batter sticks)

Café con leche

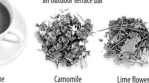

Camomile

Lime flower

Hot Drinks

Coffee served in Spanish bars is usually espresso. The traditional start to the day is a big cup of *café con leche* (with milk). *Café cortado* has a dash of milk, *café sólo* is black and *café americano* is weaker. Another popular breakfast drink is thick hot chocolate served with *churros* (fried batter sticks). A good cup of tea is hard to find, but herbal teas to try are *manzanilla* (camomile) and *tila* (lime flower).

Cold Drinks

Madrid's tap water is safe to drink and it is acceptable to ask for this in restaurants. Alternatively, bottled water (*agua mineral*), either still (*sin gas*) or sparkling (*con gas*), is available. Summer favourites include Valencian *horchata*, a sweet milky drink made from ground *chufas* (earth almonds), and *granizado de limón* (iced lemon). *Gaseosa*, or sparkling lemonade, can be drunk either on its own or as *tinto de verano*, mixed with red wine (*see Mixed Drinks*). Soft drinks and orange juice (*zumo de naranja*) are also widely available.

Sparkling and still mineral water

Horchata, made from *chufas*

Wine

Spain produces some of the best wines in the world. The key standard for the industry is the *Denominación de Origen* (DO) classification, a guarantee of a wine's origin and quality. *Vino de la Tierra* is a classification of wines below that of DO in which over 60 per cent of the grapes come from a specified region. *Vino de Mesa*, the lowest category, covers basic unclassified wines. Spanish *cavas* include bestselling sparkling wines Freixenet and Codorniú, which are *brut* (dry) or *semi-seco* (slightly sweet). In restaurants, wine is served by the glass, bottle or half-bottle. House wines are sometimes decanted into a carafe.

Penedès white wine

Rioja red wine

Sparkling wine (*cava*)

Spirits and Liqueurs

Not all of Spain's grapes go into making wine. Much of the harvest is distilled to make clear spirits, the basis of Spain's many liqueurs. These include the aniseed flavoured *anís* which can either be extremely dry (*seco* or *orujo*) or syrupy sweet (*dulce*). Brandy (*coñac*) de Jerez, an aged wine spirit, is another popular digestif; the price is a good indication of quality. Fruits are also used to flavour liqueurs. One of the most popular variations is *pacharán*, a Navarrese drink using sloes. Spain, and especially the Canary Islands, has always produced *ron* (rum) from sugar cane that grows in the south. *Ginebra* (gin) was introduced by the British when they occupied the island of Menorca in the 18th century. Whisky is also a favourite, though imported Scotch is preferred to the domestic brands. A popular drink with younger people is *cuba-libre*, a rum with cola (*see Mixed Drinks*).

Anís   *Pacharán*

Beer

Spaniards love their *cerveza* (beer) and Mahou is a popular brand in Madrid. Bars serve *cerveza del barril* (draught beer) in a *caña* (small glass) or larger *jarra*. Beer also comes in bottles of 25 cl, 33 cl or one litre (*litronas*). Alcohol-free lager (*cerveza sin alcohol*) is sold in many bars.

Bottled beers

Sherry

Sherry is produced in *bodegas* in Jerez de la Frontera, Sanlúcar de Barrameda and El Puerto de Santa María. Similar wines are produced in Montilla near Córdoba, although they are not officially called sherry. Pale *fino* is dry and light and makes an excellent aperitif. Amber *amontillado* (aged *fino*) has a strong, earthy taste while *oloroso* is full-bodied and ruddy.

Two brands of *fino* sherry

Mixed Drinks

Red wine and lemonade

Sangría is a refreshing blend of red wine and *gaseosa* (lemonade). Other ingredients include pieces of freshly chopped fruit, sugar and liqueurs. Another favourite drink is *Agua de Valencia*, which is an invigorating combination of *cava* (sparkling wine) and orange juice. A wide range of cocktails is available, including the ever-popular *cuba-libre*.

Cuba-libre   *Tinto de verano*

Sangría

How to Read a Wine Label

As well as the wine's name and its producer, the label will tell you the region it comes from, usually a *Denominación de Origen*, and the vintage year. Wines labelled *cosecha* are recent vintages and the least expensive, while *crianza* and *reserva* wines are aged a minimum of two or three years, part of that time in oak casks. *Blanco* (white) can be *seco* (dry), *semi-seco* (semi-dry) or *dulce* (sweet). *Rosado* is rosé and *tinto* is red. The label also gives the content (usually 75 cl) and the alcohol level (around 12–13 per cent volume) and sometimes specifies the grape variety.

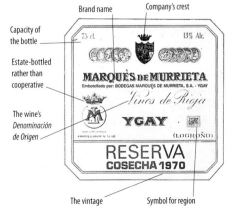

Capacity of the bottle

Brand name   Company's crest

Estate-bottled rather than cooperative

The wine's *Denominación de Origen*

75 cl.   13% Alc.

MARQUÉS DE MURRIETA
Embotellado por: BODEGAS MARQUÉS DE MURRIETA, S.A. - YGAY

Vinos de Rioja

YGAY   (LOGROÑO)

RESERVA
COSECHA 1970

The vintage   Symbol for region

Where to Eat and Drink

Old Madrid

Café de los Austrias €
Café   **Map** 4 D2
Plaza Ramales 1
Tel *91 559 84 36*
Ideal for morning coffee and
a pastry, with burnished mirrors
and marble-topped tables
inside, and a delightful terrace
outside. The café also serves a
simple menu of tapas and
traditional dishes.

La Carbonería €
Traditional Spanish   **Map** 4 E2
Calle Coloreros 5
Tel *91 354 67 27*   **Closed** *mid-Jan–
mid-Feb*
Traditional and welcoming, this
tiny restaurant is a great place
to enjoy classic Spanish dishes.
The menu is available in nine
languages and the friendly
owner will go out of his way to
help you make a good choice.

La Casa del Abuelo €
Tapas   **Map** 7 A2
Calle de la Victoria 12
Tel *91 521 23 19*
"Grandfather's house" has been
in the same family for a century,
and specializes in delicious prawns
served with a local sweet wine
and a range of tasty local tapas.

Casa Labra €
Tapas   **Map** 4 F2
Calle de Tetuan 12
Tel *91 531 00 81*
A classic since 1860, this
restaurant preserves its original
decor of plenty of wood panelling and chandeliers. It serves
one of the best cod *croquetas*
in town, along with a range of
other traditional tapas.

The vintage bar area at Delic in
Old Madrid

Casa Revuelta €
Tapas   **Map** 4 E3
*Calle de Latoneras 3 (off Plaza
Puerta Cerrada)*
Tel *91 521 45 16*   **Closed** *Sun,
Mon dinner*
Ideal for tapas if you're near the
Plaza Mayor, this long-established
favourite boasts a colourfully tiled
interior and serves tasty local
dishes to a largely local crowd.

Chocolatería San Ginés €
Café   **Map** 4 E2
*Pasadizo de San Ginés 5 (off
Calle del Arenal)*
Tel *91 365 65 46*
Hidden away in a small alley;
famously serves some of the
best chocolate *con churros* (fried
dough strips served with thick
hot chocolate) in Madrid.

La Ciudad Invisible €
Café   **Map** 4 E1
Costanilla de los Ángeles 7
Tel *91 542 25 40*   **Closed** *Mon*
Do a spot of armchair travelling
at this super-stylish travel
bookshop and café, which serves
light meals, tapas and wine, and
features changing art exhibitions.

DK Choice

Delic €
Café   **Map** 3 C3
Plaza de la Paja s/n
Tel *91 364 54 50*   **Closed** *Mon
lunch*
A hipster favourite on a
charming square, this is
perfect for a lazy breakfast or
a light lunch – perhaps of leek
tart or Japanese dumplings.
It is also ideal for tea and
cakes in the afternoons, with
wonderful tarts, muffins and
brownies. In the evenings,
enjoy delicious cocktails.

El Mollete €
Tapas   **Map** 4 D1
Calle de la Bola 4
Tel *91 547 78 20*   **Closed** *Sun*
This cosy, brick-lined bar sums
up a huge variety of tasty tapas,
from fried artichokes to Iberian
beef with a redcurrant sauce.

Malaspina €
Tapas   **Map** 4 F2
Calle de Cádiz 9
Tel *91 523 40 24*
Popular local tavern, with plenty
of traditional tapas and *tostadas* –
big slices of toasted country
bread with a huge variety of tasty
toppings – at excellent prices.

Price Guide
For a three-course meal for one,
including half a bottle of house wine,
tax and service.

€	under €35
€€	€35 to €50
€€€	over €50

La Musa Latina €
Tapas   **Map** 3 C3
Costanilla de San Andrés 12
Tel *91 354 02 55*
This stylish eatery offers a great
choice of tapas, along with deli-
cious salads and stir-fried dishes.

La Perejila €
Tapas   **Map** 4 D3
Calle de la Cava Baja 25
Tel *91 364 28 55*   **Closed** *Sun dinner,
Mon*
Paintings, chandeliers and trailing
plants make this minuscule bar a
rather atmospheric spot. Try the
speciality, meatballs (*perejilas*), or
a *rebanada* – toasted bread with
a choice of original toppings.

Le Petit Bistrot €
French   **Map** 7 A3
Plaza de Matute 5
Tel *91 429 62 65*   **Closed** *Sun,
Mon dinner*
With wooden tables, great prices
and plenty of charm; serves
classics such as French onion
soup and duck *magret*. Their great-
value set lunch is very popular.

Vietnam €
Vietnamese   **Map** 7 B3
Calle de las Huertas 4
Tel *91 755 31 26*
A simple restaurant that serves
authentic Vietnamese cuisine.
Don't miss out on some of the
classics, like *Pho Bo* noodle soup
and summer rolls.

Ana La Santa €€
Mediterranean   **Map** 7 A3
ME Madrid, Plaza Santa Ana 14
Tel *91 701 60 13*
A wide range of dishes span the
menu – from snacks and sand-
wiches to creative rice dishes.
The atmosphere is relaxed and
the lovely "greenhouse" area is
a good seating option.

Café de Oriente €€
Café   **Map** 3 C2
Plaza de Oriente 2
Tel *91 541 39 74*
This classy and elegant café
(good for tapas, or coffee and
cakes) and restaurant (for more
substantial local fare) has a
magnificent terrace facing the
Royal Palace.

Casual outdoor seating at El Estragón

Camoati €€
Argentinian Map 3 C3
Calle de Alfonso VI 3
Tel *91 366 95 50* **Closed** *Mon, Tue–Thu lunch*
Simply but artfully decorated with flea market finds, this serves delicious Argentinian and Italian favourites, including tender grilled meats and authentic pasta dishes, with international wines.

Casa Alberto €€
Traditional Spanish Map 7 A3
Calle de las Huertas 18
Tel *91 429 93 56* **Closed** *Sun dinner, Mon*
Founded in 1827, and oozing old-fashioned charm, this place offers traditional dishes such as oxtail stew, meatballs and ham *croquetas*. Excellent tapas, too. Vermouth, an alcoholic drink made from wine and herbs, is available on tap.

Casa Ciriaco €€
Madrileño Map 3 C3
Calle Mayor 84
Tel *91 548 06 20* **Closed** *Sun, Mon–Thu dinner*
An established favourite, famous for its *"callos Madrileños"* (tripe), a classic local dish, as well as the *gallina en pepitoria* (a delicious local stew made with chicken and vegetables).

Casa Jacinto €€
Madrileño Map 4 D1
Calle del Reloj 20
Tel *91 542 67 25* **Closed** *Sun dinner, Mon*
Don't be fooled by the humble exterior: this is considered by many to serve the best *cocido* (a traditional local stew) in town, and has an extensive menu of classic *Madrileño* favourites. There are lovely views from the terrace.

Casa María €€
Modern Spanish Map 4 E2
Plaza Mayor 23
Tel *91 559 10 07*
A reliable bet for lunch on the Plaza Mayor, this has a wonderful terrace and an intimate, brick-walled interior. Traditional stews, plus a choice of tapas and *raciones*.

Donnafugata €€
Italian Map 4 D2
Calle Conde de Lemos 3
Tel *91 559 31 81*
This place specializes in Sicilian dishes like seafood ravioli, and also does excellent pizzas baked in a wood-fired oven. Finish with tiramisu or rich chocolate truffles.

El Abrazo de Vergara €€
Modern Spanish Map 4 D2
Calle de Vergara 10
Tel *91 542 00 62* **Closed** *Mon*
Try delicious rice with wild mushrooms and truffles, or a selection of exquisite gourmet tapas (perhaps some spider crab *croquetas* or cherry *gazpacho*) at this sleek restaurant.

El Estragón €€
Vegetarian Map 3 C3
Plaza de la Paja 21
Tel *91 365 89 82*
One of Madrid's oldest vegetarian restaurants, with generous portions of reliable classics, such as vegetable lasagne and tofu stir fry, served out on a pretty terrace in summer.

Estado Puro €€
Tapas Map 7 A3
Calle de San Sebastián 2 (in the NH Palacio de Tepa)
Tel *91 389 64 90*
Super-stylish, with gourmet tapas by celebrated chef Paco Roncero, who takes classic recipes such as *buñuelos de bacalao* (cod puffs) and reinvents them magnificently.

Esteban €€
Madrileño Map 4 D4
Cava Baja 36
Tel *91 365 90 91* **Closed** *Sun dinner, Tue*
Visit this atmospheric tavern to tuck into roast suckling pig, *cocido* (meat and chickpea stew), *callos* (tripe) and all the *Madrileño* classics, plus plenty of tapas.

Julián de Tolosa €€
Modern Spanish Map 4 D3
Cava Baja 18
Tel *91 365 82 10* **Closed** *Sun dinner*
A handsome restaurant on two levels, with exposed brick walls. It is famous for its huge, succulent steaks (the *chuletón* is recommended), cooked on a charcoal brazier.

Matritum €€
Modern Spanish Map 4 D4
Cava Alta 17
Tel *91 365 82 37* **Closed** *Mon, Tue dinner*
Charming and intimate, this restaurant has a spectacular wine selection, and offers a range of exquisite, contemporary dishes, which include grilled turbot with scallops and steak *tartare*.

Naïa €€
Modern Spanish Map 4 D3
Plaza de la Paja 3
Tel *91 366 27 83*
Chic but relaxed bistro, popular with actors and artists, serving fresh, modern cuisine with a creative twist. Dishes might include hake and razor clams with coriander or Iberian pork with citrus.

La Ópera de Madrid €€
Modern Spanish Map 4 D2
Calle de la Amnistía 5
Tel *91 559 50 92* **Closed** *Sun, Mon dinner*
Classic Spanish cuisine is given a modern twist at this spacious, airy restaurant, but the real draw here is the musical accompaniment from opera and *zarzuela* singers.

Prada a Tope €€
Traditional Spanish Map 7 A2
Calle del Príncipe 11
Tel *91 429 59 21* **Closed** *Sun dinner, Mon during summer*
An atmospheric, wood-panelled and bottle-lined restaurant that specializes in traditional, largely meaty, dishes from León in northern Spain, and serves very decent wines from its own vineyard.

For more information on types of restaurants *see page 157*

Taberna del Chato €€
Tapas **Map** 4 F3
Calle de la Cruz 35
Tel *91 523 16 29*
Exquisite wines and beautifully presented gourmet tapas from ham *croquetas* to *nidos de langostinos* (langoustine nests) have made this a local favourite.

Taberneros €€
Tapas **Map** 4 D2
Calle de Santiago 9
Tel *91 542 21 60* **Closed** *Mon lunch*
With just a handful of tables, this elegant restaurant features a superb wine list and an array of international dishes which include wild mushroom *croquetas* or a cod and artichoke risotto.

Botín €€€
Madrileño **Map** 4 E3
Calle de los Cuchilleros 17
Tel *91 366 42 17*
The world's oldest restaurant is set in a series of rustic, interconnected dining rooms, and is justly famed for its excellent *cocinillo* (roast suckling pig).

El Club Allard €€€
Modern Spanish **Map** 1 C5
Calle de Ferraz 2
Tel *91 559 09 39* **Closed** *Sun, Mon*
Offers a choice of three set menus, each a series of sublime dishes created by chef María Marte. Her inventive approach has garnered the restaurant two Michelin stars.

El Cucurucho del Mar €€€
Seafood **Map** 4 E1
Postigo de San Martín 6
Tel *91 524 08 41* **Closed** *Mon dinner*
This classic seafood restaurant, filled with delightfully kitsch seashell decoration, bears witness to the Spanish claim that the freshest fish in Spain ends up in Madrid.

La Esquina del Real €€€
French **Map** 4 D2
Calle de la Amnistía 4
Tel *91 559 43 09* **Closed** *Sat lunch, Sun*
Arguably one of the best French restaurants in Madrid, this romantic spot serves exquisite dishes such as *magret* of duck, *escargots* and fresh seafood in an elegantly restored 17th-century building.

La Terraza del Casino €€€
Modern Spanish **Map** 7 A2
Calle de Alcalá 15
Tel *91 521 87 00* **Closed** *Sun, Mon*
Dazzling decor and a stunning terrace are matched by equally impressive contemporary cuisine by award-winning chef Paco Roncero, a disciple of Ferran Adrià.

Tastefully decorated dining room at El Club Allard

Bourbon Madrid

Café del Botánico €
Traditional Spanish **Map** 8 D3
Calle de Ruiz de Alarcón 27
Tel *91 420 23 42*
Ideal for lunch when visiting the Prado, this delightfully old-fashioned spot offers a great *menú del día* featuring traditional regional dishes. The shaded terrace is a pleasant place to sit.

Café del Círculo de Bellas Artes €
Café **Map** 7 B2
Calle del Marqués de Casa Riera 2
Tel *91 360 54 00*
This airy Art Deco café, in a beautiful cultural centre, is great for everything from morning coffee to lunch or evening cocktails. For delicious cuisine with a global flavour, head to The Tartan Room on the roof terrace.

Casa González €
Tapas **Map** 7 A3
Calle del León 12
Tel *91 429 56 18* **Closed** *Sun dinner*
Part deli, part wine bar, behind a wonderful old façade; serves platters of *charcuterie* and cheeses to go with their excellent selection of wines. They also do occasional tastings.

Pizzería Cervantes €
Tapas **Map** 7 A3
Calle del León 8
Tel *91 429 56 18*
A classic, with a long, marble bar and a great selection of traditional tapas, from platters of Iberian ham and cured Manchego cheese to *pulpo a la gallego* (tender octopus).

Pulpería Maceira €
Tapas **Map** 7 B3
Calle de Jesús 7
Tel *91 429 15 84*
Specializing in *pulpo* (succulent octopus), this scruffy but appealing tapas bar also offers a range of delicious seafood tapas and *raciones*, including *croquetas* and rice dishes.

Bocaíto €€
Modern Spanish **Map** 7 B1
Calle de la Libertad 6
Tel *91 532 12 19* **Closed** *Sun*
Squeeze into this bustling Andalusian-style eatery to enjoy tapas at the bar, where hams hang from the ceiling, or tuck into traditional Spanish cuisine in the restaurant.

Café Murillo €€
Modern Spanish **Map** 8 D3
Calle de Ruiz de Alarcón 27
Tel *91 369 36 89* **Closed** *Sun dinner*
A delightful spot which melds old and new both in its decor and on the menu. Good tapas, salads and grilled meats, as well as a great brunch.

Casa Manolo €€
Traditional Spanish **Map** 7 B2
Calle de los Jovellanos 7
Tel *91 521 45 16* **Closed** *Sun dinner, Mon*
For over a century, this charming tavern has been a local favourite, serving some of the city's best *croquetas* at the tapas bar, as well as classic dishes in the dining area.

Paradis de Madrid €€
Mediterranean **Map** 7 B2
Calle del Marqués de Cubas 14
Tel *91 429 73 03* **Closed** *Sun dinner*
Dine on delicious Mediterranean rice dishes, fresh seafood and Catalan specialities including sausages and *calçots* (seasonal leek-like vegetables).

Trattoria Sant Arcangelo €€
Italian **Map** 8 D3
Calle de Moreto 15
Tel *91 369 10 93*
A beautiful, airy restaurant, perfect for a romantic meal, serving Italian dishes from around the boot, including home-made pasta and fresh seafood.

Zerain €€
Traditional Spanish **Map** 7 B3
Calle de Quevedo 3
Tel *91 429 79 09* **Closed** *Sun dinner*
A traditional Basque restaurant, serving regional dishes prepared with remarkably fresh fish and shellfish, flown in daily, as well as succulent, chargrilled meat.

El Mirador del Museo
Modern Spanish   Map 7 C2
Paseo del Prado 8
Tel *91 429 39 84*   **Closed** *lunch, mid-Sep–mid-Jun*
Exquisite modern cuisine and fine views at this beautiful, rooftop, summer-only restaurant in the Thyssen-Bornemisza museum.

Europa Decó
Modern Spanish   Map 7 A2
Carrera de San Jeronimo 34
Tel *91 787 77 70*   **Closed** *Sat lunch, Sun, Mon*
At one of the city's hottest addresses, the glitzy Hotel Urban, this serves sophisticated dishes such as lobster *carpaccio* or rack of lamb with saffron rice.

DK Choice

Palacio Cibeles   €€€
Modern Spanish   Map 7 C1
Plaza Cibeles 1, 6th Floor
Tel *91 523 14 54*
The spectacular, neo-Gothic former post office, now the city hall, has a fantastic modern restaurant on the sixth floor, with fabulous views to go with its refined, contemporary cuisine. Book a table on the terrace and enjoy suckling pig, wild mushrooms, fine wines and perhaps the best marzipan tart in the city.

Around La Castellana

A 2 Velas
Café   €
Calle de San Vicente Ferrer 16   Map 2 F4
Tel *655 45 83 67*
Fresh, unusual salads and tasty international dishes, such as blinis with smoked salmon and Vietnamese spring rolls. A three-course picnic menu is offered as well.

La Bicicleta Café
Café   €
Plaza de San Ildefonso 9   Map 2 F5
This friendly café offers tasty organic treats from tarts to cakes in fun, bike-themed surroundings. Bike workshop and art gallery, too.

Bodegas El Maño
Tapas   €
Calle de la Palma 64   Map 2 D4
Tel *91 521 50 57*
Classic Castilian tavern, perfect for an ice-cold beer and some traditional tapas like *tortilla* and *croquetas*, as well as generous portions of local classics.

Bodega La Ardosa
Tapas   €
Calle de Colón 13   Map 2 F5
Tel *91 521 49 79*
A wonderfully old-fashioned tapas bar, where you can enjoy *salmorejo cordobés* (a chilled tomato and almond soup), *charcuterie*, *tortilla* and other traditional tapas.

La Candelita
Latin American   €
Calle de Barquillo 30   Map 5 B5
Tel *91 523 85 53*   **Closed** *Sun dinner*
Charming and stylish, this fashionable eatery serves everything from *empanadas* (small filled pies) and *ceviches* to *chupe de gallina*, a rich chicken stew.

Elcano
Traditional Spanish   €
Calle de Lagasca 7   Map 8 E1
Tel *91 127 25 24*
Pinchos, simple Basque specialities which consist of baguette slices with a range of delicious toppings, are the big draw here. Heavier dishes are also available.

Mamá Framboise
Café   €
Calle de Fernando VI 23   Map 5 B5
Tel *91 391 43 64*
A large selection of absolutely delectable French cakes and pastries. Mamá Framboise is perfect for breakfast, a light lunch or afternoon coffee.

Las Mañanitas
Mexican   €
Calle de Fuencarral 82   Map 5 A4
Tel *91 522 45 89*
Popular with locals, this eatery offers authentic Mexican dishes including *tacos, enchiladas* and *nachos*. The signature dish, *cochinita pibil* (slow-roasted pork), is highly recommended.

Maricastaña
Café   €
Corredera Baja de San Pablo 12   Map 2 F5
Tel *91 082 71 42*
Retro-chic decor and delicious sandwiches, innovative salads, great brunch options and a good-value set lunch menu make this a favourite spot in trendy Triball. Also great for a drink at night.

Mesón del Jamón
Tapas   €
Gran Vía 72   Map 2 D5
Tel *91 541 20 23*
Spanish hams are the speciality at this popular chain. Ogle the long line of hams hanging from the ceiling. Handily located for a break when shopping on the Gran Vía.

DK Choice

La Musa   €
Modern Spanish   Map 2 F3
Calle de Manuela Malasaña 18
Tel *91 448 75 58*
A classic in Malasaña since the 1990s, this popular restaurant is always lively and warm. Sample the set lunch or enjoy a light dinner with friends. The varied menu changes regularly to include new dishes or tapas. Wooden tables and large windows add to the atmosphere.

My Veg
Modern Spanish   Map 4 F1
Calle de Valverde 28
Tel *91 531 17 02*   **Closed** *Mon dinner*
Stylish interiors and a pretty terrace, where visitors can choose from a range of dishes, many of which are vegetarian. Try the baby squid with avocado.

Naif Madrid
International   €
Calle de San Joaquín 16   Map 2 F5
Tel *91 007 20 71*
A boho-chic loft-style restaurant with murals, gourmet burgers and imaginative salads. Good for lunch, afternoon coffee and cakes, and also for cocktails in the evening.

Seating at the sophisticated Palacio Cibeles

For more information on types of restaurants *see page 157*

Peggy Sue's American Diner €
American **Map** 5 B5
Calle de Belén 5
Tel *91 308 30 93*
Fun American-style diner, with colourful 1950s decor, serving milkshakes, burgers, hot dogs and ice cream. It's particularly popular with families.

Pulcinella €
Italian **Map** 5 B5
Calle de Regueros 7
Tel *91 319 73 63*
Friendly Italian restaurant serving tasty pasta dishes, prepared with authentic ingredients, and big pizzas cooked in a wood-fired oven. Finish with the fantastic tiramisu.

Ainhoa €€
Traditional Spanish **Map** 5 C5
Calle de Bárbara de Braganza 12
Tel *91 308 27 26* **Closed** *Sun,*
Mon dinner
Bacalao pil-pil (cod with a classic, herby sauce), grilled spring lamb chops and stuffed peppers are on offer at this classic Basque restaurant. Good-value mid-week dinner menu.

Al Hoceima €€
Moroccan **Map** 5 A5
Calle de la Farmacia 8
Tel *91 531 94 11* **Closed** *Mon, Tue*
One of the city's best addresses for traditional Moroccan food, including delectable *harira* soup, *couscous* with a choice of sauces and *bastilla* (meat pie).

Bar Tomate €€
Mediterranean **Map** 6 D4
Calle de Fernando el Santo 26
Tel *91 702 38 70*
Fashionable spot for market-fresh dishes such as tuna *tartare* with guacamole or hake baked with olives and tomatoes. The airy, loft-style interior is laid out with big wooden tables.

Bolívar €€
Modern Spanish **Map** 2 E3
Calle de Manuela Malasaña 2
Tel *91 445 12 74* **Closed** *Sun*
Elegant black-and-white decor and sophisticated Spanish cuisine based on seasonal produce, served with a great wine selection. Try the fresh vegetable tempura, or the sea bream in a salt crust.

Le Cabrera €€
Gastro-bar **Map** 5 C5
Paseo de Recoletos 2
Tel *91 319 94 57* **Closed** *Lunch,*
Mon, Tue
Gorgeous, designer gastro-bar, serving exquisite gourmet tapas and fabulous cocktails.

Bright, attractive decor at Con 2 Fogones

Café Gijón €€
Café **Map** 5 C5
Paseo de Recoletos 21
Tel *91 521 54 25*
One of Madrid's famous literary cafés, established in 1887. It serves classic specialities in a resplendent, wood-panelled dining room hung with oil paintings, or out on the large terrace.

Casa Perico €€
Madrileño **Map** 4 F1
Calle de la Ballesta 18
Tel *91 532 81 76* **Closed** *Sun*
This family-run spot from the 1940s has oodles of old-fashioned charm. It offers traditional local dishes, from hearty mountain stews with lentils to excellent meatballs, and classic desserts like rice pudding.

DK Choice

Casa Salvador €€
Traditional Spanish **Map** 7 B1
Calle de Barbieri 12
Tel *91 521 45 24* **Closed** *Sun,*
Mon dinner
Almost unchanged since the 1940s, this well-known establishment is decorated with bullfighting posters and historic prints. Choose from a variety of authentic local dishes, such as *callos* (tripe), meat and lentil stews, and classic desserts like *natillas* (custard pudding).

Cinco Jotas €€
Tapas **Map** 6 E5
Calle de Puigcerdá s/n
Tel *91 575 41 25*
The place for ham-lovers, specializing in the sought-after *jamón de bellota*, produced from acorn-fed pigs. Also offers a good range of classic Spanish tapas, from *croquetas* to *tortilla*.

DK Choice

Con 2 Fogones €€
Modern Spanish **Map** 2 D5
Calle de San Bernardino 8
Tel *91 559 63 26*
An attractive, warmly decorated restaurant with a weekly changing menu which could include squid meatballs with wild rice or tuna *tataki*. The set lunch, offered on weekdays, is a steal. Make sure to save room for dessert – try the refreshing mango sorbet.

Dionisos Chueca €€
Greek **Map** 5 B5
Calle de San Gregorio 11
Tel *91 319 77 31*
Decorated in blue and white, this modern Greek restaurant boasts a stylish interior and a delicious menu of tasty specialities such as *moussaka*, Greek salad and swordfish with potatoes.

El Cocinillas €€
Modern Spanish **Map** 5 A5
Calle de San Joaquín 3
Tel *91 523 29 60* **Closed** *Sun dinner,*
Mon
Intimate and charming, with a tasty selection of market-fresh dishes prepared with a creative twist. Menu could include avocado timbale with baby squid, or kid with honey and rosemary.

El Mentidero de la Villa €€
Mediterranean **Map** 5 C3
Calle de Almagro 20
Tel *91 308 12 85* **Closed** *Sat lunch,*
Sun
A series of elegant dining rooms, and a menu that melds modern French, Spanish and Italian cuisine, featuring dishes such as tuna *tartare* with truffle caviar, delicious risottos and excellent desserts.

Embassy €€
Café Map 6 D4
Paseo Castellana 12
Tel *91 435 94 80*
This is where Salamanca's ladies-who-lunch come for an elegant breakfast or afternoon tea. It also has a great deli, ideal for picking up Spanish delicacies, including organic olive oil.

La Fragua de Sebín €€
Modern Spanish Map 2 F4
Calle del Divino Pastor 21
Tel *91 445 95 97* **Closed** *Sun dinner, Mon*
Beautifully fresh cuisine, from risotto with *foie* and wild mushrooms to grilled baby squid, and a beautiful terrace which is (unusually) open year-round. The set lunch is a great bargain.

La Galette II €€
Vegetarian Map 5 C5
Bárbara de Braganza 10
Tel *91 308 54 13*
An elegant restaurant catering especially to vegetarians with dishes such as asparagus and parmesan cheese quiche or their classic apple *croquettes*. Creative non-vegetarian fare also spans the menu.

Gumbo €€
American Map 2 E5
Calle del Pez 15
Tel *91 532 63 61* **Closed** *Sun dinner, Mon*
Jambalaya, fried green tomatoes and, of course, *gumbo* are served by friendly staff in a pretty blue-and-white dining room decorated with photos of jazz greats.

La Kitchen €€
International Map 5 C5
Calle de Prim 5
Tel *91 360 49 74* **Closed** *Sun*
Airy, fashionable restaurant with a tasty menu of fusion dishes like red tuna steak with caramelized Belgian endive.

Ma Bretagne €€
French Map 2 F4
Calle de San Vicente Ferrer 9
Tel *91 531 77 74* **Closed** *Mon–Fri lunch*
Charming, romantic candlelit crêperie, serving sweet and savoury crêpes with myriad fillings. Friendly service.

Poncelet Cheese Bar €€
Gastro-bar Off Map 6
Calle de José Abascal 61
Tel *91 399 25 50*
Modern, elegant restaurant with a dazzling cheese selection from around Europe, plus fine wines.

Quintana 30 €€
Modern Spanish Map 1 A4
Calle de Quintana 30
Tel *91 542 65 20* **Closed** *Mon*
Elegantly served Basque and Navarrese cuisine prepared with the freshest ingredients, including superb fish and gourmet tapas.

Ribeira Do Miño €€
Seafood Map 5 A5
Calle de Santa Brigida 1
Tel *91 521 98 54* **Closed** *Mon*
Fabulously fresh seafood, including unusual delicacies like *percebes* (barnacles) as well as lobster, scallops and more, is served at this cheerful, rustically decorated restaurant.

La Tape €€
Café Map 2 E3
Calle de San Bernardo 88
Tel *91 593 04 22*
A bright, modern option that offers an excellent selection of craft beers and original salads, *ceviches*, tarts and cakes.

Ramón Freixa Madrid €€€
Modern Spanish Map 6 E3
Calle de Claudio Coello 67
Tel *91 781 82 62* **Closed** *Sun, Mon*
Award-winning cuisine by one of Spain's most lauded chefs, in a wonderful restaurant overlooking a garden.

DK Choice

Restaurante Lúa €€€
Modern Spanish Map 5 B2
Paseo de Eduardo Dato 5
Tel *91 395 28 53* **Closed** *Sun*
A truly exquisite restaurant, with beautiful modern decor and artworks on the walls, Lúa prides itself on its creatively updated versions of classic Spanish recipes, which are served in a choice of two set menus (plus a great lunch menu) conceived according to what's in season. They are accompanied by a fine selection of wines.

Sergi Arola €€€
Modern Spanish Map 5 C2
Calle de Zurbano 31
Tel *91 310 21 69* **Closed** *Sun, Mon*
Sergi Arola, a disciple of Ferran Adrià, creates culinary fireworks at his eponymous, Michelin-starred restaurant.

La Tasquita de Enfrente €€€
Modern Spanish Map 4 F1
Calle de la Ballesta 6
Tel *91 532 54 49* **Closed** *Sun*
There's no menu here, just a selection of dishes based on whatever is freshest in the market.

Further Afield

Bodegas Rosell €
Traditional Spanish
Calle del General Lacy 14
Tel *91 467 84 58* **Closed** *Sun dinner, Mon*
This traditional tavern opened in 1920 and serves a variety of classic tapas, along with some excellent wine from the barrel

Los Caracoles €
Tapas Map 1 B3
Calle de Toledo 106
Tel *91 366 42 46*
An old-fashioned 1940s tavern offering a varied menu that includes *caracoles* (snails), prepared with a selection of sauces. Locals often drop in for tapas after visiting the nearby Rastro flea market..

Casa de Asturias €
Traditional Spanish Map 7 A5
Calle de Argumosa 4
Tel *91 527 27 63*
This typical Asturian *sidrería* (cider-house) serves great tapas to go with delicious cider, along with traditional dishes such as fried hake or grilled chops.

Casa Mingo €
Traditional Spanish
Paseo de la Florida 34
Tel *91 547 79 18*
Cavernous, old-fashioned *sidrería* with a terrace. The roast chicken and cider are worth the excursion.

Casa Mono €
Modern Spanish Map 1 B3
Calle Tutor 37
Tel *91 452 95 52*
Spacious, airy, modern restaurant, offering tasty dishes like bream stuffed with prawns, or *confit* of duck. Also good for breakfast.

Diners at the bustling Casa Mingo, popular for its cider

For more information on types of restaurants *see page 157*

El Jalapeño €
Mexican
Calle Pedro Muguruza 4
Tel *91 142 79 94*
Spicy, authentic Mexican
quesadillas, *nachos* and *tacos*
served up in colourful surround-
ings. There is a good-value set
menu and great margaritas too.
Friendly, helpful staff.

El Vergel €
Vegetarian
Paseo de la Florida 53
Tel *91 547 19 52*
Organic produce rules at this
simple veggie restaurant located
by the river, which has plenty
of vegan options. The menu
changes daily. There is also a
shop on site.

Lateral €
Tapas **Map** 6 D1
Paseo de la Castellana 89
Tel *91 561 33 37*
This airy, modern restaurant, with
its long, shared wooden tables,
specializes in Basque *pinchos*.
Lovely outdoor seating area.

Aroy Thai €€
Thai
Calle del Comandante Zorita 3
Tel *91 554 23 88*
Prettily decorated, this place
serves great curries and noodle
dishes. Tailor your dish to suit
your own needs: ask if you
want it spicy.

Café Saigon €€
Vietnamese **Map** 6 D1
Calle de María de Molina 4
Tel *91 563 15 66*
The decor evokes French Indo-
china, with wooden and bamboo
furnishings and leafy palms. The
French-influenced Vietnamese
cuisine includes glass noodles
with scallops and duck curry.

Casa Valencia €€
Mediterranean **Map** 1 A3
Paseo del Pintor Rosales 58
Tel *91 544 17 47* **Closed** *Sun dinner*
One of the best places to try
an authentic *paella*. Serves a
fantastic range of Mediterranean
rice dishes, including rice cooked
in squid ink, plus plenty of meat
and seafood dishes.

La Castela €€
Modern Spanish
Calle del Dr Castelo 22
Tel *91 573 55 90* **Closed** *Sun dinner*
Classic restaurant with a mixture
of contemporary and traditional
dishes – tapas at the front, and
full service at the back, with fried
artichokes, wild mushrooms and
fresh turbot on the menu.

Cosme €€
Mediterranean
Calle del Duque de Sesto 25
Tel *91 431 67 80* **Closed** *Sun*
Chic and inviting, with modern
interpretations of traditional
Mediterranean recipes, such as
hake with squid ink pasta or duck
with asparagus risotto, as well as
particularly good rice dishes.

El Brote €€
Modern Spanish
Calle Javier Ferrero 8
Tel *91 110 31 39* **Closed** *Sat, Sun,
mid-Jun–mid-Sep*
Wild mushrooms are the speciality
here, available in myriad varieties,
along with delicacies such as
stuffed courgette flowers.

La Gabinoteca €€
Modern Spanish
Calle Fernández de la Hoz 53
Tel *91 399 15 00* **Closed** *Sun*
Stylish, minimalist decor and
creative, beautifully presented
dishes such as *"el potito"*, layers
of egg, potato and truffle.

DK Choice

La Gilda €€
Modern Spanish
Calle Víctor Andrés Belaúnde 56
Tel *91 344 00 26* **Closed** *Sun &
Mon dinner*
Bright, modern restaurant,
dominated by a huge mural of
Rita Hayworth, serving delicious
creative cuisine, with unusual
specialities like vegetable
tempura and ostrich steaks. The
set lunch is excellent. It is also a
popular place for drinks and
tapas. Locally sourced produce
is used as much as possible.

Warm, intimate seating at the stylish
Metro Bistró

Lakasa de César €€
Modern Spanish
*Calle de Raimundo Fernandez
Villaverde 26*
Tel *91 533 87 15* **Closed** *Sun dinner,
Mon*
This restaurant is located near the
Bernabéu stadium. Come here to
enjoy exquisitely presented
contemporary dishes such as
seafood *millefeuille* or roast pigeon
at the bar or in the dining area.
Book ahead.

Metro Bistró €€
Modern Spanish **Map** 1 B4
Calle Evaristo San Miguel 21
Tel *91 542 95 21* **Closed** *Sun dinner*
Fresh, tasty, inventive cuisine
including stuffed baby squid
with black rice or sweet and sour
beef, served with a thoughtfully
selected wine list in a bright,
stylish bistro near the park.

Paolo €€
Italian
Calle del General Rodrigo 3
Tel *91 554 44 28* **Closed** *Sun; Mon &
Tue dinner*
Near the Canal Isabel II park
(which has sports facilities), Paolo
serves copious portions of freshly
made pasta and pizzas cooked
to perfection in a wood-fired
oven. Offers traditional Spanish
dishes as well.

Sal Gorda €€
Modern Spanish
Calle Beatriz de Bobadilla 9
Tel *91 553 95 06* **Closed** *Sun &
Mon dinner*
White linen tablecloths and
sparkling crystal set the scene
at this elegant restaurant, where
you can try modern Spanish
dishes such as stuffed baby squid
and a phenomenal apple pie.

Taberna de la Daniela €€
Traditional Spanish
Calle del General Pardiñas 21
Tel *91 575 23 29*
With colouful tiles and wooden
tables, this is regularly voted one
of the best restaurants in town
for authentic *cocido Madrileño*
(served daily, unlike in other
restaurants which traditionally
serve it on Wednesdays).

Urkiola Mendi €€
Traditional Spanish
Calle de Arturo Soria 51
Tel *91 367 52 94* **Closed** *Mon dinner*
Sophisticated Basque fare, with
a seasonal menu that might
include spider crab *canelones*,
sautéed wild mushrooms with
caramlized *foie gras* or tender
mountain lamb. Occasional
live jazz.

Rustic decor of the Mesón Cuevas del Vino, Chinchón

La Vaca Argentina €€
Argentinian   Map 1 B1
Calle de Gaztambide 50
Tel *91 543 53 83*
One of a small chain, this large, loft-style restaurant offers a good choice of succulent Argentine steaks, salads and pasta dishes. A good option for groups or families.

Aldaba €€€
Traditional Spanish
Avenida Alberto Alcocer 5
Tel *91 359 73 86*   **Closed** *Sun, public hols*
A favourite with business travellers, this place has classic Spanish cuisine, prepared to perfection and matched with great wines.

DK Choice

DiverXO €€€
Modern Spanish
NH Madrid Eurobuilding, Calle de Padre Damián 23
Tel *91 570 07 66* **Closed** *Sun, Mon*
With three Michelin stars to its credit, DiverXO is a fantastic contemporary restaurant run by David Muñoz, one of Spain's youngest and most adventurous chefs. Guests can choose from one of two equisite tasting menus, and experience David's theatrical, imaginative cuisine.

Santceloni €€€
Modern Spanish
Paseo de la Castellana 57
Tel *91 210 88 40*   **Closed** *Sat lunch, Sun, public hols*
The late great Santi Santamaria is mourned, but his legacy lives on at this spectacular, multi-award winning restaurant with talented chef Óscar Velasco at the helm.

Beyond Madrid

ALCALÁ DE HENARES: Hostería del Estudiante €
Traditional Spanish
Calle Colegios 3
Tel *918 88 03 30*
The regional delicacies here have become an institution. Try the *migas* (fried breadcrumbs with garlic) and *duelos y quebrantos* (a Manchegan dish with scrambled eggs, chorizo and bacon).

DK Choice

ARANJUEZ: Casa José €€€
Modern Spanish
Calle de Abastos 32
Tel *91 891 14 88*   **Closed** *Sun dinner*
This enchanting restaurant, in a beautifully restored mansion, serves sophisticated dishes, such as leek with broccoli foam and sea anenome, or marinated grouper. Locally sourced produce is used wherever possible, and the wine list features more than 250 labels, including some interesting boutique wineries.

CHINCHÓN: Mesón Cuevas del Vino €€
Traditional Spanish
Calle de Benito Hortelano 1
Tel *91 894 02 06*   **Closed** *Sun dinner*
Set in a 17th-century mill, this rustically decorated restaurant is the perfect setting for traditional dishes like lamb chops.

EL ESCORIAL: Montia €
Modern Spanish
Calle Calvario 4
Tel *91 133 69 88*   **Closed** *Mon*
This Michelin-starred restaurant serves creative dishes made using organic regional products.

EL ESCORIAL: La Rueda €€
Modern Spanish
Avenida de la Constitución
Tel *91 890 27 82*
Two-in-one: a classic *mesón* for tapas, and a more modern restaurant for succulent stews.

NAVACERRADA: El Rumba €€
Modern Spanish
Plaza del Doctor Gereda
Tel *91 856 04 05*   **Closed** *Mon, Tue; Wed & Thu lunch; Sun dinner*
Wonderful charcoal-grilled local meats and a sprinkling of interesting modern dishes such as scallops with citrus and *salmorejo*.

SEGOVIA: La Almuzara €
Café
Calle Marqués del Arco 3
Tel *921 46 06 22*   **Closed** *Mon & Tue lunch*
Charming, friendly café, with a great menu featuring pizzas, pastas and salads, as well as plenty of vegetarian options.

SEGOVIA: Casa Zaca €€
Traditional Spanish
Calle Embajadores 6, La Granja de San Ildefonso
Tel *921 47 00 87* **Closed** *dinner, Mon*
This former coaching inn now houses the town's most elegant restaurant, featuring classic fare such as *cocido* and lamb stew.

SEGOVIA: El Bernardino €€
Traditional Spanish
Calle Cervantes 2
Tel *921 46 24 77*
Updated Castilian cuisine in a graceful town house, with the town's star dish, roast suckling pig, the house speciality.

SIGÜENZA: El Doncel €€
Modern Spanish
Paseo de la Alameda 3
Tel *94 939 00 01* **Closed** *Sun dinner, Mon*
A beautiful 18th-century mansion provides a sublime setting for exciting contemporary cuisine.

TOLEDO: Adolfo €€
Modern Spanish
Calle Hombre de Palo 7
Tel *925 22 73 21* **Closed** *Sun dinner*
Dine under a splendid *artesanado* ceiling on sophisticated versions of Toledano dishes, accompanied by excellent wines.

TOLEDO: La Mar Salá €€
Seafood
Calle Honda 9
Tel *925 25 47 85*   **Closed** *Mon; Tue & Wed dinner*
An atmospheric eatery with just a few tables. The mixed seafood platter is a highlight. Book ahead.

For more information on types of restaurants *see page 157*

SHOPPING IN MADRID

From sherry to seafood, the finest goods in Spain have always made their way across the country to the capital. Madrid still lives off that heritage, despite increasing competition from other parts, especially archrival Barcelona. Many products are basic Castilian commodities – Manchego cheese, olive oil and leather goods – whose quality lies in the excellent raw materials. Since the swinging 1980s, fashion design has flourished in Madrid. New-look, home-grown fashion outlets now dot Madrid's different shopping areas from the city centre to the upmarket district of Salamanca (see p101). The latest streetwear is available in the Chueca (see p96) and Las Salesas areas. There are colourful food markets all over the city, and in the heart of Old Madrid you'll find superb speciality food and wine stores. Don't miss the El Rastro flea market (see p65) on Sundays.

Opening Hours

Spanish shopping hours are not like anywhere else in Europe, thanks to Spanish mealtimes. Most shops are open from 10am to 2pm and from 5pm to 8:30pm, with only shops in the very centre, department stores and shopping centres staying open during the lunch break. Small shops often close on Saturday afternoons. Sunday opening hours vary; however, all shops tend to open on the first Sunday of each month as well as every Sunday in December and during the sales. Shopping centres are open every Sunday and most public holidays.

How to Pay

Both cash and credit cards are popular methods of payment in Madrid, whereas cheques are hardly ever accepted. Small shops may sometimes reject credit cards which charge them high commission, so it's always worth double-checking that your card is acceptable. A passport or photo ID will be required when you pay by credit card. Some tourist shops accept payment in US dollars.

VAT Exemption and Tax

A value-added tax (IVA) is applied to most goods. The standard rate of 18 per cent is charged on clothes and most other products, while the rate for most foodstuffs is 7 per cent. A reduced rate of 4 per cent is applied to basic foods such as cheese and fruit, as well as printed matter and materials for the disabled. At shops with a "Tax-free for Tourists" sign, non-EU residents can claim tax refunds on all purchases over €90, except food, drink, tobacco, motorbikes, cars and medicines.

Sales

Spanish sales are a popular institution, taking place in January and July. Beginning after the Feast of the Epiphany on 6 January, the New Year sales go on well into February. In July the summer fashion sales can turn up some real bargains, especially useful as Madrid's hot season often lasts well into September. Look out for signs advertising *Rebajas, Ofertas* or *Liquidación*.

High fashion on Calle de Serrano, Madrid's smartest shopping street

Shopping Centres

Shopping centres, or *centros comerciales*, have grown rapidly in Madrid. Among the best for upmarket fashion are the **Jardín de Serrano** and **ABC Serrano**, both set in the elegant neighbourhood of Salamanca, where you will also find many specialist luxury shops and the top international designer stores in and around the Calle de Serrano (see p100). If you want to find everything under one roof, go to the huge **Príncipe Pío** mall on the west side of Madrid.

The department store **El Corte Inglés** is a national institution. Gigantic branches all over the city sell clothes, food, household goods and almost everything else. They offer photo-developing and shoe repair services, too.

Madrid also boasts a number of hypermarkets, mostly located off the M30 ring road.

Museo del Jamón (see p178) sells a range of cured hams

Display of hand-painted ceramics in Toledo

Markets

The legendary **El Rastro** flea market is held on Sundays and public holidays. It is located between the Plaza de Cascorro and streets leading off the Ribera de Curtidores. Do not expect to stumble across a painting by Velázquez, but you will find everything else from valuable antiques to second-hand clothes, jewellery, records, collector items, mountain gear and statues for your garden. This is probably the only market in Madrid where it is possible to knock two-thirds off the starting price. Many shops and stalls in the area are open on weekdays for more relaxed browsing.

Open on Sundays only, the **Mercadillo de Sellos y Monedas** is a small coin, stamp and postcard market held under the arches of the Plaza Mayor. For a browse through old books, visit the **Mercado del Libro** on the south side of the Real Jardín Botánico *(see p86)*. Both new and second-hand books are sold here. On Sundays the stalls are thronged, but most open on weekdays, too.

Annual Fairs

For many *Madrileños*, the passing of the year is marked by popular annual fairs, many of them outdoors.

The contemporary art fair **ARCO** takes place in February. Whether you want to buy or just browse, it provides a great opportunity to catch up on the latest trends in the art world. In the week prior to Madrid's Fiestas de San Isidro *(see p38)*, which begin on 15 May, you can buy earthen cookware and wine jugs at the **Feria de Cerámica** in the colourful district of Conde Duque *(see p106)*. A sure sign that summer is just around the corner is the arrival of hundreds of book stalls along the leafy avenues of Parque del Retiro *(see p81)*, where publishers and book-shop owners exhibit their wares at the **Feria del Libro** over two weeks, beginning at the end of May.

On the Paseo de Recoletos the **Feria de Artesanos** takes place every December. Craft items from ceramics and jewellery to leather goods, glassware and silks make it ideal for Christmas shopping. Throughout December, the Plaza Mayor is the venue for a traditional Christmas fair, the **Mercado de Artículos Navideños**. Christmas trees are for sale, as well as cork-wood and moss for use in home-made nativity scenes. Stallholders also sell all the traditional figurines.

Sunday morning in the busy El Rastro flea market

DIRECTORY

Shopping Centres

ABC Serrano
Calle de Serrano 61.
Map 6 E3.
Tel 91 577 50 31.
w abcserrano.com

El Corte Inglés
Calle de Preciados 1–3.
Map 4 F2.
Tel 91 379 80 00.
One of several branches.
w elcorteingles.es/
centroscomerciales/es

Jardín de Serrano
Calle de Goya 6–8.
Map 6 E4.
Tel 91 577 00 12.
w jardindeserrano.es

Príncipe Pío
Paseo de la Florida.
Map 3 A1.
Tel 91 758 00 40.
w ccprincipepio.com

Markets

El Rastro
Calle de la Ribera de Curtidores. **Map** 4 E4.

Mercadillo de Sellos y Monedas
Plaza Mayor. **Map** 4 E3.

Mercado del Libro
Calle de Claudio Moyano. **Map** 8 D4.

Annual Fairs

For information on outdoor events call city information: **Tel** 010.

ARCO
Parque Ferial Juan Carlos I. **Tel** 90 222 15 15.
w ifema.es

Feria de Artesanos
Paseo de Recoletos.
Map 6 D5.

Feria de Cerámica
Plaza de las Comendadoras.
Map 2 D4.

Feria del Libro
Paseo de Coches del Retiro, Parque del Retiro.
Map 8 F1.

Mercado de Artículos Navideños
Plaza Mayor.
Map 4 E3.

What to Buy in Madrid

If flamenco frills and kitsch bulls are not to your taste, you can find a satisfying reminder of your visit in many traditional Spanish goods. Strongly scented saffron, matured ewe's cheese or a fruity extra virgin olive oil all make prized gifts. Leather goods are particularly sought after. The beautifully crafted Loewe bags are in a league of their own, but most leather, especially shoes, is extremely good value. Traditional crafts, such as woven baskets, are harder to find, but lovely and inexpensive ceramics are widely available. By looking around, you may even pick up an original piece of clothing.

Chulapo Dolls
These typically Spanish dolls with their endearing pout are dressed in the traditional costume of Madrid's *castizos* (*see p107*).

Spanish T-shirt
T-shirts make great gifts, and Madrid's shops offer a wide range of unique designs.

Leather Handbag
The best bags come from Mallorca, and are stocked at Piamonte (*see p176*), although many other shops sell leather, too.

Mantón de Manila
Classical, beautifully embroidered silk shawls, like this one, are easy to find and come in a wide range of colours.

Turrón
Luxury nougat and almond paste comes in a wooden gift box at Casa Mira (*see p178*).

Saffron (Azafrán)
Hand-picked *azafrán* comes from the autumn crocus. Introduced by the Moors, it is the world's most expensive spice.

Queso Manchego
Used in tapas or served with quince jelly (*membrillo*) at the end of a meal, Manchego cheese also makes an ideal gift. It is widely regarded as Spain's finest cheese.

Barquillera
Filled with wafer biscuits, this old-fashioned cookie (biscuit) tin has a children's roulette game on the lid. *Barquilleras* are sold in the pastry departments of El Corte Inglés and Mallorca *(see p178).*

Modern Fan
A wide range of fans, from the traditional delicate lace variety to colourful, simple modern versions, can be found throughout Madrid.

Modern fan

Traditional Ceramics
The art of hand-painting ceramics with traditional colours and designs continues to thrive in Madrid. The attractive plates and tiles make memorable keepsakes.

Antique ceramic tiles

Painted modern candlesticks

Decorative ceramic plates

Modern Ceramics
Those in search of 20th-century ceramics will not need to look far. As well as traditional designs, Madrid offers a wide range of entirely modern craftwork.

Sausages and Hams

Spain has a deep-rooted tradition of pork products, ranging from whole hams to sausages of every shape and size. The annual *matanza*, when pigs were killed and families spent the day preparing food for the months ahead, was an important date on the country calendar. Today, most products are made in a factory. *Jamón serrano* is cured ham, served thinly sliced as a *tapa* or used diced as an ingredient in numerous recipes. The best, and most expensive ham, is *ibérico*, from the small, black-hoofed, free-ranging Iberian pig. Many sausages are seasoned with Spain's favourite spice – paprika; they are called chorizo. Those without paprika are called *salchichón*. Other types of sausage are *longaniza* (long, thin sausages), *morcilla* (blood sausage or black pudding, made with rice, onions or potatoes) and *chistorras* (small Basque sausages, often flambéed). *Caña de lomo* is cured pork loin.

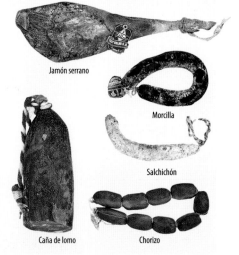

Jamón serrano

Morcilla

Salchichón

Caña de lomo

Chorizo

Fashion and Accessories

Spaniards are celebrated for their elegance. No woman will leave the house, even if it is simply to go to the market, without dressing impeccably. The most popular styles tend towards classic cuts, with the occasional Baroque flounce. Madrid's cultural boom in the 1980s impacted the fashion world with a look based on sleek, understated design and sophisticated accessories. Footwear and clothing boutiques carry all the well-known international designer labels but, if you want something a little bit different, look out for the Spanish designers.

Shoes

The best shoes are made in Mallorca, with classic footwear by Yanko at the very top of the range. Yanko shoes are so soft and comfortable that they feel like slippers. **Bravo** shoe shops carry many top Mallorcan makes, including Yanko, Lotusse and Barratts.

Another Mallorcan export is the young and comfortable **Camper** shoe. Outlets exist all over Madrid, with customer-friendly displays.

For sophisticated designs – and prices – look for Farrutx in El Corte Inglés.

If you forgot your trainers, or need to get out of rain-soaked shoes cheaply, try the shops along the Calle de Fuencarral, or go to **Los Guerrilleros** in the heart of Madrid's "kilometre 0" – the area around the Puerta del Sol. Jot down the reference number of the shoe in the showcase and you will get efficient service inside.

Brightly coloured espadrilles are sold in most areas but, for an old-world feel, visit **Casa Hernanz** off the Plaza Mayor.

Handbags and Other Leather Goods

The ultimate in Spanish bags and leather clothing goes by the prestigious name of **Loewe**, established in 1872 by a German tanner who settled in Spain. Loewe bags are sold all over the world. At the Loewe shop in Calle de Serrano, you can feast your eyes, if nothing else. Around the corner you will find **Lotusse** selling wallets, bags and coats, as well as its

famous shoes. The Mallorcan connection continues nearby at **Boxcalf**, with an enticing range of quality leather clothing and accessories.

Piamonte, in the Salamanca district, has become synonymous with attractive bags at affordable prices. They also have belts and an interesting selection of jewellery.

For a touch of Andalusian chic, see the handbags and belts for sale by **El Caballo** in El Corte Inglés.

Manuel Herrero offers value for money in what feels like a bazaar crammed with leather and suede, visitors and persuasive salespeople.

A delightful outlet for classic gloves is the small, but well-stocked **Guante Varadé**.

Jewellery

Madrid is full of small shops, stacked with trays of 18-carat gold studs, chains and bracelets, and grand jewellers – whether you walk down the Gran Vía or Calle de Serrano. Most Spanish women adore gold – the heavier the better – and pearls. Popular, man-made "Majorica" pearls, as well as the cultivated variety, can be found all over Madrid. **Casa Yustas**, spread over three floors, stocks Majorica pearls as well as Lladró porcelain.

Del Pino on Calle de Serrano is fun for its variety of costume jewellery across the price range, and the Catalans' innovative **Tous** outlet in Madrid should not be missed.

If you are interested in new creations, visit internationally acclaimed jeweller **Joaquín Berao**. His shop is like a

miniature art gallery devoted to thoughtfully understated and tasteful design.

Helena Rohner, whose silver, bronze and enamel jewellery can be found in **Piamonte** (see Handbags), is also becoming a popular name. You can visit her workshop, but it is best to call first.

Women's Fashions

The best of Spanish and international fashion is located on Calle de Serrano and Calle de José Ortega y Gasset, as well as in adjacent streets. The best place to find the work of young designers is the Chueca district, in and around Calle del Almirante, with shops such as **Ararat**. If you want original "street" fashion, go to **Glam** in busy Calle de Fuencarral, a street full of fun shops for the young.

In the designer category, **Adolfo Domínguez** – doyen of Madrid's minimalist look – and **Roberto Verino** offer excellent value for money. The more eccentric should try **Agatha Ruíz de la Prada**'s unique creations – also for children in her shop in Calle de Serrano. For a combination of designer clothes and leather goods, try **Loewe**, but be prepared for high prices.

Another creation in a league of its own is the traditional **Seseña** cape, exclusive to the Madrid fashion house of the same name which also makes more modern versions.

The chain store **Zara** has become an international phenomenon, offering easy-to-wear clothes for women, men and children at very good prices. **Bimba y Lola** has a wonderful collection of bags, leather goods and women's clothing as well.

Fine lingerie is part of a Spanish tradition, and lingerie shops – called corseterías in the more popular parts of town – are everywhere. A cotton nightdress can be an expensive affair but, for a select choice of sleepwear as well as bed linen, visit ¡Oh que luna! for original and attractive designs. Don't forget that Spain is big on babies, and **Prenatal** is well worth a visit for pregnant women and for anyone with very young children.

Menswear

Men's fashions can be found in the same areas of Madrid as women's. The traditional tailored look lives on, but Spanish men also like styles from abroad. You will find that many shops which sell off-the-peg clothes have Italian- or English-sounding names, but only sell home-produced merchandise. Prices and quality vary.

For a more interesting purchase, check out the menswear at **Adolfo Domínguez** or **Zara**. **Roberto Verino**, an icon of national fashion for both men and women, is also worth a look. His men's and women's ranges, as well as accessories, are all stocked at his elegant store on Calle de Serrano. At the top end, **Loewe**'s store for men has beautiful clothes, adapting fashion trends to its own look. A Loewe silk tie with a Spanish art motif makes a rewarding purchase.

Another name to look out for is Antonio Miró and his famous shirts, available in **Gallery**, which hosts a range of top international labels.

For casual wear, **Custo Barcelona** is extremely popular and there are clothes for women, too. Its outlets throughout the city offer quality cottonwear with original designs that come in attractive colours. If you are looking for younger and more affordable men's fashion, head to **Caramelo** with several branches in Madrid.

For outdoor clothes, which cater for anything between a walk in the park and a safari, go to **Coronel Tapioca** for comfort at a reasonable price.

DIRECTORY

Shoes

Bravo
Calle de Serrano 42.
Map 6 E4.
Tel 91 435 27 29.

Camper
Gran Vía 54.
Map 4 E1.
Tel 91 547 52 23.
w camper.es

Casa Hernanz
Calle de Toledo 18.
Map 4 E3.
Tel 91 366 54 50.

Los Guerrilleros
Puerta del Sol 5.
Map 4 F2.
Tel 91 521 27 08.

Handbags and Other Leather Goods

Boxcalf
Calle de Jorge Juan 14.
Map 6 E5.
Tel 91 435 33 42.

El Caballo
Calle de Lagasca 55.
Map 6 E5.
Tel 91 576 40 37.

Guante Varadé
Calle de Serrano 54.
Map 6 E3.
Tel 91 575 67 41.

Loewe
Calle de Serrano 26.
Map 6 E4.
Tel 91 577 60 56.
w loewe.es

Lotusse
El Jardin de Serrano, Calle de Goya 6–8.
Map 6 E4.
Tel 91 577 20 14.

Manuel Herrero
Calle de Preciados 7 & 16.
Map 4 F2.
Tel 91 521 29 90.

Piamonte
Marqués de Monasterio 5.
Map 5 C5.
Tel 91 702 55 61.

Jewellery

Casa Yustas
Plaza Mayor 30.
Map 4 E2.
Tel 91 366 50 84.

Del Pino
Calle Ayala 46.
Map 6 E3.
Tel 91 435 22 67.

Helena Rohner
Calle del Almendro 4.
Map 4 D3.
Tel 91 365 79 06.

Joaquín Berao
Calle Lagasca 44.
Map 6 E5.
Tel 91 577 28 28.

Piamonte
See Handbags and Other Leather Goods

Tous
Calle de Serrano 46.
Map 6 E4.
Tel 91 431 92 42.
w tous.es

Women's Fashions

Adolfo Domínguez
Calle de Serrano 5.
Map 8 D7.
Tel 98 839 87 43.

Agatha Ruíz de la Prada
Calle de Serrano 27.
Map 6 E4.
Tel 91 319 05 01.

Ararat
Calle del Almirante 10.
Map 5 C5.
Tel 91 531 81 56.

Bimba y Lola
Calle de Serrano 22.
Map 6 E5.
Tel 91 576 11 03.

Glam
Calle de Fuencarral 35.
Map 7 A1.
Tel 91 516 11 90.

Loewe
See Handbags and Other Leather Goods

¡Oh que luna!
Calle de Ayala 32.
Map 6 F4.
Tel 91 431 37 25.

Prenatal
Calle Goya 99.
Map 7 A1.
Tel 91 431 59 30.
w prenatal.es

Roberto Verino
Calle de Serrano 33.
Map 6 E4.
Tel 91 426 04 75.

Seseña
Calle de la Cruz 23.
Map 7 A2.
Tel 91 531 68 40.

Zara
Calle de Serrano 23.
Map 6 E4.
Tel 91 436 31 58.

Menswear

Adolfo Domínguez
See Women's Fashions

Caramelo
Calle de Serrano 19.
Map 6 E5.
Tel 91 435 01 77.

Coronel Tapioca
Calle del Carmen 12.
Map 4 F2.
Tel 91 826 80 04.

Cortefiel
Gran Vía 27.
Map 4 F1.
Tel 91 531 88 69.

Custo Barcelona
Calle Mayor 37.
Map 4 E2.
Tel 91 354 00 99.

Gallery
Calle de Jorge Juan 38.
Map 6 E5.
Tel 91 576 79 31.

Loewe
See Handbags and Other Leather Goods.

Roberto Verino
See Women's Fashions.

Zara
See Women's Fashions.

Antiques, Crafts and Gifts

Spain's rich and varied popular art makes it relatively easy to pick up an original piece of handicraft. It is often possible to obtain the same item, be it a ceramic mortar or a silk shawl, as an antique, a reproduction or even a stylized update. Genuine articles at good prices can still be found, but many rural crafts are fast disappearing. Fortunately, they do not include the age-old arts of producing Manchego cheese, cured ham and wines. Spain's musical tradition is very much alive, and a CD of flamenco-jazz fusion can be a spellbinding gift.

Antiques

Along Calle de Claudio Coello, in the elegant Salamanca district, are some outstanding antique shops. The streets around are also full of specialist outlets for rare antiques, ranging from 18th-century lacquered furniture at **María Gracia Cavestany**, to 15th-century Flemish paintings at **Theotokopoulos**. Some of Madrid's top dealers, such as Codosero and Zenón Sierra, can be found under one roof at the **Centro de Anticuarios**.

Calle del Prado is lined with antique shops crammed with Castilian-style furniture, books, old tiles, religious artifacts and antique jewellery. Shops on neighbouring Calle de las Huertas deal in old prints. **Alcocer**, located in Santa Catalina, is one of the oldest antique dealers, with a great collection of European furniture.

Palacios in El Rastro (see p65) sells collectors' items such as keys and corkscrews, while reasonably priced bric-a-brac (including some reproductions) can be found at **La Trastienda de Alcalá**, just northeast of the Parque del Retiro (see p81).

Casa Postal, near Plaza de Cibeles, specializes in old postcards and has a great selection of old signs and posters.

Modern Art, Prints and Photographs

When it comes to modern art, new trends and new talent, the galleries around Calle de Claudio Coello are well worth visiting. The **Juan Gris** gallery always has works from established as well as up-and-coming artists. **Juana de Aizpuru** has rapidly become one of the most influential galleries in Madrid. Also well known for promoting young artists is **Fúcares**. You can find sketches by artists such as Picasso, Chillida, Tàpies and Miró at **Galería Pilar Serra**. Most galleries are closed on Mondays.

Crafts

A wide choice of ceramics is offered at **Cántaro**, near the Plaza de España (see p57). Well stocked in regional styles, the shop also carries so-called "extinct" ceramics – pottery which is no longer produced. **Antigua Casa Talavera** opened in the late 19th century and sells hand-painted ceramics including vases, trays and pots produced in different regions of Spain.

The Spanish are proud of their embroidered linen, but hand-embroidered tablecloths or shawls at ridiculously low prices probably come from China. **Casa de Diego** is run by the fourth generation of the same family and sells quality embroidered shawls.

One of the best shops for *mantones* (silk shawls) and linen – hand- and machine-made – is **Borca**, just off the Puerta del Sol (see p48).

For a wide selection of hats, including top hats, bowlers and berets, try **La Favorita**. And for fine handmade guitars, visit **Guitarrería F Manzanero**.

Books and Music

There is an ample stock of foreign-language titles at **Casa del Libro** on Gran Vía. French-owned **FNAC**, nearby, offers a wide choice of books both in English and other languages. **Booksellers**, a little further afield, has classics but only a limited choice of new books. The second-hand bookstalls of the **Mercado del Libro** behind the Ministerio de Agricultura (see p86) are good for cheap paperbacks and, sometimes, rare volumes.

A curated selection of books can be found at **Desperate Literature**, while **Gaudí**, near Chueca, specializes in art books.

For all types of music, go to FNAC or **El Corte Inglés** branches in Calle de Preciados or Paseo de la Castellana. Flamenco buffs should visit **El Flamenco Vive**.

Gifts

Food gifts from Madrid are always appreciated, and olive oil or "green gold" from Catalonia to Andalusia is available at **La Chinata**, a specialist olive oil shop near Plaza Mayor. The **El Corte Inglés** Club du Gourmet in the basement of its Calle de Serrano branch also carries a wide selection of olive oil and other typical Spanish produce, such as sherry vinegar.

At **Casa Mira** you can get *turrón* – Spain's traditional Christmas sweet – all year round. An almond speciality, *turrón* comes in a hard or a soft version. For a less sticky, bite-size treat of soft *turrón* pressed into almond-shaped wafer shells, try *almendras imperiales* (imperial almonds).

For assorted cakes in the centre of Madrid go to **Horno de San Onofre**; for a first-class selection of wines visit **Mariano Madrueño**. Various categories of ham and preserved gourmet food are available at **Petra Mora**. One of the best cheese shops is **La Boulette** inside the Mercado de la Paz, just off Calle de Serrano. **Mallorca**, Madrid's finest delicatessen, carries the very best of foodstuffs to eat in or take away.

El Arco Artesanía is one of Madrid's most tasteful gift shops, with jewellery, leather goods and ceramics, while **Así**, conveniently located in the city centre, sells all kinds of dolls as well as reasonably priced household goods. The Spanish share a national passion for cologne, and there are *perfumerías* (toiletry and cosmetic shops) everywhere.

Souvenirs

The streets around Plaza Mayor are full of souvenir shops, but for something original, visit **Kukuxumusu**, which has cards, T-shirts and mugs with cute cartoon bulls commemorating the San Fermín fiesta.

Barquilleras (traditional biscuit or cookie tins) are sold at **El Corte Inglés** pastry shops and **Mallorca** *(see Gifts)*.

Dolls in typical Madrid costume are available at the **Sanatorio de Muñecas**.

Between the Puerta del Sol and Plaza Mayor, especially on Calle de Postas, are outlets for religious artifacts. **Palomeque** specializes in postcards and reproductions of religious art.

Monsy, on the Plaza Mayor, sells a vast range of fans. For a T-shirt that reminds you of your stay without feeling too touristy, try **El Tintero** in Chueca.

DIRECTORY

Antiques

Alcocer
Calle Santa Catalina 5.
Map 7 B3.
Tel 91 429 79 19.

Casa Postal
Calle de la Libertad 37.
Map 7 B1.
Tel 91 532 70 37.

Centro de Anticuarios
Calle de Lagasca 36.
Map 6 E5.

María Gracia Cavestany
Calle Ayalla 6.
Map 6 E4.
Tel 91 577 76 32.

Palacios
Plaza de General Vara del Rey 3.
Map 4 E4.
Tel 91 527 31 70.

Theotokopoulos
Calle de Alcalá 97.
Map 8 E1.
Tel 91 575 84 66.

La Trastienda de Alcalá
Calle de Alcalá 64.
Map 8 F1.
Tel 91 576 34 86.

Modern Art, Prints and Photographs

Fúcares
Calle Doctor Fourquet 28.
Map 7 A5.
Tel 91 319 74 02.
W fucares.com

Galería Pilar Serra
Calle Santa Engracia 6.
Map 5 A1.
Tel 91 308 15 69.
W estiarte.com

Juan Gris
Calle de Villanueva 22.
Map 6 E5.
Tel 91 575 04 27.
W galeriajuangris.com

Juana de Aizpuru
Calle de Barquillo 44.
Map 5 B5.
Tel 91 310 55 61.

Crafts

Antigua Casa Talavera
Calle Isabel la Católica 2.
Map 4 D1.
Tel 91 547 34 17.

Borca
Calle del Marqués Viudo de Pontejos 2.
Map 4 E2.
Tel 91 532 61 53.

Cántaro
Calle de la Flor Baja 8.
Map 2 D5.
Tel 91 547 95 14.

Casa de Diego
Puerta del Sol 12.
Map 4 F2.
Tel 91 522 66 43.

La Favorita
Plaza Mayor 25.
Map 4 E2.
Tel 91 366 58 77.

Guitarrería F Manzanero
Calle de Santa Ana 12.
Map 4 D4.
Tel 91 366 00 47.

Books and Music

Booksellers
Calle Fernández de la Hoz 40.
Map 5 C1.
Tel 91 442 79 59.

Casa del Libro
Gran Vía 29.
Map 4 F1.
Tel 90 202 64 02.
W casadellibro.com

Desperate Literature
Calle de Campomanes 13.
Map 4 D2.
Tel 91 188 80 89.

El Corte Inglés
Calle de Preciados 1–3.
Map 4 F2.
Tel 91 379 80 00.

El Flamenco Vive
Calle Conde de Lemos 7.
Map 4 D2.
Tel 91 547 39 17.

FNAC
Calle de Preciados 28.
Map 4 E1.
Tel 90 210 06 32.
W fnac.es

Gaudí
Calle de Argensola 13.
Map 5 C4.
Tel 91 308 18 29.

Gifts

El Arco Artesanía
Plaza Mayor 9.
Map 4 E2.
Tel 91 365 26 80.

Así
Calle del Arenal 20.
Map 4 E2.
Tel 91 521 97 55.

La Boulette
Mercado de la Paz (Calle de Ayala 28). **Map** 6 E4.
Tel 91 431 77 25.

Casa Mira
Carrera de San Jerónimo 30. **Map** 7 A2.
Tel 91 429 88 95.

La Chinata
Calle Mayor 44.
Map 4 D2.
Tel 91 152 20 08.

El Corte Inglés
Calle de Serrano 70.
Map 6 E3.
Tel 91 432 54 90.

Horno de San Onofre
Calle de San Onofre 3.
Map 7 A1.
Tel 91 532 90 60.

Mallorca
Calle de Serrano 6.
Map 8 D1.
Tel 91 577 18 59.

Mariano Madrueño
Calle del Postigo de San Martín 3.
Map 4 E1.
Tel 91 521 19 55.

Petra Mora
Calle de Ayala 21.
Map 6 E4.
Tel 98 063 53 90.

Souvenirs

Kukuxumusu
Calle Mayor 47.
Map 4 E2.
Tel 66 397 97 87.

Monsy
Plaza Mayor 20.
Map 4 E2.
Tel 91 548 15 14.

Palomeque
Calle del Arenal 17.
Map 4 E2.
Tel 91 548 17 20.

Sanatorio de Muñecas
Calle de Preciados 19, 1st Floor.
Map 4 E1.
Tel 91 521 04 47.

El Tintero
Calle de Gravina 5.
Map 5 B5.
Tel 91 308 14 18.

ENTERTAINMENT IN MADRID

Few European cities take their entertainment as seriously as Madrid. The city is an international mecca for cultural events, putting a great deal of energy into providing its citizens and visitors with the best in traditional and modern entertainment throughout the year. World-famous orchestras, ballets and operas, including Madrid's own *zarzuela*, are daily staples. Dozens of mainstream and alternative theatres offer everything from Spanish Golden Age classics to experimental drama. The country's best flamenco acts bring their southern Spanish art to Madrid's

international audiences. Some of Europe's liveliest cafés and bars are found here. The afternoon siesta, once a civilized way to escape the Spanish heat, is now either an excellent remedy for the previous night's revelry, or a way to prepare for the one ahead. Most bars and dance clubs are crowded four nights a week, from Thursday through Sunday, and smaller venues offer jazz, rock, salsa and world music on an almost nightly basis. Be prepared for late nights, however, because most activities begin well after midnight and often continue until after breakfast.

Elegant façade of the Teatro Caser Calderón *(see p182)*

Practical Information

The first stop for visitors to Madrid should be at one of several tourist information offices, where English will be spoken and free information can be obtained. A Madrid Card (www.madridcard.com) can be bought there, giving access to museums, tours, shows and sightseeing buses. For those interested in exploring Madrid with a professional guide, contact **A.P.I.T.** or **COSITUR**. These agencies supply guides with an intimate knowledge of the city.

Most Spaniards speak some English and are usually willing to help confused foreigners. Unfortunately, however, most of the city's entertainment guides are published exclusively in Spanish. *Lookout* is one informative English-language magazine relied upon by Madrid's expatriate community. Another is *In Madrid*, a free

monthly publication found in bookshops, record shops and some bars. You can also pick up a copy at embassies and at the tourist information office at the Adolfo Suárez Madrid-Barajas Airport *(see p200)*.

Of the Spanish options, the most complete entertainment guide is the weekly *Guía de Ocio*, which hits newsstands and bookstores on Friday and is usually sold out by Sunday.

Madrid's top three daily newspapers – *El Mundo*, *El País* and *ABC* – have weekly entertainment supplements. These are more geared towards entertainment features, but their listings are broad and sometimes include last-minute events that you may not find in the *Guía de Ocio*. The *El Mundo*, *El País* and *ABC* supplements appear on Friday, covering information on music, theatre, cinema and books.

Booking Tickets

The easiest way to purchase tickets to major events, especially theatre, opera and concerts, is by telephone or over the internet. **Entradas.com** and **Tel-Entrada** are the two main agents. Both accept Visa and MasterCard. Their services are provided free of charge and your tickets will be waiting for you at the venue's ticket booth. Many other reliable internet sites also sell tickets. Check the websites of venues too, since many of them offer online booking services.

The megastore **FNAC** sells most big-venue concert tickets, while the **TEYCI** agency sells tickets for bullfighting at Plaza de Toros de Las Ventas, but charges up to 20 per cent commission.

Another agency that sells tickets for a wide variety of events is **El Corte Inglés**, by telephone, or directly from the stores.

The impressive interior of Madrid's opera house, Teatro Real *(see pp62–3)*

Children enjoying the adventure playground in the Plaza de Oriente

Seasons

While there is never a shortage of top events year-round in Madrid, the main concert and theatre seasons run from September to June. During May's Fiestas de San Isidro *(see p38)* and the Festival de Otoño a Primavera *(see p40)*, from October to May, the authorities book top Spanish and international names in music, theatre and dance. Special events listings can be picked up at tourist offices and at most branches of the Caja Madrid bank.

Facilities for the Disabled

To find out about wheelchair accessibility, you are advised to telephone the venue itself. *El País* provides a 1–4 rating for some venues in its daily listing: "1" means totally accessible while "4" indicates considerable difficulty.

Getting to and from events is easier. Each bus route runs several low-level vehicles with a wheelchair symbol. **Radio-teléfono Taxi** (91 547 82 00) provides special cars – book well in advance and ask for Eurotaxis. Only the new Metro stations have elevators.

Children's Activities

There is no shortage of activities in Madrid for visitors with children. To give them some space, head for the Casa de Campo *(see p116)*. Simply getting to this park can be fun if you take the high-flying **Teleférico** cable car. The park is home to the **Zoo-Aquarium**, the modern **Parque de Atracciones** amusement park, a boating lake and several swimming pools. In the centre of Bourbon Madrid is the popular Parque del Retiro *(see p81)* with magic shows, jugglers, clowns and a lake. The main children's theatre is **Sala San Pol**, but numerous fringe theatres also hold performances for young people.

Flamenco guitarist in the Parque del Retiro

Relaxing at a street café in the Plaza del Dos de Mayo *(see p105)*

DIRECTORY

Tickets

El Corte Inglés
Tel 90 222 44 11.
w elcorteingles.es/entradas

Entradas.com
Tel 90 248 84 88 (theatre)
90 222 16 22 (cinema).
w entradas.com

FNAC
Calle de Preciados 28.
Map 4 E1. Tel 90 210 06 32.

Tel-Entrada
Tel 90 210 12 12.
w telentrada.com

TEYCI
Vilafranca 4. Tel 91 366 88 10.
w ticketstoros.com

Tourist Offices

Adolfo Suárez Madrid-Barajas Airport (Terminals 2 & 4).
Tel 91 454 44 10.
Calle del Duque de Medinaceli 2.
Map 7 B3. Tel 90 210 00 07.
w turismomadrid.es
Plaza Mayor 27. Map 4 E3.
Tel 91 758 55 28.
Plaza de Colón. Map 6 D4.
w esmadrid.com

Tourist Information

Tel 010 (local; calls from Madrid).
w esmadrid.com

Tourist Guides

A.P.I.T.
Calle Jacometrezo 4, 9th floor.
Map 4 E1. Tel 91 542 12 14.
w apit.es

COSITUR
Gran Vía 69, 6th Floor.
Map 7 B2. Tel 91 429 89 65.
w cositur.com

Children's Activities

Parque de Atracciones
Casa de Campo. Tel 90 234 50 01.
w parquedeatracciones.es

Teleférico
Paseo del Pintor Rosales at Calle del Marqués de Urquijo. Tel 90 234 50 02. w teleferico.com

Teatro San Pol
Plaza de San Pol de Mar 1.
Tel 91 541 90 89.
w teatrosanpol.com

Zoo-Aquarium
Casa de Campo. Tel 90 234 50 14.
w zoomadrid.com

Traditional Entertainment

The Spanish take particular pride in their cultural heritage, and attending a performance at one of Madrid's theatres, opera houses, music auditoriums or cabarets is one of the best ways of sharing the experience and traditions of Spain. Madrid plays host to a wide variety of classical art performances, which equal the best on offer in other European cities, but also provides plenty of opportunities for savouring the traditional art forms of the Spanish people. These include the spontaneity of flamenco, the three-act drama of the *corrida* or bullfight *(see p113)*, and *zarzuela*, Madrid's particular version of the Spanish operetta *(see p79)*.

Classical Music

The **Teatro Real** *(see p62)* is probably best known as the home of the city's opera company, but it is also the venue for top national and international classical music concerts.

The two concert halls of the **Auditorio Nacional de Música** also host international classical music performances, along with programmes by the national orchestra, the Orquesta Nacional de España. The Orquesta Nacional is frequently accompanied by Spain's national choir, the Coro Nacional de España.

The **Teatro Monumental** is the main venue for the excellent Orquesta Sinfónica y Coro de RTVE, the orchestra and choir of Spain's state radio and television company.

Theatre

Madrid's most prestigious theatres are the **Teatro de la Comedia** and the **Teatro María Guerrero**. The former is the home of the Compañía Nacional de Teatro Clásico, which stages classic works by Spanish playwrights. The Teatro María Guerrero hosts foreign productions as well as modern drama in Spanish. Many other theatres, including **Teatro Cofidis Alcázar**, **Teatro Español**, **Teatro Pavón**, **Teatro Muñoz Seca** and **Teatro Reina Victoria**, also stage drama productions.

As well as drama, Teatro Muñoz Seca and Teatro Reina Victoria also offer comedy productions, as do **Teatro**

Lara and **Teatro La Latina**, which specializes in *Madrileño* comedy productions. **Teatro Fernán Gómez** (previously called Centro Cultural de la Villa) presents popular theatre. Madrid also has a thriving network of alternative venues, most notably **Cuarta Pared** and **Teatro Alfil**. **Teatro Caser Calderón**, **Teatro Lope de Vega** and **Teatro Nuevo Apolo** often stage musicals.

The cultural centre **La Casa Encendida** hosts alternative theatre and dance.

A vast range of established and radical Spanish and international theatrical talent gathers in the city during the annual Festival de Otoño *(see p40)*.

Opera and Zarzuela

A visit to the Spanish capital would not be complete without spending a night at the *zarzuela*, Madrid's own variety of comic opera, the origins of which can be traced back to the 17th century. The best productions are those staged at the **Teatro de la Zarzuela**.

The best place to see national opera, as well as touring international productions is the **Teatro Real**, next to the Ópera Metro station. Productions of *zarzuela* are also staged here.

Dance

There are several venues in Madrid that stage performances of classical and modern dance, in addition to those that put on

larger flamenco productions. The **Teatros del Canal** is the main place to see good international dance companies as well as the top national acts. The two other major venues are the **Nuevo Teatro Alcalá** and the **Teatro de la Zarzuela**.

Flamenco

A spontaneous musical art form, flamenco has its roots in the gypsy culture of Andalusia. However, many of the best exponents are now based in the capital.

Flamenco is an art form with shows usually taking place through the evening and into the early hours of the morning. Most venues offer dinner and a show, which may be singing only, or both singing and dancing. Although the familiar rhythmic dancing is often a part of flamenco, the purest form of the art consists of a solo singer accompanied by a guitar.

Casa Patas is still the best place to catch the raw power of genuine flamenco guitar and *cante* singing. Dancing often, but not always, accompanies the singing. Both music and dance can be enjoyed at **Café de Chinitas**. Other venues offering high-quality flamenco performances are **Arco de Cuchilleros**, **Corral de la Morería**, **Candela** and **Torres Bermejas**.

Bullfighting

Bullfighting continues to be a popular spectacle in Madrid *(see p113)*, as throughout the country, but it is not for the squeamish. The **Plaza de Toros de Las Ventas** bullring is the most important in the world, and holds *corridas* every Sunday from March through to October. During the May Fiestas de San Isidro *(see p38)* there are fights every day. Each fight is made up of six 15-minute *faenas* of three acts, the last of which ends with the killing of the bull or, on very rare occasions, the matador.

Football

Winners of the European Cup on many occasions, **Real Madrid** are the local aristocrats of football. Their Bernabéu stadium, which has a capacity of 105,000, is one of the great theatres of the game. Real Madrid's cross-town rivals are **Atlético de Madrid**. They play at the Vicente Calderón stadium, a smaller and cheaper venue along the Manzanares river. Madrid's third team is **Rayo Vallecano**, who are constantly shifting up and down between the first and second divisions. Tickets are available at the stadiums or through the clubs themselves, but to see the massively popular Real Madrid, you may need to book ahead. Numerous websites offer ticketing services for Real Madrid and other teams' games – expect a hefty booking fee. Once in Madrid, try the ticket agents *(see p181)*.

DIRECTORY

Classical Music

Auditorio Nacional de Música
Calle del Príncipe de Vergara 146.
Tel 91 337 01 34.

Teatro Monumental
Calle de Atocha 65.
Map 7 A3.
Tel 91 429 81 19.

Teatro Real
Plaza de Oriente.
Map 4 D2.
Tel 91 516 06 60 (info).
90 224 48 48 (tickets).
w **teatro-real.com**

Theatre

La Casa Encendida
Ronda de Valencia 2.
Tel 90 243 03 22.

Cuarta Pared
Calle de Ercilla 17.
Tel 91 517 23 17.

Teatro Alfil
Calle del Pez 10.
Map 2 F5.
Tel 91 521 45 41.

Teatro Caser Calderón
Calle de Atocha 18.
Map 4 F3.
Tel 91 429 43 43.

Teatro Cofidís Alcázar
Calle de Alcalá 20.
Map 7 A2.
Tel 91 532 06 16.

Teatro de la Comedia
Calle del Príncipe 14.
Map 7 A3.
Tel 91 521 49 31.

Teatro Español
Calle del Príncipe 25.
Map 7 A3.
Tel 91 360 14 84.

Teatro Fernán Gómez
Plaza de Colón.
Map 6 D5.
Tel 91 436 25 40.

Teatro Lara
Calle Corredera Baja de San Pablo 15.
Map 2 F5.
Tel 91 523 90 27.

Teatro La Latina
Plaza de la Cebada 2.
Map 4 D4.
Tel 91 365 28 35.

Teatro Lope de Vega
Gran Vía 57.
Map 4 E1.
Tel 91 547 20 11.

Teatro María Guerrero
Calle de Tamayo y Baus 4.
Map 5 C5.
Tel 91 310 29 49.

Teatro Muñoz Seca
Plaza del Carmen 1.
Map 4 F1.
Tel 91 523 21 28.

Teatro Nuevo Apolo
Plaza de Tirso de Molina 1.
Map 4 F3.
Tel 91 369 06 37.

Teatro Pavón
Calle Embajadores 9.
Map 4 E4.
Tel 91 539 64 43.

Teatro Reina Victoria
Carrera de San Jerónimo 24.
Map 7 A2.
Tel 91 369 22 88.

Opera and Zarzuela

Teatro Príncipe – Gran Vía
Calle de las Tres Cruces 8.
Map 4 F1.
Tel 91 531 85 14.

Teatro Real
See Classical Music.

Teatro de la Zarzuela
Calle de Jovellanos 4.
Map 7 B2.
Tel 91 524 54 00.

Dance

Nuevo Teatro Alcalá
Calle Jorge Juan 62.
Map 6 D5.
Tel 91 435 34 03.

Teatro de la Zarzuela
Calle de Jovellanos 4.
Map 7 B2.
Tel 91 524 54 00.

Teatros del Canal
Calle de Cea Bermúdez 1.
Tel 913 08 99 99.
w **teatroscanal.com**

Flamenco

Arco de Cuchilleros
Calle de Cuchilleros 7.
Map 4 E3.
Tel 91 364 02 63.

Café de Chinitas
Calle de Torija 7.
Map 4 D1.
Tel 91 547 15 02.

Candela
Calle del Olivar 7.
Map 7 A4.
Tel 91 467 33 82.

Casa Patas
Calle de Cañizares 10.
Map 7 A3.
Tel 91 369 04 96.

Corral de la Morería
Calle de la Morería 17.
Map 3 C3.
Tel 91 365 11 37.

Torres Bermejas
Calle de Mesonero Romanos 11.
Map 4 F1.
Tel 91 532 33 22.

Bullfighting

Plaza de Toros de Las Ventas
Calle de Alcalá 237.
Tel 91 356 22 00.

Football

Atlético de Madrid
Estadio Vicente Calderón, Paseo de la Virgen del Puerto 67.
Tel 90 226 04 03.
w **clubatletico demadrid.com**

Rayo Vallecano
Estadio Teresa Rivero, Calle Payaso Fofó.
Tel 91 478 22 53.
w **rayovallecano.es**

Real Madrid
Estadio Santiago Bernabéu, Avenida de Concha Espina.
Tel 91 398 43 00.
w **realmadrid.com**

Modern Entertainment

Madrid's nightlife starts to rumble at dusk in the city's numerous tapas bars and cafés. After a quick bite and yet another *caña* (small glass of beer), you may decide to head off to one of the city's palatial movie houses to see a film, or perhaps you would prefer to hit a lively night spot for a little rock, jazz or salsa to warm up your dancing shoes. The younger *Madrileños*, who may well have to go to school the next day, begin to head for the Metro stations at about 1:30am to catch the last train home, clearing the way for the multitudes of over-20s to take over the dance clubs until daybreak.

Cinema

Spanish cinema has undergone a renaissance as a new crop of film-makers tries to follow in the footsteps of internationally acclaimed film director Pedro Almodóvar, famous for his *Women on the Verge of a Nervous Breakdown (see p106)*.

For those with a grasp of the language, Spanish cinema is a rewarding experience, especially if enjoyed at one of the vast movie houses along Gran Vía *(see p52)*, such as the **Capitol** or **Callao City Lights**. At the weekends some cinemas have late-night film programmes which begin only after midnight.

For those with no knowledge of Spanish, Hollywood productions and independent films can be seen in their original-language version at **Golem**, **Ideal**, **Princesa** and **Renoir** among others. These cinemas have sprung up over the years to cater to Madrid's foreign residents and Spaniards who wish to enjoy productions in their purest form with Spanish subtitles. Films shown in their original version are listed in the film section of newspapers and various listings magazines as *VO (versión original)*.

Cafés and Bars

With such a vast array of cafés and bars in Madrid, you'd think supply would outstrip demand. But Madrid's social life revolves around the city's endless watering holes, which are also great places for people-watching and encounters. The **Café del Círculo de Bellas Artes** is a cultural institution overlooking the busy Calle Alcalá, and the view of the Palacio Real *(see pp58–61)* from the **Café de Oriente** is without equal.

Overlooking the lively Plaza de Santa Ana *(see p51)* are the well-established **Cervecería Alemana** and **Cervecería Santa Ana** bars. Two quite different bars can be found in the La Latina district. **El Almendro 13** offers sherry on the crowded first floor and popular Spanish cuisine in the basement. **Café del Nuncio** is an old-style café with a beautiful outdoor terrace on an old stone staircase over Calle Segovia. And then, of course, there are the *tabernas (see pp34–5)*, the quintessential ingredient of any visit to Madrid. **Viva Madrid** draws in a healthy crowd of young *Madrileños* attracted by the nightly activity around the Plaza de Santa Ana. **Taberna Alhambra**, next to Santa Ana, is like an old Andalusian tavern, and is perfect for a quiet drink, while nearby **La Casa del Abuelo** serves superb sweet red wine. **Taberna de Ángel Sierra**, in the gay district of Chueca, is a good place from which to people-watch. **Bodega La Ardosa** is another favourite and has been open since 1892. It offers Spanish wines, beers and vermouth and, since the 1980s, Guinness and other Irish beers. La Ardosa is not a restaurant but it does have a good selection of tapas. **Casa Labra** was the birthplace of the Spanish socialist party in the late 19th century and, as well as its clandestine history, you can savour its tasty tapas. **Vinícola**

Mentridana is another great place for tapas and it also serves excellent Spanish wines. For sheer character born from centuries-old history, visit **Casa Alberto**, **La Bola** and **Taberna Antonio Sanchez**. The elegant surroundings of the **Taberna Casa Domingo** exude a more modern feel, whereas the *belle époque* decor of **El Parnasillo** can be admired while enjoying a delicious coffee or cocktail.

Nightclubs

There is a high price to pay for dancing until dawn at one of Madrid's many nightclubs as entrance fees tend to be expensive. Two that are very much in vogue at the moment are **Kapital** and **Joy Eslava**. Both these clubs are housed in old theatres and have kept the original interior structures. For something slightly different, however, you might like to try **Berlín Cabaret** where dance is mixed with cabaret acts and plays some nights.

The roomy and somewhat upmarket dance club **Teatro Barceló** contrasts with the rest of the music bars in Malasaña, which tend to be reasonably priced but rather claustrophobic.

Famous Spanish actor Javier Bardém many years ago opened the nightclub **El Torero**, where you can dance to Latin and Flamenco-style music upstairs, or head downstairs for some funky house music. Flamenco enthusiasts can try **Cardamomo** where there are also live flamenco nights. Nightclubs stay open until after 3am.

Rock, Jazz and World Music

For those who would rather seek out good live music, there is no shortage of venues in Madrid. For rock music, **Sala el Sol**, which opened in 1979 in time for *La Movida (see p106)*, has hosted some internationally famous bands. Located in a narrow street, close to the Puerta del Sol, this venue offers club nights with featured DJs as well as live concerts. **Moby Dick** and **Siroco** are good places to see some of the vibrant local and national talent. **Café Central** is considered the best place to enjoy jazz in a wonderfully elegant setting. The nearby **Populart** is an excellent venue, too. Formerly a pottery shop, it is a relaxed and busy venue. Both the Café Central and Populart are also near to some of the Latin music clubs in Madrid,

where you can see live bands and dance to the sinuous rhythms of salsa into the early hours of the morning. The much larger **Clamores** hosts a range of musical performers, from jazz and tango to pop and blues.

Honky Tonk holds some of the city's best rock concerts, so keep an eye out for posters advertising forthcoming events.

Gay Clubs

The heart of the gay scene is located in the Chueca district (*see p96*) of central Madrid. **Why Not** is a small bar that caters mostly to locals and plays music from the 1970s and 1980s. There is not much in the way of leather available at the **Leather Club**, but it is still one of the most popular male gay bars in the city.

DIRECTORY

Cinema

Callao City Lights
Plaza del Callao 3.
Map 4 E4.
Tel 91 522 58 01.

Capitol
Gran Vía 41.
Map 4 E1.
Tel 90 233 32 31.

Golem
Calle de Martín de los Heros 14. **Map** 1 A1.
Tel 91 559 38 36.

Ideal
Calle Doctor Cortezo 10.
Map 4 F3.
Tel 90 222 09 22.

Princesa
Calle de la Princesa 3.
Map 1 C5.
Tel 91 541 41 00.

Renoir
Calle Martin de los Heros 12.
Map 1 C5.
Tel 91 541 41 00.

Cafés and Bars

El Almendro 13
Calle Almendro 13.
Map 4 D3.
Tel 91 365 42 52.

Bodega La Ardosa
Calle Colón 13.
Map 2 F5.
Tel 91 521 49 79.

La Bola
Calle Bola 5.
Map 4 D1.
Tel 91 547 69 30.

Café del Círculo de Bellas Artes
Calle del Marqués de Casa Riera 2.
Map 7 B2.
Tel 91 360 54 00.

Café del Nuncio
Calle Segovia 9.
Map 4 D3.
Tel 91 366 08 53.

Café de Oriente
Plaza de Oriente 2.
Map 3 C2.
Tel 91 541 39 74.

La Casa del Abuelo
Calle de la Victoria 12.
Map 7 A2.
Tel 91 521 23 19.

Casa Alberto
Calle de las Huertas 18.
Map 7 A3.
Tel 91 429 93 56.

Casa Labra
Calle de Tetuán 12.
Map 4 F2.
Tel 91 531 00 81.

Cervecería Alemana
Plaza de Santa Ana 6.
Map 7 A3.
Tel 91 429 70 33.

Cervecería Santa Ana
Plaza de Santa Ana 10.
Map 7 A3.
Tel 91 429 43 56.

El Parnasillo
Calle San Andrés 33.
Map 2 F3.
Tel 91 447 00 79.

Taberna Alhambra
Calle Victoria 9.
Map 7 A2.
Tel 91 521 07 08.

Taberna de Ángel Sierra
Plaza de Chueca, Calle Gravina 11.
Map 5 B5.
Tel 91 531 0126.

Taberna Antonio Sanchez
Calle Mesón de Paredes 13.
Map 4 F5.
Tel 91 539 78 26.

Taberna Casa Domingo
Calle de Alcalá 99.
Map 8 F1.
Tel 91 431 18 95.

Vinícola Mentridana
Calle de San Eugenio 10
Map 7 B4.
Tel 91 527 8760

Viva Madrid
Calle de Manuel Fernández y González 7.
Map 7 A3.
Tel 91 420 35 96.

Nightclubs

Berlín Cabaret
Costanilla de San Pedro 11.
Map 4 D3.
Tel 91 366 20 34.

Cardamomo
Calle Echegaray 15.
Map 7 A2.
Tel 91 805 10 38.

El Torero
Calle de la Cruz 26.
Map 4 F3.
Tel 91 523 11 29.

Joy Eslava
Calle del Arenal 11.
Map 4 E2.
Tel 91 366 37 33.

Kapital
Calle de Atocha 125.
Map 7 B4.
Tel 91 420 29 06.

Teatro Barceló
Calle de Barceló 11.
Map 5 A4.
Tel 91 447 01 28.

Rock, Jazz and World Music

Café Central
Plaza del Angel 10.
Map 7 A3.
Tel 91 369 41 43.

Clamores
Calle de Alburquerque 14.
Map 5 A3.
Tel 91 445 54 80.

Honky Tonk
Calle de Covarrubias 24.
Map 5 B3.
Tel 91 445 61 91.

Moby Dick
Avenida del Brasil 5.
Tel 91 555 76 71.

Populart
Calle de las Huertas 22.
Map 7 A3.
Tel 91 429 84 07.

Sala el Sol
Calle Jardines 3.
Map 7 A1.
Tel 91 532 64 90.
W elsolmad.com

Siroco
Calle de San Dimas 3.
Map 2 E4.
Tel 91 593 30 70.

Gay Clubs

Leather Club
Calle de Pelayo 42.
Map 5 B5.
Tel 91 308 14 62.

Why Not
Calle de San Bartolomé 7.
Map 7 A1.
Tel 91 521 88 03.

OUTDOOR ACTIVITIES

A vast wilderness, ranging from the gentle to the dramatic, lies on the doorstep of Madrid. A scant hour's drive from the city centre will bring you to granite peaks, pine forests, glacial lakes and wild pastureland. Against this backdrop there are endless possibilities for hiking, climbing, horse riding, camping, swimming, skiing or simply finding tranquillity. Stretching across central Spain, the Sierra de Guadarrama and the Sierra de Gredos form a 250-km (155-mile) chain of craggy peaks dipping down to lush pastureland, where you can track a mountain stream in spring, ski in winter or picnic in the wilderness in summer. Within Madrid, golf and tennis facilities are on hand, and water parks have begun to appear everywhere in response to the hot summers. Beyond Madrid, the area surrounding Toledo is famous for its hunting and, further afield, Cuenca's river gorges and ravines are an ideal setting for adventure sports. Details on all outdoor activities are available at **Comunidad de Madrid Tourist Information** offices.

Enjoying a game of golf in the attractive countryside of El Escorial

Golf and Tennis

Madrid's finest sports grounds are to be found at the semi-private **Club de Campo**. The entrance fee for nonmembers is high, but the excellent facilities and lovely setting make it well worth the cost for weary tourists who need a day away from the museums. Tennis, squash and golf are all on offer here. The club also provides designated play areas for children. Tennis courts can be reserved over the telephone, but for golf you must turn up at the club in person. When deciding which day to plan your activities, it is worth bearing in mind that admission prices rise at the weekends.

El Olivar de la Hinojosa is a golf course just off the road to Adolfo Suárez Madrid-Barajas Airport (see p200). It accepts reservations over the telephone. At both the Club de Campo and El Olivar you can rent golf equipment.

If you want a game of tennis in the centre of town, you can reserve a court at the **Canal de Isabel II** sports centre. This modern, attractively designed complex, which is conveniently located in north-central Madrid, boasts excellent facilities as well as a pleasant bar and restaurant. The **Puerta de Hierro** sports complex, alongside the Río Manzanares (see p116), also has tennis courts and a swimming pool.

Walking and Cycling

For keen walkers, there are numerous day hikes within easy access of the city – even if you don't have a car. Just an hour away by train, Cercedilla is an excellent starting point for trails into the Valle de la Fuenfría. One such trail is the old Roman road (calzada romana). Dating from around the 1st century AD, the road once ran over the mountain to Segovia. A tram which links Cercedilla with the area's ski resorts climbs to the Puerto de Navacerrada for more substantial trails higher up.

Further east, the regional park which encompasses Manzanares el Real (see p132) leads into a valley of fast-flowing streams and pools, climbing sharply to the source of the Río Manzanares. The valley tends to attract large numbers of picnickers – one good reason for an early start.

Because only limited roadside bicycle trails are available, many cyclists opt for mountain biking instead. **Karacol Sport** near Atocha Station (see p87) rents bicycles which can then be taken by train to Cercedilla.

People head towards a walking trail at Cercedilla

A sunny day for cyclists at the Madrid Río Park

For other destinations, check with RENFE first (see p204).

Specialist outlets provide bikes and transport at weekends to areas such as the Sierra Pobre, east of the Guadarrama.

Remember to take sensible precautions when walking or cycling in the intense Spanish summer heat. It is essential to wear a hat and a high-factor sun cream and to take an adequate supply of water with you. Walkers venturing into high-mountain areas should always check the weather forecast first, as conditions here can change very rapidly.

Horse Riding

The sierras and cañadas (old sheep trails) surrounding Madrid are ideal for horse riding. Spaghetti westerns were once filmed in this wild region of the country. At the **Club de Campo**, on the edge of the city, horses can be hired for rides through Madrid's expansive Casa de Campo (see p116) from the adjoining equestrian centre. You can also hire a steed by the hour or even for the day at **El Potril**.

Centro Equestre Alameda del Pardo is situated in the village of El Pardo about 5 km (3 miles) northwest of Madrid and offers

routes through the extensive forest surrounding the famous Palacio de El Pardo (see p140).

High up on the route from Cercedilla to the Puerto de Navacerrada, set back from the tram line, **Centro Hípico los Ciruelos** offers a wide choice of day horse-riding routes or even longer outings. The stunning peaks of the Sierra de Guadarrama can be admired on the riding tours provided by **Picadero Las Suertes** that explore the area around Rascafría and Lozoya.

For an overnight stay or longer stays, the Sierra de Gredos offers superb horse riding set against imposing peaks. Further down the road from the Parador Nacional de Gredos, **Gredos Rutas a Caballo (GRAC)** organizes day- or week-long outings. **Turismo Ecuestre Almanzor** are also based in this area and offer day tours.

During holiday periods, especially the Easter week, visitors should book their accommodation well in advance. Also make sure the riding centre is open on the day you plan to go, and remember to specify your riding level.

Rugged terrain of the sierras – perfect for horse riding

Skiing at the popular resort of Puerto de Navacerrada

Skiing

In a year of good snowfall, skiing through pine trees under an azure sky can be a glorious experience. The most popular resort near Madrid is the **Puerto de Navacerrada**. It has 15 slopes and a daunting chairlift up to the "Bola del Mundo" at 2,200 m (7,200 ft). Further away, **Valdesquí** offers better snow conditions and 24 slopes, while **La Pinilla** in the Segovia region is probably the least crowded. All the equipment you need, including skis, snowboards and sleds, can be rented at the resorts.

On weekends during the skiing season, the route to the Puerto de Navacerrada tends to be congested with traffic. Avoid driving if you can and take the tram from Cercedilla. A reliable source of information is **ATUDEM** (Asociación Turística de Estaciones de Esquí y Montaña), a group that specializes in alpine skiing and will provide details on any of the resorts.

Mountaineering and Climbing

Some perfect drops for novice climbers can be found at La Pedriza de Manzanares, as well as at La Cabrera at the eastern end of the Guadarrama mountains. Patones, in the Sierra Pobre, offers ideal rock

Climbing at Escalada en Patones

faces. For the experienced mountaineer, the huge granite needles and walls in the Sierra de Gredos present a greater challenge. Information on courses and guides is available at the **Federación Madrileña de Montañismo. A Tu Aire** organizes hiking tours through the countryside of Madrid and nearby provinces. One-day or weekend excursions (some with a hot picnic) to beautiful villages and nature reserves in the Sierra de Madrid, Guadalajara and Segovia are available. **Gente Viajera** organizes weekend courses near Cuenca in which those with a seriously robust constitution can be taught the exciting art of rappelling (abseiling) down river gorges.

Shooting

Like the rest of Spain, the rugged terrain surrounding Madrid is ideal for hunting. But, unless you are fortunate enough to hunt on one of the many private estates, you will not find much game in the remaining free shooting zones. The best option is to go to Toledo or Ciudad Real, both of which are rich in game, from birds to wild boar and deer. To avoid hassles for permits, contact **Cacerías Ibéricas** in advance. They will do the paperwork, organize the outing and provide equipment.

Watersports

Madrid's sizzlingly hot summers make watering holes a dire necessity. There is a splendid swimming pool at the **Club de Campo Villa de Madrid** although, in spite of its great size, it can be uncomfortably full on a hot day. The sports complex at **Puerta de Hierro** has a huge, neck-deep basin just for cooling off, as well as a proper lane pool for swimmers. By far the best pool in Madrid is the **Centro de Natación M-86**, but it is only open to the public from June to the end of August. The **Canal de Isabel II** sports complex, which is also conveniently situated in town, has a much-appreciated outdoor pool, as well as a children's pool. There are also

One of the reservoirs on the outskirts of Madrid – ideal for canoeing

Causing a splash outside Madrid

a number of large reservoirs outside Madrid, which are perfect for sailing, windsurfing and canoeing. Contact **Asociación Sport Natura**, which provides equipment and transport at weekends to its centre at Embalse del Atazar near El Berrueco.

Theme Parks

Nearly 500 animals run wild at **Safari Madrid** outside Aldea del Fresno, making this a great outing for children. There is also a daily show of birds of prey. A nearby added attraction is the park and beach along the Alberche river.

Aquópolis, a 40-minute drive from the city, is Madrid's most complete water park, with slides and innumerable other water features. Bring a picnic, and enjoy a day out for the family.

For an alternative form of nature park visit **Faunia**, a biological park that recreates the world's ecosystems and natural surroundings to suit the different species of animals.

The thrilling **Parque de Atracciones** (see p116) has the latest stomach-churning rides from rollercoasters to vertical drops, as well as all the old favourites. There is also a zone for small children. A **Warner Bros. Park** in Madrid has rollercoaster rides, recreations of film sets and a Hollywood Boulevard.

DIRECTORY

Comunidad de Madrid Tourist Information
Calle del Duque de Medinaceli 2.
Map 7 B3.
Tel 90 210 00 07.
🆆 madrid.org/turismo

Golf and Tennis

Canal de Isabel II
Avenida de Filipinas 54.
Tel 91 533 17 91.

Club de Campo Villa de Madrid
Carretera de Castilla, km 2.
Tel 91 550 20 10 (tennis).
Tel 91 550 20 27 (watersports). **Tel** 91 550 20 10 (riding school).

El Olivar de la Hinojosa
Campo de las Naciones,
Via de Dublin.
Tel 91 721 18 89.

Puerta de Hierro
Carretera de la Coruña,
km 7. **Tel** 91 376 80 91.

Walking and Cycling

Karacol Sport
Calle de Tortosa 8.
Map 7 C5.
Tel 91 539 96 33.

Horse Riding

Centro Ecuestre Alameda del Pardo
Carretera Fuencarral, km
2.3, El Pardo.
Tel 91 372 09 58.

Centro Hípico los Ciruelos
Camino los Ciruelos 26,
Carretera Camorritos,
Cercedilla.
Tel 60 861 32 72.

Club de Campo
See Golf and Tennis.

El Potril
Avenida de las
Caudalosas, Brunete.
Tel 69 611 32 98.

Gredos Rutas a Caballo (GRAC)
Calle Trigueras 4, Hoyos
del Espino (Ávila).
Tel 920 34 90 85.

Picadero Las Suertes
Avenida de Cascajales 53,
Rascafría.
Tel 69 235 79 84.

Turismo Ecuestre Almanzor
Calle Pajizo s/n, Navarredonda de Gredos (Ávila).
Tel 920 34 80 47.

Skiing

ATUDEM
Calle del Padre Damián 43.
Tel 91 359 15 57.
🆆 atudem.org

La Pinilla
Tel 90 287 90 69.

Puerto de Navacerrada
Tel 90 288 23 28.

Valdesquí
Tel 91 570 12 24.

Mountaineering and Climbing

A Tu Aire
Plaza del Ángel, 11
(1st Floor).
Map 7 A3.
Tel 91 523 26 02.

Federación Madrileña de Montañismo
Avenida Salas de los
Infantes 1.
Tel 91 527 38 01.

Gente Viajera
Calle de Santa Alicia 19.
Tel 91 478 01 11.

Shooting

Cacerías Ibéricas
Calle de San Pedro el
Verde (3rd Floor),
Toledo.
Tel 92 521 22 55.

Watersports

Asociación Sport Natura
Avenida Donostiarra 4
posterior.
Tel 91 403 61 61.

Canal de Isabel II
See Golf and Tennis.

Club de Campo
See Golf and Tennis.

Centro de Natación M-86
Calle de José Martínez de
Velasco 3.
Tel 91 409 53 51

Puerta de Hierro
See Golf and Tennis.

Sport Natura
See Walking and Cycling.

Theme Parks

Aquópolis
Avenida de la Dehesa,
Villanueva de la Cañada.
Open mid-Jun–mid-Sep.
Tel 90 234 50 06.

Faunia
Avenida Comunidades
28. **Tel** 90 253 55 45.

Parque de Atracciones
Casa de Campo.
Tel 90 234 50 01.

Safari Madrid
Motorway A5, Exit 32,
Aldea del Fresno.
Tel 91 862 23 14.

Warner Bros. Park
Carretera A4, Exit 22,
San Martín de la Vega.
Open Mar–Oct and
weekends through
the year.
Tel 90 202 41 00.

SURVIVAL GUIDE

PRACTICAL INFORMATION

Spain boasts an excellent tourist infrastructure. As well as helpful advice and information through websites (including www.spain.info and www.esmadrid.com), there are tourist offices in Madrid and in the surrounding towns. All offer help finding accommodation, restaurants and activities in their area. Madrid's main tourist information office is in the Plaza Mayor.

August is Spain's vacation (holiday) period, during which many businesses close. Roads are busy at the beginning and end of the month. Find out in advance whether your visit coincides with one of Madrid's many fiestas; although these are attractions, they often entail widespread closures. Plan leisurely lunches, as most of Spain stops from 2pm to 5pm.

Tourist office, Plaza Mayor

Visas and Passports

Spain is part of the Schengen common European border treaty. Visas are not currently required for citizens of the EU, but check entry requirements before you go. A list is available from Spanish embassies detailing the rules for 50 countries, including Canada, Australia and the US, whose nationals do not need a visa for visits of less than 90 days. For an extension, apply to the *Gobierno Civil* (a local government office) with proof of employment or of sufficient funds to cover a long stay. Visitors from all other countries need a visa.

Tourist Information

Madrid and all major historic towns in the vicinity have *oficinas de turismo* (tourist information offices), which provide maps, transport details and hotel and restaurant lists. On arrival, it is worth visiting the tourist office at **Adolfo Suárez**

Madrid-Barajas Airport's Terminal One, where there is also a hotel reservation desk and a RENFE *(see p204)* desk offering information on rail travel; there is another tourist information office in Terminal Four. Tourist kiosks can be found in Plaza de Cibeles, Plaza del Callao and Plaza de Colón. Tourist information offices are usually open daily from 9:30am to 8:30pm.

Customs Information

Non-EU residents can reclaim IVA (VAT) on most items worth over €90 and bought in shops with "Tax-free for Tourists" signs.

EU citizens travelling between EU countries do not have to declare goods imported into Spain if they are for personal use. Non-EU citizens are restricted on what they can take home: those from the US are allowed duty-free goods worth US$800, including 250 cigarettes or 50 cigars, plus 1 litre (33.8 fl oz) of alcohol. For more information, check with your home customs authorities.

Sign indicating tax-free goods

Admission Fees

Admission fees are charged at most museums and sights. The tourist information office can provide details of various discount tickets, such as the *Madrid Card* or the *Abono paseo del Arte*, which includes admission to the Prado, Thyssen-Bornemisza and Reina Sofía. Most museums offer free admission once a week, but sometimes more often.

Opening Hours

Most museums and monuments close on Sunday afternoons and all day Monday (the Reina Sofía closes on Tuesdays). Major art museums do not close over lunch. Churches have more restricted opening hours; some open only for services.

Language

Spain's official language is *castellano* (Castilian). It is spoken by everyone and is the language you will hear most frequently in Madrid. Places that deal with tourists – hotels, information offices, restaurants – usually employ people who speak English.

Etiquette and Smoking

It is common for the Spanish to greet and say goodbye to strangers at bus stops and in elevators (lifts), shops and other public places. They often talk to people they do not know. It is customary to shake hands when introduced. Women kiss on both cheeks when they meet; friends and family embrace or kiss.

Smoking is illegal inside public spaces, though outdoor smoking areas (terraces) are usually provided. Locals do not always tip, but it is expected of visitors. Tip between 5 and 10 per cent for good service in restaurants and tapas bars; it is not necessary to tip in bars or cafés. Give a euro or two to a helpful taxi driver.

Access to Public Conveniences

Public conveniences are rare in Madrid. Most people walk into a bar, café or store and ask for *los servicios*, although it is preferable to be a customer.

Travellers with Special Needs

Spain's national association for the disabled, **Confederación Coordinadora Estatal de Minusválidos Físicos de España (COCEMFE)**, operates a tour company which offers a guide to disabled facilities and assistance planning a vacation (holiday) to your requirements. Alternatively, the travel agent **Ilunión Viajes** can do the work for you. Maps and other information in Braille are available from the Spanish national organization for the blind, **Organización Nacional de Ciegos (ONCE)**.

Travelling on a Budget

For those travelling on a budget, most museums offer free admission at least once a month, and usually once a week. Check museum websites for details. The *menú del día*, a set lunch menu served by many restaurants from Monday to Friday, is a superb bargain: usually, it offers three courses including drinks for €9–15.

Fruit and vegetables on sale in Mercado Cebada

Holders of the International Student Identity Card (ISIC) are entitled to discounts on travel and admission to museums. Contact the government-run youth information centre, **Centro Regional de Información y Documentación Juvenil (CRIDJ)**. The **Turismo y Viajes Educativos (TIVE)** also specializes in student travel.

Time

Madrid is one hour ahead of Greenwich Mean Time (GMT) and 6 hours ahead of Eastern Standard Time (EST).

Electricity

Spain's electricity supply is 220 volts. Plugs have two round pins.

Responsible Tourism

Environmental issues don't have the same urgency in Spain as in some other places in Europe, although green awareness is growing. Visitors can reduce their impact by shopping at local markets, using the excellent public transport system, eating local food and using the recycling collection points located around the city. Spanish people traditionally choose seasonal produce, and markets are a part of daily life. Visitors can stock up on local produce at La Cebada market in La Latina, or Antón Martin, off Calle de Atocha. Hotels are conscious of Spain's chronic water shortages. Choose showers over baths, and ask house-keepers not to change sheets and towels daily.

DIRECTORY

Embassies

Australia
Torre Espacio, Paseo de la Castellana 259D.
Tel 91 353 66 00.
w spain.embassy
.gov.au

Canada
Torre Espacio, Paseo de la Castellana 259, level 24.
Tel 91 382 84 00.
w canadainternational
.gc.ca

New Zealand
Calle Pinar 7, 3rd Floor.
Map 6 E1.
Tel 91 523 02 26.
w nzembassy.com

United Kingdom
Torre Espacio, Paseo de la Castellana 259.
Tel 91 714 63 00.
w gov.uk

United States
Calle de Serrano 75.
Map 6 E2. **Tel** 91 587 22 00.
w spanish.madrid
.usembassy.gov

Tourist Information

Adolfo Suárez Madrid-Barajas Airport
Terminals 2 & 4.
Tel 91 454 44 10.

Estacíon de Atocha
Tel 90 232 03 20.

Estacíon de Chamartín
Tel 90 243 23 43.

Municipal Tourist Office
Plaza Mayor 27. **Map** 4 E3.
Tel 91 758 55 28.

Travellers with Special Needs

COCEMFE
Calle de Luis Cabrera 63.
Tel 91 744 36 00.
w cocemfe.es

ONCE
Calle del Prado 24.
Map 7 B3. **Tel** 91 589
46 00. w once.es

Ilunión Viajes
Calle Pechuán 1,
Castellana 228. **Tel** 91 323
25 23. w viajes2000
accesibles.es

Travelling on a Budget

CRIDJ
Paseo de Recoletos 7–9.
Map 6 D5. **Tel** 90 151 06
10. w madrid.org/
inforjoven

TIVE
Calle de Fernando el
Catóilico 88. **Map** 1 B1.
Tel 91 543 74 12.
w madrid.org/
inforjoven

Personal Security and Health

In Madrid, as in other cities with large numbers of tourists, you should take steps to guard against theft. Carry credit cards, money and a photocopy of your passport in a money belt, and never leave anything visible in your car when you park it. If you lose your documents, contact your embassy *(see p193)* and the police. If you are unwell, there is always a pharmacy *(farmacia)* open.

Police

There are essentially three types of police in Spain. The *Guardia Civil* (paramilitary Civil Guard) mainly police rural areas, country roads, highways and state buildings. They also take part in some anti-terrorist operations. Their uniform is olive green in colour. The *Policía Nacional* wear a dark blue uniform, and they deal with national security and take the main respsonsibility for terrorism. They also police immigration, work permits and residence documents. There is a service for tourists who have been victims of crime (SATE, Servicio de Atención al Turista Extranjero). This is based at the police station on Calle Leganitos 19, just off the Plaza de España, and is open daily from 9am to 10pm. You can contact them and/or make telephone incident reports *(denuncias)* on 90 210 21 12, which has English-speaking operators. You will still have to go to the station to sign telephone statements, but you will avoid the inevitable queues. The *Policía Municipal* are involved with traffic regulation, the imposition of fines and the policing of local communities. Their uniform is dark blue with fluorescent yellow jackets.

What to be Aware of

Although violent crime is rare in Madrid, it is wise to take sensible precautions. Pickpocketing is rife: be wary of "helpful" strangers, who might point out dirt on your clothing or tell you've dropped your keys.

To guard against theft, wear your bag or camera strapped across your body and always keep your possessions in sight, especially at the airport and on public transport.

At night, avoid walking alone in poorly lit areas and, if possible, take a taxi back to your lodgings.

Avoid carrying large sums of money around with you. It should not be necessary as Spain has numerous ATMs (cashpoints); more, in fact, than any other country in Europe.

In an Emergency

The telephone number for all emergency services is 112, which also has English-speaking operators. Depending on the nature of the problem you have, ask for *policía* (police), *ambulancia* (ambulance) or *bomberos* (fire brigade). In medical emergencies, hospitals accept admissions to the *urgencias* (casualty/emergency department).

Lost and Stolen Property

If you discover a loss or theft, report it to the local *comisaría* (police station). It is essential that you make a *denuncia* (formal statement) via the tourist police, SATE *(see Police)*, and ensure that you get a copy for your insurers as without one you cannot make a claim. It is advisable to do this as soon as you can.

If you lose your passport, your embassy will be able to supply a replacement but cannot provide financial assistance. Items that are found on public transport will be sent to the Lost and Found Office *(Oficina de Objetos Perdidos)*, Paseo Molino 7, Tel 91 527 95 90, Metro Legazpi (only mornings). For any items that are lost at the airport call 91 393 61 19 (Terminal 1) or 91 746 64 39 (Terminal 4).

Logo of Madrid's health service, which has hospitals around the city

Medical Treatment

In an emergency, head for the casualty (emergency) department *(urgencias)* at the nearest hospital *(see Directory)*. There are both private and public hospitals: ensure that you are going to the latter unless you are certain that your travel insurance covers the former. The European Health Insurance Card (EHIC, *see Travel and Health Insurance*) is only accepted at public hospitals.

For non-emergencies, a pharmacist *(farmacéutico)* can advise and, at times, prescribe without a doctor's consultation. The *farmacia* sign is a green cross. The addresses of those open at night or at weekends are displayed in the windows of local pharmacies. Should you need a dentist *(see Directory)*, note services are expensive.

Guardia Civil   Policía Municipal

Patrol car of the Policía Nacional

Fire engine

Ambulance

Travel and Health Insurance

All EU nationals are entitled to short-term emergency health care cover. To claim, you must obtain the European Health Insurance Card (EHIC) from a post office or apply online in sufficient time before you travel. It is completely free of charge and is valid for five years. The card gives you free health cover at all public Spanish hospitals. It comes with a booklet, *Health Advice for Travellers*, which explains what care you are entitled to and how you can claim. Not all treatments are covered by the EHIC and some are costly, so for more peace of mind, arrange for medical cover before travelling. If you want private health care, ask at your hotel, embassy or tourist office for the name of a doctor. Visitors from the US should check with their insurance companies before leaving home to be sure they are covered if medical care is needed. Some private medical facilities require payment for treatment in full at the time of service. Get an itemized bill to submit to your insurance company. Travellers may wish to take out extra travel insurance for emergency hospital care, doctors' fees and repatriation. Have your policy to hand when requesting medical assistance.

Legal Assistance

Some insurance policies cover legal costs, for instance after an accident. If you are in need of assistance and are not covered, telephone your embassy. They should be able to provide you with a list of bilingual lawyers.

If you are arrested, you have the right to telephone your embassy. The *Colegio de Abogados* (Lawyers' Association) can also advise you of where to obtain legal advice or representation.

If you require an interpreter, consult your embassy *(see p193)* or the *Páginas Amarillas* (Yellow Pages) telephone directory under *Traductores* (Translators) or *Intérpretes* (Interpreters). Both *Traductores Oficiales* and *Traductores Jurados* are qualified to translate legal and official documents.

Outdoor Hazards

Spain is prey in summer to forest fires fanned by winds and fuelled by bone-dry vegetation. Avoid fire hazards by extinguishing cigarettes and taking empty bottles away with you as sun shining on the glass can cause flames.

The sign *coto de caza* in woodland areas identifies a hunting reserve where you must follow the country code. *Toro bravo* means "fighting bull" – do not approach. A *camino particular* sign indicates a private driveway.

If climbing or hiking, go properly equipped and tell someone when you expect to return. You can keep in touch by mobile phones, which work in most parts of the country.

DIRECTORY

Emergency Services

Ambulance, Fire & Police
Tel 112.

Ambulance (Ambulancia)
Tel 061.

Fire Brigade (Bomberos)
Tel 112.

Police (Policía)
Tel 091.

Red Cross
Tel 91 532 55 55.

Medical Treatment

Antigua Farmacia de la Reina Madre
Calle Mayor 59.
Map 4 D3.
Tel 91 548 00 14.
🚇 Sol, Opera.

Clínica Dental Cisne
Calle de Magallanes 18.
Map 2 E2.
🚇 Quevedo.
Tel 91 446 32 21.

Clínica Dental Plaza Prosperidad
Plaza Prosperidad 3, 2-B.
Tel 91 415 81 97.
🇼 clinicadentalplaza prosperidad.com.

Farmacia El Globo
Calle de Atocha 46.
Map 7 A3.
Tel 91 369 20 00.
🚇 Anton Martín.

Farmacia Rebollo Abbad
Calle de Goya 89.
Tel 91 435 49 58.
🚇 Goya.

Hospital Clínico San Carlos
Calle del Profesor Martín Lagos.
Tel 91 339 00 01.
🚇 Moncloa.
🇼 madrid.org/ hospitalclinicosancarlos

Hospital General Gregorio Marañón
Calle del Doctor Esquerdo 46.
Tel 91 586 80 00.
🚇 O'Donnell.
🇼 hggm.es

Banking and Local Currency

You may enter Spain with any amount of money, but if you plan to export more than €10,000, you must declare it. Travellers' cheques may be exchanged at banks, *cajas de cambio* (foreign currency exchanges), some hotels and some shops. Banks generally have better exchange rates. The cheapest rate may be offered on your credit or debit card, which you can use in cash dispensers (ATMs) with the appropriate logo. Prepaid holiday cards can be used like debit or credit cards.

A branch of the Caja Madrid Bank

Banks and Bureaux de Change

As a general rule, banks are open from 8am–2pm on weekdays. Many banks have a foreign exchange desk with the sign *Cambio* or *Extranjero*. Remember to always take your passport with you as ID to complete any transaction. You can draw up to €300 on major credit cards at a bank. If you bank with either **Barclays Bank** or **Citibank**, you can cash a cheque in the usual way at one of their branches in Spain.

Foreign currency exchange offices (*bureaux de change*), with the sign *Caja de Cambio* or "Change", may state that they charge no commission, but their exchange rates are invariably worse than those found at banks. One benefit is that they are often open outside normal banking hours. There are several offices on Gran Vía around the Plaza del Calleo as well as in many popular tourist areas. *Cajas de ahorro*

(savings banks) also exchange money. They open from 8:30am–2pm on weekdays.

Credit Cards and Travellers' Cheques

The most widely accepted cards in Spain are **Visa** and **MasterCard**, although **American Express** is also used. **Diners Club** is also widely accepted in Madrid, but less so outside the city. All cash dispensers accept most foreign credit and debit cards, however the commission charged on your withdrawal will depend on your own bank's rates and some credit cards may charge an additional fee.

When you pay with a card, cashiers will pass it through a card reader and you usually need to enter your pin number. In shops you will always be asked for additional photo ID. Since leaving your passport in the hotel safe is preferable, make sure you have an alternative original document on hand (not a photocopy), such as a driving licence. As with the rest of Europe, cards are not always accepted in smaller bars and restaurants. Check in advance or take some cash with you.

An increasingly popular and convenient way to pay is to use a prepaid currency card. These cards function like bank debit/ credit cards and can be used to withdraw money from ATMs or to pay for services in shops, restaurants and so on. These cards are available through

Logo for BBVA, the Banco Bilbao Vizcaya Argentaria

several providers, including **Thomas Cook** and **Travelex**, and can be reloaded through their websites. Look for one that offers fair exchange rates, no ATM fees and no charges for purchases.

The use of travellers' cheques is declining and it is not always easy to find places to cash the cheques. Banks require 24 hours' notice to cash cheques larger than €3,000. If you cash more than €600 in travellers' cheques, you may be asked to show the purchase certificate.

ATMs

If your card is linked to your home bank account, you can use it with your PIN to withdraw money from cash dispensers (ATMs). Nearly all take Visa or MasterCard (Access). Cards with Cirrus or Maestro logos can also be used in many cash machines.

When you enter your PIN, instructions are displayed in English, French, German and Spanish. Many dispensers are inside buildings, so customers must swipe their card through a door-entry system.

DIRECTORY

Banks and Bureaux de Change

Barclays Bank
Carrera de San Jeronimo 17.
Tel 91 360 13 10.

Citibank
Calle de Velázquez 31.
Tel 91 426 07 82.

Credit Cards and Travellers' Cheques

American Express
Tel 900 10 32 96 (toll free).

Diners Club
Tel 90 240 11 12.

MasterCard
Tel 900 97 12 31 (toll free).

Travelex/T Cook MC
Tel 900 94 89 71 (toll free).

Visa
Tel 900 99 11 24 (toll free).

The Euro

The euro (€) is the common currency of the European Union. It went into general circulation on 1 January 2002, initially for 12 participating countries. Spain was one of those countries, with the Spanish *peseta* phased out in

2002. EU members using the euro as sole official currency are known as the Eurozone. Several EU members have opted out of joining this common currency. Euro notes are identical throughout the Eurozone countries, each one including designs of fictional

architectural structures and monuments. The coins, however, have one side identical (the value side), and one side with an image unique to each country. Notes and coins are exchangeable in all participating euro countries.

Banknotes

Euro banknotes have seven denominations. The €5 note (grey in colour) is the smallest, followed by the €10 note (pink), €20 note (blue), €50 note (orange), €100 note (green), €200 note (yellow) and €500 note (purple). All notes show the 12 stars of the European Union.

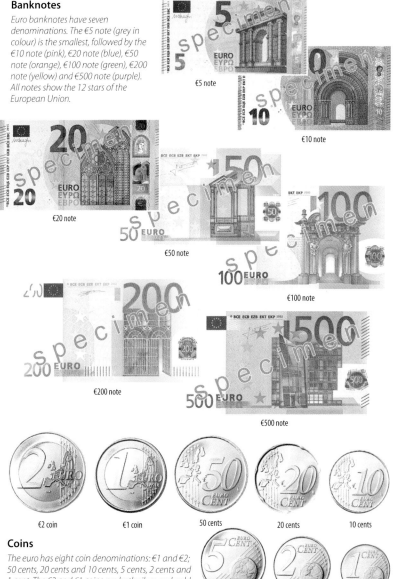

€5 note

€10 note

€20 note

€50 note

€100 note

€200 note

€500 note

€2 coin

€1 coin

50 cents

20 cents

10 cents

Coins

The euro has eight coin denominations: €1 and €2; 50 cents, 20 cents and 10 cents, 5 cents, 2 cents and 1 cent. The €2 and €1 coins are both silver and gold in colour. The 50-, 20- and 10-cent coins are gold. The 5-, 2- and 1-cent coins are copper coloured.

5 cents

2 cents

1 cent

Communications and Media

The telecommunications company Movistar dominates the industry in Spain, but companies like Orange and Vodafone also compete for the mobile phone market. Most public phones, operated by Telefónica, take a phonecard or credit card. International calls are expensive. Registered mail can be sent from Correos (postal service) offices; they also sell stamps, as do *estancos* (tobacconists). Wi-Fi is widely available in restaurants, bars, cafés and hotels, and computer terminals for internet access are usually found in cybercafés and in some hotels.

Logo of Movistar

Spanish payphone with on-screen instructions in English

Telephoning in Spain

When calling from a fixed line, there are four charge bands for international calls: EU countries which cost around 13 cents per minute; non-EU European countries and north-west Africa costing around 26 cents; North and South America costing 37 cents; and the rest of the world, which costs around 58 cents. International calls can be quite expensive, especially when made from a hotel, which may add a surcharge.

Though now harder to find, there are still some public telephone boxes (*cabinas*) in Madrid and there are nearly always payphones in bars. *Cabinas* take phonecards and credit cards, while bar phones take coins. There will be a high minimum connection charge, especially for international calls. Phonecards can be purchased at tobacconists, supermarkets and newsstands and cost either €5 or €10. Calling from a *cabina* can cost as much as 35 per cent more than from a private phone, though using a phonecard gives much cheaper rates. Collect calls within the EU may be dialled directly, but most others must be made through the operator.

To call Madrid from abroad, first dial your country's international access code, then Spain's country code (34), and then Madrid's area code (91).

Mobile Phones

If you are bringing your mobile phone to Spain, check with your home service provider that international roaming is enabled. Travellers from North America should ensure that their phones are GSM-compatible.

International roaming rates can vary greatly among the different providers, however, mobile phones have become a more reasonable option if your operator offers a special fixed rate. The EU has tried to standardize the cost of using a mobile phone within its borders.

If you are planning to make a lot of calls, the best option is to buy a Spanish SIM card (available at the El Corte Inglés department store and phone shops); these will only work in unlocked phones. Other options include buying a pay-as-you-go package (available from all phone shops), or a Bic "disposable" phone, which costs €29 and includes €12 of calls.

Internet

There are scores of cybercafés and *locutorios* across the city offering internet access. They tend to be concentrated around train and bus stations, and just off the Gran Vía. The **Work Center** chain (www.workcenter.es) has several branches around Madrid and provides internet access, as well as copying, printing and courier services. Many hotels and cafés have Wi-Fi, although, it tends to be the smartest hotels that charge for the service. More modest hotels usually have an internet connection in the reception area for guests to use.

Postal Services

The postal service, Correos, can be slow in Spain. Urgent items can be sent by *urgente* (express) or *certificado* (registered) mail. To be sure of fast delivery, it is advisable to use a private courier such as **MRW**, **DHL** or **FedEx**. Mail can be registered at all Correos offices. Stamps

---

Useful Spanish Dialling Codes

- For calls within and between provinces, first dial the area code (beginning with 9).
- To make an international call, dial 00, wait for the tone, then dial the country code, the area code and the number. Country codes are: UK 44; Eire 353; US and Canada 1; New Zealand 64; Australia 61; South Africa 27.
- To call Spain from another country, dial that country's international access code, the code for Spain (34) and the full area code.
- For operator/directory service, dial 11818.
- For international directories, dial 11825.
- To make a collect (reversed-charge) call within the EU, dial 1005 followed by the country code; to the US or Canada, dial 1005 followed by 11 or 15 respectively.

for letters and postcards can be bought from an *estanco*. Postal rates fall into four price bands: the EU; the rest of Europe; the USA; and the rest of the world. Parcels need to be weighed and stamped at a post office and must be securely tied with string or a charge may be made to have them sealed by a clerk.

Main Correos offices are open 8:30am to 8:30pm Monday to Friday and 9am to 1pm on Saturday. Branches in the suburbs and in smaller towns and villages are open 9am to 2pm Monday to Friday and 9am to 1pm on Saturday. In an emergency, go to the post office in El Corte Inglés at Sol, which has longer opening hours and is open on Saturdays and Sundays too.

Madrid has yellow pillar boxes, while other towns and villages normally have small, wall-mounted mailboxes. *Poste restante* letters should be addressed care of the *Lista de Correos*, Madrid. You will be able to collect them from the main post office *(see Directory)*. In order to send and receive money by mail, ask for a *giro postal*.

Spanish mailbox

Addresses

In Spanish addresses, the house number follows the name of the street. For example, to get to Calle de Goya 46, 4-2°, go to Calle de Goya, find the building at No. 46, head to the fourth floor and find the door marked No. 2. The system for labelling floor levels can be confusing: ground-floor apartments are called *bajos* (abbreviated as *bjos*); above *bajos* there may be one further floor – *entresuelos (entl)* – before you arrive at the numbered floors. The letters s/n stand for *sin número*, which means "no number", and is usually used for large or isolated buildings that don't require a street number. All postcodes have five digits, with the first two standing for the province.

Television and Radio

Televisión Española, Spain's state TV company, has two general channels, TVE1 and TVE2, the news channel 24H, Teledeporte for sport and Clan TV for children's programmes.

Several regions have their own television stations. Madrid's is called Telemadrid and is a useful source of news. There are four national independent TV stations in Spain: Antena 3, Tele-5 (Telecinco), Cuatro and La Sexta. There are also several satellite channels.

Most foreign films shown on Spanish television (and in cinemas) are dubbed. Subtitled films appear in listings as V.O. *(versión original)*.

The state radio station, Radio Nacional de España, has four channels. Radio 2 and 3 play music, while Radio 1 and 5 air news programmes.

Newspapers and Magazines

Most of the newspaper kiosks around Puerta del Sol, Gran Vía, Calle de Alcalá and Paseo de la Castellana stock foreign periodicals. English-language newspapers available on the day of publication are the *International Herald Tribune*, the *Financial Times* and *The Guardian Europe*. Other English-language and European titles are available one day after publication.

The most widely read of the Spanish newspapers, in descending number of sales, are *Marca*, *El País*, *El Mundo* and *ABC*. *Marca* is a sports newspaper, while the others cover international news.

The main weekly listings magazines for arts and events are the *Guía del Ocio*, which appears on Fridays; *Metrópoli*, free in *El Mundo* on Fridays; and *On Madrid*, free with *El País*, on Fridays.

Local newspapers in Spanish can be a useful source of detailed information about events in the city and throughout the region.

A kiosk selling a range of magazines

Publications in English are *Guidepost*, with business and general information; *In Madrid*, with restaurant and nightlife listings; and *Lookout*, with articles about Spanish life. The web-only Map Magazine, www.mapmagazine.com, is also a useful resource.

DIRECTORY

Internet

La Fugitiva
Calle de Santa Isabel 7.
Map 7 B4.
Tel 91 468 24 53.
🚇 Antón Martín.

Lolina Vintage Café
Calle del Espíritu Santo 9.
Tel 667 20 11 69.
Map 2 E4.
🚇 Tribunal.
🌐 lolinacafe.com

Work Center
Calle Sevilla 4.
Tel 90 211 50 11.
Map 7 A2.
🚇 Sevilla.
🌐 workcenter.es

Postal Services

DHL
Tel 90 212 24 24.
🌐 dhl.es

FedEx
Tel 91 520 99 10.
🌐 fedex.com

Main Post Office
Correos, Paseo del Prado 1.
Tel 91 523 06 94. **Map** 7 C2.
🌐 correos.es

MRW
Tel 91 782 34 40.
🌐 mrw.es

TRAVEL INFORMATION

Spanish road and rail links are excellent, particularly since the extensions to the high-speed AVE train line. Madrid is also a good starting point for trips to other destinations, whether Spanish, European or international. While Adolfo Suárez Madrid-Barajas Airport, one of Europe's busiest, caters for domestic and European travel, it is also one of the main gateways to South America. By road, there are seven main entry points to Madrid, and trains offer regular services to many European cities, as well as high-speed links with destinations all over Spain.

Arriving by Air

Adolfo Suárez Madrid-Barajas Airport is served by many international airlines and charter companies. **Iberia**, the national carrier, has daily flights linking all Western European capitals except Dublin and Berlin, and once- or twice-weekly flights to those of Eastern Europe. Aer Lingus operates direct flights from Dublin to Madrid. **Air Europa** also flies between London and Madrid. **British Airways** and **easyJet** offer direct scheduled flights from the UK. **Ryanair** flies from Stansted Airport in the UK and from Ireland. **Vueling** links Madrid with Paris, Rome and Venice, among other European destinations. US airlines **United** and **Delta Air Lines** link Madrid to New York, while **American Airlines** links Madrid to Miami. Iberia flies direct to New York, Montréal and Toronto.

Tickets and Fares

Airfares to Madrid vary throughout the year. They are generally at their highest in the summer months due to high demand. Special deals for weekend breaks in the city are often offered during winter and may include a number of nights at a hotel with vouchers to visit the sights. Iberia and British Airways invariably have some cheap return-flight deals on offer throughout the year. Air Europa, Spanair and easyJet also offer competitive deals worth looking out for.

Internal Flights

Iberia operates a frequent shuttle service (*puente aéreo*) between Madrid and Barcelona. It flies every quarter of an hour, and passengers can buy tickets just 15 minutes prior to departure.

Vueling and Air Europa also have scheduled services between Madrid and Barcelona. **Air Nostrum**, Spanair and Air Europa operate flights between both Madrid and Barcelona and the regional capitals and, though they are not as frequent as the *puente aéreo*, their prices tend to be lower. The earlier you book a flight, the greater the discount. For the cheapest tickets, book at least a week in advance.

Sign for the shuttle service linking Madrid and Barcelona

Transport from Airport to Town

It takes about 30 minutes by taxi to reach the city centre from Barajas Airport. Taxis should cost no more than €35. It takes only 12 minutes on the Metro to reach the central station of Nuevos Ministerios from the airport. Local buses provide a regular service from the airport to Avenida de América station. Bus 200 picks passengers up from each terminal (although the return service does not stop at Terminal 3). They run every 12 minutes between 6am and 11:30pm and the journey costs around €1.50. Journey times depend on traffic, but can be lengthy. The 24-hour Airport Express bus service (*express aeropuerto*) leaves roughly every 20 minutes (25–35 minutes after midnight) from Terminals 2 and 4 and heads directly to the centre, with stops at Plaza de Cibeles (not far from the Prado museum) and Atocha train station. The journey takes approximately 40 minutes and costs €5 (pay the driver). From the city, you can only pick up the Airport Express at Atocha, except after midnight, when the service begins and ends at Plaza de Cibeles.

Arriving by Train

The Spanish national rail network, RENFE (*Red Nacional de Ferrocarriles Españoles*), has two long-distance train stations in Madrid – **Atocha** (*see p87*) south of the centre and **Chamartín** in the north. Atocha receives trains from Portugal and the south

National carrier, Iberia, connecting Spain with the rest of Europe

Atocha station, one of Madrid's first glass and wrought-iron structures

and west of Spain, as well as the high-speed AVE lines from Seville, Córdoba, Valencia, Zaragoza, Toledo, Barcelona, Lleida, Málaga, Valladolid, Girona and Alicante. Trains coming from France or northern and eastern Spain go to Chamartín station. Since the two stations are linked by a tunnel under the city, some trains stop at both stations and often the intermediate stations, Nuevos Ministerios and Recoletos.

The AVE service between Madrid and Barcelona via Guadalajara and Zaragoza has recently been extended to the French border. This links the AVE network with the TGV and similar lines throughout the rest of the European Union network.

There are also TALGO expresses, which use both AVE and European tracks, and slower, long-distance (*largo recorrido*) trains. TALGO high-speed services mean that it is now possible to travel

between the main cities extremely quickly.

Overnight sleeper trains arrive from Lisbon, Paris and parts of Spain. Cars can be booked in advance to travel with the train. Bicycles can be carried only in the sleeping compartments of these trains and must be dismantled and packaged up before you board.

Arriving by Car

Many people drive to Spain via the French highways (motorways). From the UK there are also car ferries from Plymouth to Santander and from Portsmouth to Bilbao. From whichever direction you approach Madrid, make sure you are able to identify your highway (motorway) turn-off by its street name. Madrid has two major ring roads, the outer M40 and the inner M30. If you need to cross the city, it is

advisable to take one of the two and get as close as possible to your destination before turning off. All highways (motorways) lead to the M30 but most do not continue into the city. For information on Spanish driving law, *see p203*.

Arriving by Bus

Travelling by bus (coach) is usually a relatively cheap form of travel and, in Spain, it can quite often be a quicker way to get around than trains, especially from destinations such as the *costas* (coast). Buses offer travellers a modern airline-style service on fast highways. **Eurolines** operates regular bus services throughout Europe.

There are three main long-distance bus stations in Madrid. The **Estación Sur de Autobuses**, situated just southeast of the city centre, serves the whole of Spain. The second is Estación Auto-Res, which operates services to Valencia, eastern Spain, Lisbon and northwest Spain. The third, **Estación de Avenida de América**, located east of the city centre, serves towns in northern Spain. The transport interchange at Calle de Méndez Álvaro also offers convenient access to buses and trains, linking three local railways, the Estación Sur de Autobuses and line 6 of the Metro.

DIRECTORY

Arriving by Air

Adolfo Suárez Madrid-Barajas Airport
Tel 91 321 10 00.
w aena.es

Air Europa
Tel 90 240 15 01.
w air-europa.com

Air Nostrum
Tel 90 111 15 00.
w airnostrum.es

American Airlines
Tel 90 211 55 70 (Spain).
w aa.com

British Airways
Tel 90 211 13 33 (Spain).
w britishairways.com

Delta Air Lines
Tel 90 281 08 72 (Spain).
w delta.com

easyJet
Tel 90 259 99 00 (Spain).
w easyjet.com

Iberia
Tel 90 111 15 00 (Spain).
w iberia.com

Ryanair
Tel 00 44 871 246 00 11
(UK). w ryanair.com

United
Tel 90 081 39 96 (Spain).
w continental.com

Vueling
Tel 90 210 42 69
(Spain).
w vueling.com

Arriving by Train

Atocha
Plaza del Emperador
Carlos V.
Map 7 C5.
Tel 90 232 03 20.
w renfe.com

Chamartín
Calle de Agustín
de Foxá.
Tel 90 232 03 20.

Arriving by Bus

Estación Sur de Autobuses
Calle de Méndez
Alvaro.
Tel 91 468 42 00.

Estación de Avenida de América
Avenida de América 9.
Tel 90 242 22 42.

Eurolines
Tel 91 506 33 60
(Madrid).
w eurolines.es

Getting Around Madrid

Most of the major sights are clustered together in the centre of Madrid, within walking distance of each other. There are also other interesting attractions further afield, which can be reached easily by train or bus. Plan your day in advance, bearing in mind that some museums and shops close between 2pm and 5pm, and try to cover one area at a time. The Metro is by far the most efficient way to travel around Madrid – the trains are quick and clean. However, if you have more time and prefer to see where you are going, the city bus service is excellent, and there is no shortage of taxis in Madrid if you don't mind spending a bit extra.

One of Madrid's local buses

Green Travel

Madrid, like many capitals, suffers from traffic congestion and a shortage of on-street parking. You can help to reduce congestion by strolling around the city centre on foot, and by using the excellent public transport network. The Metro is efficient, and the buses, though slower, are good for short hops. There are also some electric minibuses running on a couple of lines. It is not recommended to use bicycles to get around, owing to the lack of bike lanes, but the city's parks are perfect for recreational cycling.

Buses

Buses are an excellent way to see the city. Bus stop signs display the bus numbers stopping there and basic route maps. Either pay the driver with change or a small note or put your Metrobús ticket in the machine. Request a stop by pressing a button next to the exit doors.

People in wheelchairs can board buses displaying the words *piso bajo* (low floor).

Some useful bus routes include: 2, which crosses central Madrid east to west; 5, which starts at Calle Alcalá going northwest to Chamartín railway station via Plaza de Cibeles; 27, which travels from north to south the length of the Paseo de la Castellana from Plaza de Castilla to Glorieta de Embajadores via Paseo del Prado and Calle de Atocha; and C, which makes a circuit around Madrid via Ronda de Atocha. An express bus service runs to the airport from Atocha.

Buses run from 6am to 11:30pm. Twenty night buses, or *búhos* (owls), run every 15 minutes at weekends and every 30 minutes until 4am on weekdays. All leave from the Plaza de Cibeles.

Bus Tours

A sightseeing service operated by **EMT** (*Empresa Municipal de Transportes*), **Bus Turístico**, allows you to hop on or off at major sights multiple times in one day. Buses run from 10am

to 9pm. Tickets can be purchased on board or at the Tourist Information Office on Plaza Mayor.

Juliá Travel also offers a variety of bus trips around the city, which can include visits to a *corrida* or bullfight *(see p113)* or an evening flamenco performance *(see p182)*.

Metro

The Metro is the quickest, cheapest and easiest way to travel around Madrid, avoiding the madness of the city's traffic at street level. Many of the main Metro stations have shops and bars, and Retiro station even boasts an art gallery.

The Metro is open from 6am to 2am and consists of over 200 stations, linked by 12 colour-coded lines plus the Ópera-Príncipe Pío link. For a map of the Metro, see the inside back cover of this book.

The Metro also provides easy and convenient links with the IFEMA Parque Ferial exhibition centre and Barajas Airport. Tickets to or from the airport cost €4.50.

Tickets

A single ticket on the bus (purchase directly from the driver) costs €1.50. The most useful and convenient ticket for visitors is the Metrobús – a 10-trip ticket which can be shared and used on both buses and the Metro. It costs €12.20.

Metrobús tickets are available at *estancos* (tobacconists), news kiosks, the EMT booths in Plaza de Colón, Plaza de Cibeles, Plaza del Callao, Plaza de Manuel Becerra and Puerta del Sol and all Metro stations.

Sign for a Metro station

Driving

In Spain you must carry a valid driver's licence with you when you are driving, as well as your insurance documents. If you are not an EU citizen, it is essential to have an international driver's licence. In the US, these are available through the AAA.

Driving around Madrid is quite an experience for the uninitiated as *Madrileños* tend to drive aggressively. Signs are often misleading or missing altogether, service stations are few and parking is usually difficult. Read the map before setting off, and watch out for one-way systems, tunnels and freeway overpasses (flyovers).

In rush hour, traffic hardly moves and the M30 inner ring road often comes to a standstill. If you get lost while you are driving, hail a taxi, shout the address and follow the driver to your destination.

In urban areas the speed limit is 50 km/h (31 mph), while it is 90 km/h (50 mph) on main roads and 120 km/h (75 mph) on motorways.

Parking

Parking in Madrid is difficult, so you may want to select a hotel with parking. There are underground car parks, which charge by the hour. Parking illegally can result in being towed away, with a fine of up to €200 plus towing fee (min € 147). To locate your car if it has been towed call 91 787 72 92.

Madrid's taxis are recognizable by their red door stripes

Car Rental

To rent a car in Spain you should have an international driver's licence (if you are an EU citizen your ordinary licence is usually sufficient) and be over 21 years of age.

On the ground floor of Barajas Airport's International Terminal 1 are various car rental firms, including **Avis**, **Europcar**, **Hertz** and **National Atesa**. Cars can also be rented at Atocha and Chamartín railway stations. You are strongly advised to take out full insurance, and air conditioning is recommended.

Walking

The centre of Madrid is suprisingly small, and exploring the old streets on foot is a delight. Most of the main sights are clustered closely together, and a stroll between them will reveal myriad tiny details – colourful tiling, a flower-filled balcony, a hidden café.

Taxis

Madrid's taxis are identifiable by the red diagonal stripe on the door. If they are available, the green light on the roof will be illuminated and a card in the window will say *libre*. The initial charge is between €2.40 and €2.90, but there are various additional charges.

You can order a cab by telephone through **Radio Taxi** or **Radioteléfono Taxi**. For a car specially adapted for the disabled, call **Eurotaxi**.

Cycling

Cycle lanes have been added to Madrid's main streets, and **BiciMad**, a public bicycle hiring service, with over 120 stations in the city. However, it is safer to stick to parks like the Retiro or the Casa de Campo. The enormous Parque Juan Carlos I has several bike trails and a bike rental service. Centrally located companies which offer bike tours and rentals include **Trixi** and **Bike Spain**.

DIRECTORY

Travelling Outside Madrid

The main sites around Madrid can be visited in a day, but if you plan to visit several, you might consider staying outside Madrid. The most convenient way to travel is by car, but trains are also very easy to use, with services to all the main historic towns and cities. Even Córdoba, Seville, Barcelona and Valencia are accessible using the AVE and Alaris high-speed trains, which afford superb views of the countryside. Tour companies offer coach trips to Toledo, El Escorial and Segovia. The cost of a trip usually includes the main sites and a meal. If you use a scheduled bus service, choose the most direct route, as some buses stop at every village.

A high-speed AVE train arriving at Atocha station

Train Services

Madrid is served by five types of train: *cercanías* (commuter), *regional* (local), *largo recorrido* (long-distance), TALGO (long-distance express and AVE (high-speed link to Ciudad Real, Puertollano, Córdoba, Seville, Guadalajara, Zaragoza, Calatayud, Lleida, Málaga, Barcelona, Toledo, Segovia, Valencia and Valladolid).

There are frequent services to Alcalá de Henares and Guadalajara on the *cercanías* C-2 from Chamartín, Nuevos Ministerios, Recoletos and Atocha *(see pp200–1)*. *Cercanías* leave from Atocha to Aranjuez every half-hour.

During weekends from mid-April to mid-July and mid-September to mid-October, a "Strawberry Train" (*Tren de las Fresas*), pulled by a steam engine, serves Aranjuez from Atocha. Strawberries are

included; booking is required through **RENFE**.

To Puerto Navacerrada and the ski resorts, take *cercanías* C-8b from Atocha to Cercedilla and then change to *cercanías* C-9. Use *cercanías* C-8a or C-3 for San Lorenzo de El Escorial, and *cercanías* C-8b or the *regional* from Atocha station or the AVE from Chamartín for Segovia. Sigüenza is served by *regional* trains from Chamartín, with three or four trains a day. Toledo is served by *regional* and express trains as well as the AVE from Atocha.

Tickets and Fares

Information and tickets can be obtained by phoning RENFE, from RENFE offices and stations or from travel agents. Rail fares depend on the speed and quality of the train – therefore, TALGO and AVE trains are more expensive.

Bicycles can be taken only on *regional* trains on weekends and

public holidays and at specified non-peak times in the week. *Largo recorrido* and TALGO trains will take bicycles if they are dismantled and kept in the sleeping compartments.

Fares rise on weekends and public holidays. Children aged four to 11 get a 40 per cent discount, while students aged 12 to 25 get a 20 per cent discount. Return tickets are valid for 15 days and carry the same discounts. For long journeys, RENFE may offer special rates on certain days. **Iberrail** also offers economical rail-plus-hotel deals. For a one-way journey, ask for *ida* and for a return, request *ida y vuelta*.

Driving

Check with your insurance provider about extending your comprehensive cover to Spain. In the UK, the RAC, AA and Europ Assistance offer rescue and recovery policies with European coverage.

By law you must always carry with you your vehicle's registration document, a valid insurance certificate and your driving licence. Always be ready to show a passport or a national ID card, and if using your own car you must display a country of registration sticker on the rear of the vehicle.

The headlights of right-hand-drive vehicles must be adjusted. This can be done with stickers sold at ferry ports or on ferries. You also risk on-the-spot fines if you do not carry a red warning triangle, spare light bulbs and a first-aid kit.

Driving along a mountain road through Spain's spectacular countryside

In winter you should carry chains if you intend to drive in mountain areas. In summer, take drinking water if you are travelling in a remote area.

Spain's fastest roads are its *autopistas*, which are highways (motorways) and almost all *autopistas* have tolls (*peajes*) at some point. The *carretera nacional* is the network of main roads prefixed by "N".

Madrid is served by six main *autovías*, numbered A1 to A6, which fan out in different directions, and the A42, which goes to Toledo. In addition, there are two ring roads with links between the highways. The inner ring road is the M30 and the outer one, with direct access to and from the airport, is the M40, which links four toll highways – the R2, R3, R4 and R5.

For road and traffic information in Spanish, call the toll-free number for **Información de Tráfico de Carreteras**. For car breakdown services, call **RACE**.

In Spain *gasolina* (gas/petrol) and *gasóleo* (diesel) are sold by the litre. *Gasolina sin plomo* (unleaded gas/petrol) is available everywhere.

Speed Limits and Fines

Speed limits in Spain for cars without trailers are: 120 km/h (75 mph) on *autopistas* (toll highways/motorways); 100 km/h (62 mph) on *autovías* (non-toll highways/motorways); 90 km/h (55 mph) on main roads

Juliá Travel tour buses lined up at the bus station

and *carreteras comarcales* (secondary roads); 50 km/h (30 mph) in built-up areas. There are instant fines for driving over the limit. The BAC (Blood Alcohol Concentration) limit is 0.5 g/l, and 0.3 g/l for new drivers. Tests and fines for drinking and driving are common, and some prison sentences have been given for dangerous driving.

Tour Buses and Local Buses

By far the easiest and most relaxing way to visit sights outside Madrid is by tour bus. The main tour bus company, Juliá Travel (*see p203*), will take direct bookings. **Pullmantur** and **Madrid Tourist Bus** also offer sightseeing tours.

Major towns and many villages are served by local buses. Buses from Madrid to

the following destinations depart from Estación Sur de Autobuses, south of the city centre (Metro station Méndez Álvaro).

Aranjuez and Sigüenza are served by **Autocares Samar**, San Martín de Valdeiglesias by **Autocares Cevesa**, Segovia by **La Sepulvedana** and Toledo by **ALSA**.

Alcalá de Henares is served by Continental-Auto (Avenida de América), Chinchón by **La Veloz** (Plaza de Conde Casal), Manzanares el Real by **Hijos de J Colmenarejo** (Plaza de Castilla), Puerto de Navacerrada by **Larrea SA** (Metro Moncloa), San Lorenzo de El Escorial by **Autocares Herranz** (Metro Moncloa).

Buses can often be quicker than trains. **Alsa** operates a competitively priced service to Madrid from the *costas*, for example.

DIRECTORY

Tickets and Fares

Iberrail
Tel 90 210 80 23.
🔲 iberrail.es

RENFE
Tel 90 232 03 20.
🔲 renfe.es

Driving

Información de Tráfico de Carreteras
Tel 011.
🔲 dgt.es

RACE
Calle Eloy Gonzalo 32.
Tel 91 594 73 00.
🔲 race.es

Tour Buses and Local Buses

Alsa
Estación Sur de Autobuses.
Tel 90 242 22 42.
🔲 alsa.es

Autocares Cevesa
Tel 90 239 31 32.
🔲 cevesa.es

Autocares Herranz
Tel 91 896 90 28.
🔲 autocaresherranz.com

Autocares Samar
Tel 91 723 05 06.
🔲 samar.es

ALSA
Avenida de América station. Tel 90 242 22 42.
🔲 alsa.es

Hijos de J Colmenarejo
Tel 91 846 91 44.
🔲 hjcolmenarejo.com

Larrea SA
Tel 91 851 55 92
🔲 autobuseslarrea.com

Madrid Tourist Bus
Tel 90 202 47 58.
🔲 emtmadrid.es/bus_turistico

Pullmantur
Tel 90 209 55 12.

La Sepulvedana
Tel 90 11 96 99.
🔲 lasepulvedana.es

La Veloz
Tel 90 255 15 80.
🔲 samar.es.

MADRID STREET FINDER

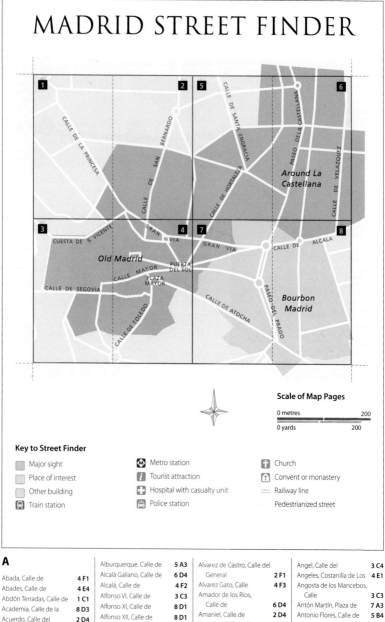

Around La Castellana

Old Madrid

Bourbon Madrid

Scale of Map Pages

0 metres 200
0 yards 200

Key to Street Finder

- Major sight
- Place of interest
- Other building
- Train station
- Metro station
- Tourist attraction
- Hospital with casualty unit
- Police station
- Church
- Convent or monastery
- Railway line
- Pedestrianized street

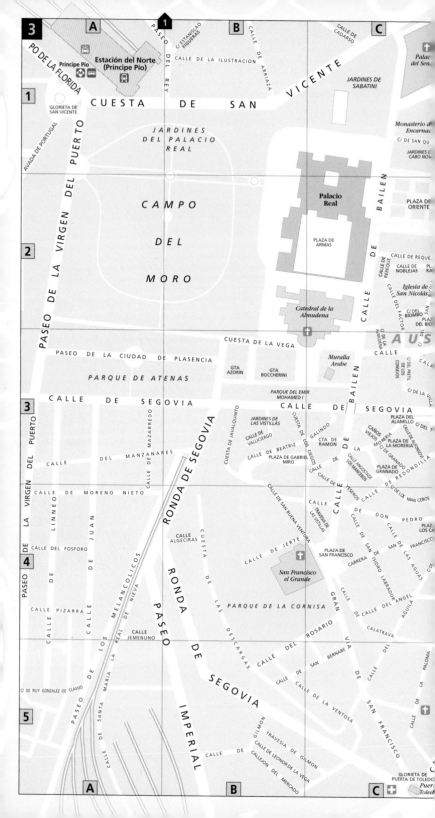

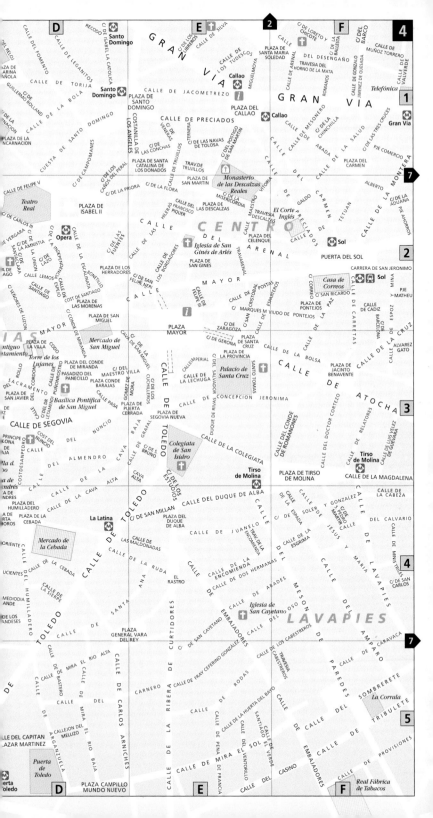

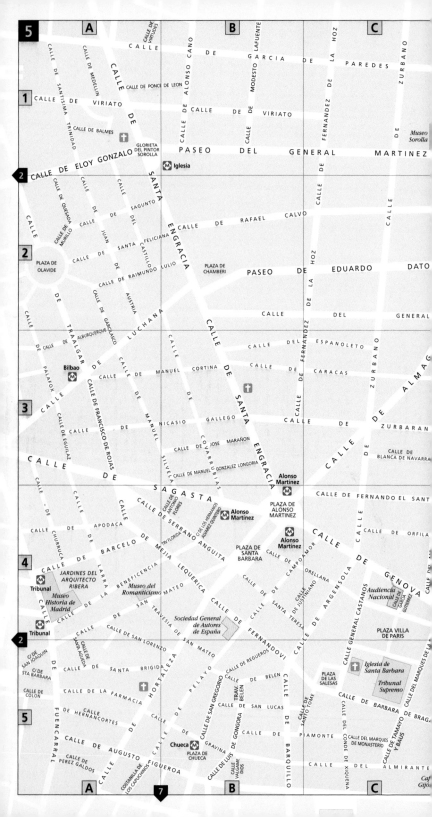

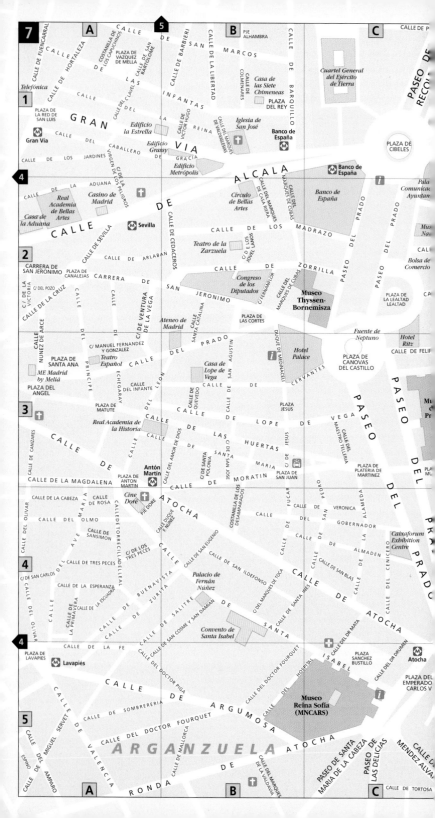

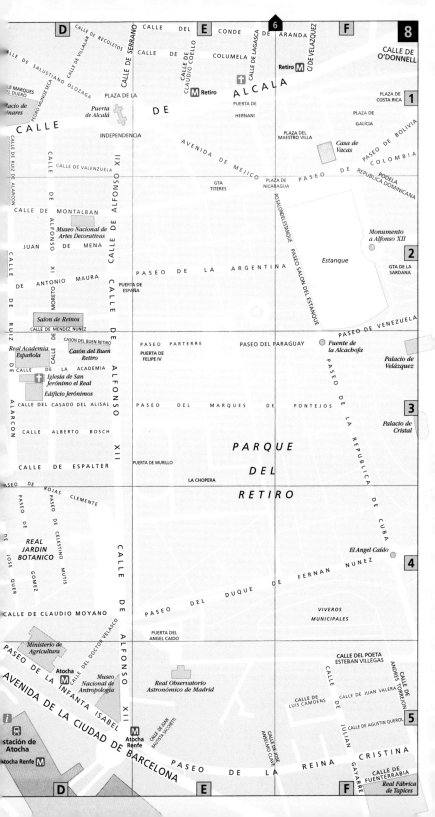

General Index

Acknowledgments

Dorling Kindersley would like to thank the following people whose contributions and assistance have made the preparation of this book possible.

Contributor
Adam Hopkins is an indefatigable travel writer and author of *Spanish Journeys: A Portrait of Spain*.

Mark Little, an American who grew up in Spain, is a freelance writer based in southern Spain. For many years he was the editor of *Lookout* magazine.

Edward Owen has been, for many years, a foreign correspondent based in Madrid, contributing to *The Times* and *The Express* in London and *Time Magazine* among other publications.

James Russo, a freelance journalist, is also a staff writer for Spain's state news agency, EFE. He has lived in Spain since the 1980s.

Kathy White is a freelance journalist who has contributed to *The Christian Science Monitor* and *Newsweek*. She also worked for the French Service of the BBC and was foreign desk assistant at Channel 4 News.

Revisions Team
Special thanks to Helen Peters for preparing the index, Juan Fernández for providing feedback on the content of the guide, Joy Fitzsimmons for visualizing the artworks, Elly King for the final design check, ERA Maptech for creating the maps, Graphical Innovations for outputting the text film, Barbara Minton for support from DK Publishing, Inc., Roberto Rama, Victoria Cano (Word on Spain) and Cristina Barrallo for fact checking, Mary Sutherland for providing feedback on the Survival Guide.
Namrata Adhwaryu, Tora Agarwala, Marta Bescos, Sonal Bhatt, Samantha Cook, Neha Dhingra, Vidushi Duggal, Caroline Elliker, Anna Freiberger, Rhiannon Furbear, Mary-Ann Gallagher, Camilla Gersh, Lydia Halliday, Christine Heilman, Michael Hornsby, Stuart James, Claire Jones, Juliet Kenny, Sumita Khatwani, Priya Kukadia, Shikha Kulkarni, Priyanka Kumar, Rahul Kumar, Alison McGill, Casper Morris, Marianne Petrou, Tom Prentice, Mani Ramaswamy, Ellen Root, Zoë Ross, Azeem Siddiqui, Meredith Smith, Susana Smith, Lynda Warrington and Hugo Wilkinson for design and editorial assistance and Stewart Wild for proofreading. Project assistance given by Fay Franklin, Annette Jacobs, Vivien Crump, Gillian Allen, Douglas Amrine, Joanne Blackmore, Monica Allende, Candela Garcia Sanchez-Herrera, Ankita Sharma, Pamela Shiels, Rituraj Singh, Joanna Stenlake, Avantika Sukhia.

Additional Photography
Ian Aitkin, Isabel Real Martinez, Ian O'Leary, Rough Guides/Time Draper, Conrad van Dyk.

Photography Permissions
© Patrimonio Nacional, Madrid: Monasterio de las Descalzas Reales; El Escorial; La Granja de San Ildefonso; Palacio Real; Palacio Real Aranjuez; Palacio de Fernán Núñez propriedad de Renfe Sede de la Fundación de los Ferrocarriles Españoles.

Dorling Kindersley would like to thank all the cathedrals, churches, museums, restaurants, hotels, shops, galleries and other sights too numerous to thank individually.

Picture credits
Key: a-above; b-below/bottom; c-centre; f-far; l-left; r-right; t-top.

Works of art have been reproduced with the permission of the following copyright holders:

Gernika Picasso © Succession Picasso/DACS 2011 89br; *Lugar de Encument* Chillida © DACS 2011 101c.

The publisher would like to thank the following individuals, companies and picture libraries for their kind permission to reproduce their photographs:

4Corners: SIME/Paolo Giocoso 180cl; **6 TOROS 6 magazine**: 113cr.

El Abrazo de Vergara: 158cl; **Ace Photo**: Bill Wassman 182br; **ADIF**: 203tl; **Agencia Efe, Madrid**: 39br, 40br; **AISA, Barcelona**: 23bc, 27bl, 27cb, *Retrato de Camilo Jose Cela* Alvaro Delgado © DACS 2011 32tr, 33t, 60cla, 80b, 82tr, 84tr, 85bl, *La Tertulia del Café de Pombo* Jose Gutiérrez Solana © DACS 2011 89bl, 106b. **Alamy Images**: Age Fotostock 73cb; Jon Arnold Images Ltd 44; Dan Atkin 158cl; Peter Eastland 65c; Robert Fried 159tl; Peter Horree 124, 193tr; imagebroker 92, 112tl; John Kellerman 58cl; David Kilpatrick; La Belle Aurore/ Steve Davey 122tr; David Pearson 13bl; PjrTravel 10cla; Prisma Archivo 8–9; Sagaphoto.com 203tr; Alex Segre 162tr, 187tl; **Max Alexander**: 120cla; **Museo Arqueológico Nacional, Madrid**: 98–9 all. **The Art Archive**: Museo del Prado, Madrid/ Dagli Orti (A) - St Cecilia Patron Saint of Music, Nicholas Poussin (1594–1665) 85cr; **Ayuntamiento de Madrid**: 197cla, 195cl, 199tr.

Bridgeman Picture Library: *The Adoration of the Shepherds* El Greco 82cla, *The Annunciation* Fra Angelico 83crb, *The Clothed Maja* Goya 83cra, *The Naked Maja* Goya 83cr, *The Three Graces* Rubens 82cb, *The Martyrdom of St Philip* Jose Ribera 83c, *St Dominic of Silos Enthroned as Abbot* Bermejo 84cl.

Caja Madrid: 196cla; **La Casa del Abuelo**: 35bl; **Casa Perico**: 34tr; **El Club Allard**: The Second Fraction/Nez Molina & Alberto Ruiz L. 166tc; **Con 2 Fogones**: 168tl; **Corbis**: Demotix/Lawrence JC Baron 186bc; Rudy Sulgan 47bc; Patrick Ward 81tc; **Joe Cornish**: 134cl; **Cover**: Quim Llenas 33br; Matias Nieto 41c.

Delic: 164bc; **El Deseo:** 104tr; **Dirección General de la Policía y de la Gurdia Civil:** 197tl; **Dreamstime.com:** Denis Dolkens 190–91; Freesurf69 138–9; Matej Kastelic 2–3; Anibal Trejo 42–3; Vinicius Tupinamba 148–9; Tupungato 72br; Robert Zehetmayer 48br, 108; Oleg Znamenskiy 28.

EMT: 202cla; **El Estragon Vegetariano:** 156br, 165tl; **European Commission:** 197; **Mary Evans Picture Library:** 20br.

Fundación Lázaro Galdiano: 31tl, 102–3.

Hostal Gala, Madrid: 153tr; **Hulton Getty:** 137b; **Getty Images:** Scott E Barbour/The Image Bank 54–5; **Godo Fotos:** 137bl; **Grupo Juliá:** 205tr.

Roland Halbe: 118bl, 122cla; **Robert Harding Picture Library:** James Strachan 57tr; **Hospital Universitario Ramón y Cajal:** 194cr.

Images Colour Library: A.G.E. Fotostock 29cra, 113ca; Horizon 113c; **Index, Barcelona:** 19b, 20cr, 22bc, 24bl, 26ca, 26clb, 27tl, 27tc, 27br, 32cla, 32clb, 33cl;.

Anthony King: 80tl.

Lonely Planet Images: Guy Moberly 123bl; Richard Nebesky 118cra; Damien Simonis 121br; **Restaurante Lúa:** 157br..

Arxiu Mas, Barcelona: 26br; **Mercado de San Miguel:** 49tr; **Meson Cuevas Del Vino:** 171tl; **Metró Bistro:** 170bc; **Museo Del Prado, Madrid:** 82bl; **Museo Thyssen Bornemisza, Madrid:** 29cr, 74tr; *Harlequin with Mirror*, Picasso © Succession Picasso/DACS 2011 74cl; 74bl; *Portrait of Baron Thyssen-Bornemisza* © Lucian Freud 74bc; 75tl, 75ca, 75crb; *Autumn Landscape in Oldenburg*, Karl Schmidt-Rottluff © DACS 2011 75bl; 76 (3), 77 (2).

Naturpress, Madrid: J.L. González Grande 187b; A. Ibanñez & Fco González 188c; Diana Kvaternik 29bc; W Kvaternik-R. Olivas 40cla, 186cl, 188tl, 189tl; Luis Olivas 38br; Petro Retamar 188br; Jaime Villanueva 1c, 25crb, 29c, 38cla, 115tr; Museo Naval, Madrid: 69crb.

Oronoz, Madrid: 20tl, 21tc, 21clb, 21br, 23c, 25tl, 26tl, 26tr, 26crb, 30tr, 30c, 30bl, 51br, 60tr, 60bl, 61tr, 61clb, 61br,

71crb, 79ca, 79b, 84bl, 85tc, 120br; Moro Cabeza Crispolo 123tr; *Portrait II* Miró © ADAGP, PARIS and DACS, London 2011 88clb, *Woman in Blue* Picasso © Succession Picasso/ DACS 2011 88ca, 104br, 105b, 113cla.

Palacio Cibeles: 167bl; **Hotel Plaza Mayor:** 154br; **Prisma, Barcelona:** 11tl/br, 18, 22tc, 22crb, 24tl, 24cr, 27tr, 27crb; **Hotel Puerta de la Santa:** 155tr.

Centro de Arte Reina Sofía, Madrid: *Retrato de Josette* Juan Gris © ADAGP, PARIS and DACS, London 2011 31bc; *Landscape in Cadaqués* Dalí © Salvador Dalí – Foundation Gala – Salvador Dalí/DACS 2011 89cra, 89tl; *Toki-Egin* (*Homenaje a San-Juan de la Cruz*), 1952 Eduardo Chillida © DACS 2011 88ca; *Guitarra ante el Mar* Juan Gris © ADAGP, PARIS and DACS, London 2011 90tr; *El Profeta* Pablo Gargallo © ADAGP, PARIS and DACS, London 2011 90c; *Minotauromaquia* Picasso © Succession Picasso/ DACS 2011 90br; *Muchacha en la Ventana* Dalí © Salvador Dalí – Foundation Gala – Salvador Dalí/ DACS 2011 91tc; **Robert Harding Picture Library:** Maria Galan 39cr.

M Angeles Sanchez: 107b; Juan Carlos Martínez Zafra 56br; **Archivo Del Senado:** Oronoz 57bc. **Taberna Antonio Sanchez:** 34bc; **Tony Stone:** 172bl; **Superstock:** Marka 66.

Teatro Real: Javier del Real 180br; **Telefónica:** 198tr, 198cla.

Hotel Único Madrid: 151br; **Hotel Urban Madrid:** 150br, 152bl.

Vinícola Mentridana: 35crb.

World Pictures: 173crb.

Map cover: **Alamy Images:** Sean Pavone.
Jacket: Front and Spine: **Alamy Images:** Sean Pavone.

Front End Paper: **Alamy Images:** Jon Arnold Images Ltd Lcl; Peter Horree Rc imagebroker Ltr; **Dreamstime.com:** Robert Zehetmayer Rcr; **Superstock:** Marka Rbc.

All other images © Dorling Kindersley. For further information see www.DKimages.com

Special Editions of DK Travel Guides

DK Travel Guides can be purchased in bulk quantities at discounted prices for use in promotions or as premiums. We are also able to offer special editions and personalized jackets, corporate imprints, and excerpts from all of our books, tailored specifically to meet your own needs.

To find out more, please contact:

in the US **specialsales@dk.com**

in the UK **travelguides@uk.dk.com**

in Canada **specialmarkets@dk.com**

in Australia **penguincorporatesales@ penguinrandomhouse.com.au**